110669136

A to Z of Philosophy

Also available from Continuum

A Brief History of Philosophy, by Derek Johnston
Great Thinkers A–Z, edited by Julian Baggini and Jeremy Stangroom
The Twenty Greatest Philosophy Books, by James Garvey
What More Philosophers Think, edited by Julian Baggini
    and Jeremy Stangroom
What Philosophers Think, edited by Julian Baggini and Jeremy Stangroom
What Philosophy Is, edited by Havi Carel and David Gamez

DISCARDED
LIBRARY

A to Z of Philosophy

Alexander Moseley

continuum

BOWLING GREEN STATE
UNIVERSITY LIBRARIES

Continuum International Publishing Group

The Tower Building
11 York Road
London SE1 7NX

80 Maiden Lane
Suite 704
New York NY 10038

www.continuumbooks.com

© Alexander Moseley 2008

All rights reserved. No part of this publication may be reproduced or transmitted in any form or by any means, electronic or mechanical, including photocopying, recording, or any information storage or retrieval system, without prior permission in writing from the publishers.

British Library Cataloguing-in-Publication Data
A catalogue record for this book is available from the British Library.
ISBN: HB: 0-8264-9947-3
          978-0-8264-9947-9
       PB: 0-8264-9948-1
          978-0-8264-9948-6

Library of Congress Cataloging-in-Publication Data
Moseley, Alexander, 1967–
The A to Z of philosophy/Alexander Moseley.
   p. cm.
   Includes bibliographical references and index.
   ISBN-13: 978-0-8264-9947-9 (HB)
   ISBN-10: 0-8264-9947-3 (HB)

   ISBN-13: 978-0-8264-9948-6 (pbk.)
   ISBN-10: 0-8264-9948-1 (pbk.)
   1. Philosophy–Encyclopedias. I. Title.

B51.M67 2008
103--dc22   2008016782

Typeset by Newgen Imaging Systems Pvt Ltd, Chennai, India
Printed and bound in Great Britain by MPG Books Ltd, Bodmin, Cornwall

To my wife, Moira, and our son, Charles

Contents

Preface

Philosophy is the love of wisdom. But what it means to be wise depends on what one is thinking about or looking at. The unwise prefer to turn off their minds, emotions or senses, and prefer not to look, feel or think. Once we begin thinking, we find that wisdom takes many roads, some less travelled than others. This is not to say that there is a plurality of paths that may be deemed equally wise or that all roads lead to the same Truth – examining that problem is one of philosophy's tasks! What the philosopher can say is that beginning any path to deeper thinking is highly rewarding – and if an end is reached, an answer apparently secured, then we should begin another route and see where we end up.

This work presents what can only be a highly selective and personal consideration of a variety of topics which I believe can whet the appetite for more philosophy. I sincerely hope that the essays may act as a springboard into further reading and thinking; I also hope that the range of thinkers and perspectives presented encourages the reader to question and analyse the authorities, traditions, expectations and preconceptions that are found in all walks of life and thought.

Caveat emptor: thinking differently can upset people though, so tread softly on others' philosophies – unless they are trying to impose theirs on yours!

Alexander Moseley

Absolute

'There's no such thing as absolutes' is a common fallacy, for the very statement presupposes at least one absolute; nevertheless, if we skip the pedantic retorts, relativism holds that truths cannot be guaranteed across time and place – that moral absolutes such as 'murder is wrong' are not universally binding.

Beyond the logical playground, the term 'Absolute' has a deeper and more mysterious meaning: the Absolute is, for philosophers such as Hegel and Bradley, the ultimate spiritual grounding to all that exists, or, for Sprigge, the totality of all experiences. The Absolute exists in itself and is independent of all other things or relations. As such, it can be considered to be everything or the whole of things, from which we can read different ideas depending on what kind of metaphysical vision of the universe we lean towards. Monism helps to sustain an Absolute for it holds that there is only one nature to the universe to which all aspects reduce; compare that with a dualist vision – that there are material and immaterial entities, which cannot logically be reduced to an underlying absolute substratum. Monists, however, divide into different species: materialists, who espouse the reduction of all things to matter, and who may be found vibrantly alive in their search for an all-encompassing Theory of Everything; or idealists, for whom all is ideal, or immaterial. The latter monists are more prone to embrace theories of the Absolute as Mind or God, enjoying the use of capitals to accentuate that they think their discovery worth Respect.

The Absolute is a vague notion, it is 'everything, man . . .', which reeks of worthlessness, as Ayer noted, for it is non-verifiable and hence of no significance. Yet is that a fair retort? Can that which underlies everything, the ultimate substratum to existence, be verified by observation? For instance, it is impossible for science to validate the existence of the universe while being in it. Or consider that particular entities form relations to one another, such as the moon orbiting the earth; for the absolutist, these possess only non-absolute status, they necessitate an underlying commonality on which all depend for their existence, just as the content of my thoughts requires a thinker. Unsurprisingly, absolute idealists posit this commonality as Mind, an all-encompassing mental entity which controls (or dreams?) the entire universe and its peculiar and apparent material entities such as you and I. That you think is a reflection of this Absolute. Some naturally lean towards describing the Absolute as God, while others avoid the theological overtones that they may otherwise disagree with, preferring to understand the concept of the 'Absolute' as philosophically more valid or interesting than that of 'God'.

An intriguing argument is that for the Absolutist there is no history as such, just Being. This resolves a horrendous problem concerning time and the logic of the past, present and future: all exist in the Absolute – there is posited the events of the past, the great and tragic, and so too are the events of the future, all ready to emerge as what we consider as the present rushes towards them.

Action

Philosophers split the world into events and actions and then the fun begins. The former explains what happens to the physical processes of the universe. For example, when comet Shoemaker-Levy 9 plummeted into Jupiter in 1994: this action involved no will, it just happened, unless an omnipotent God's will directs events. But God's acts may logically be called events as they are beyond human ken. Human acts acknowledge or imply that people are capable of choosing their next move, that is, they are not determined by prior causes and so permit what we generally refer to as freedom.

Assuming free will, philosophers then ask what constitutes an action – is it the free movement of a person? Free that is of any external cause such as being tied to a hurtling train; can it include mental acts, as when I imagine and work through jumping a fence on my horse; should it include speech acts, the verbalizations of intention, indications, demands, wishes and other subtleties of language? There is also doing nothing on purpose: omitting a positive act in order to attain a certain end, such as not attending a party to express disdain. Acts thus divide into acts of omission and commission, which raise ethical concerns about responsibility. That I did not go to Hank's country and western party was a slight on my part which may show me to be peevish or snobbish, or alternatively expressive of taste, depending on others' judgements. More seriously, if I failed to read a warning sign while driving, I may endanger others and myself for my lack of attention.

Ethically, what acts I choose seem to depend on my intentions: by failing to give Great Aunt Dotty her medication, I bring about her swift demise. Was my failure intentional, a court of law would wish to know, or a mere oversight on my part given that the old cantankerous woman was constantly berating me for not serving her well enough in other regards. And if I had a large fortune to inherit, should that make a difference on how I am judged?

If I cannot act otherwise than I did, am I still responsible for my action? Frankfurter argues that I am, for the lack of alternatives may not play a role in my choice.

Clearly the philosophy of action begins to swell – what is the relationship between intention and action, what is the logical or ethical status of omission versus commission, what is the nature of internal acts or speech acts? Should only externally validated behaviour count here as behaviourists claim, so that we can appreciate an actor's performance even though, unbeknownst to us, he was thinking of his next shopping trip? Intention and action are entwined, for to reject intention is to reject the psychological dimension that action presumes. Think about something desirable in the fridge – you can act on that desire, or choose not to at present. Do read on, though.

Aesthetics

When the word 'beautiful' is uttered or thought, a host of philo-sophical issues quickly rush in. If I say, 'X is beautiful', then I seem to imply that X is beautiful in the same sense that I would say X is cuboid or large; or I may be implying that X is beautiful to me in the sense that it provokes a certain aesthetic feeling. Alternatively, I may be noting an intrasocial agreement between others around me of the form, 'we, who are gathered here, ought to respect X as being beautiful', which would entail that beauty is cultural and historical.

The Greeks equated beauty with the good – which still finds its echoes in ugly dastardly characters and beautiful heroes in film and literature. While some such as Eco are keen to emphasize the his-torical characteristic of beauty, others stress the eternal nature of beauty and perhaps agree with Plato that beauty is a suprasensible Ideal, a perfect Form from which all sensible beauties are mere reflections. Kant offered a rationalistic description of beauty (a dis-interested pleasure) giving us quaint summaries of what is sublime and what is beautiful, while Santayana prefer to remind us of the subjective emotional quality of beauty:

> To feel beauty is a better thing than to understand how we come to feel it. (Santayana, *The Sense of Beauty*, 31)

But in sensing beauty, should I do so with disinterest and with a contemplative attitude, or should I permit myself to be immersed in the emotions that may be generated? For instance, look at an object near you. I am looking at a moveable horse shelter – a very utilitarian wooden object, cuboid with a hip-roof, the entrance gate open. Is there anything pleasing to the eye about it? At first glimpse, no, but if I alter the way that I am perceiving the object and imagine that I am going to sketch and paint it, then I can make it more pleasing to the eye. In that respect, am I removing extraneous, unpleasing things, ignoring the horse fence, for example, or the water bucket? Not necessarily, because I can do the same for them – I can begin to appreciate them as aesthetic objects. So what is it that is altering here? Since I alter my perception to see 'a potential work of art' it would be easy to say that the aesthetic is a mental experience, requiring a shift in focus from a non-aesthetic vision to an aesthetic, just as we can look at a series of numbers as just a series of numbers 2, 5, 10, 17, 26, 37, . . . or as a mathematical pattern $n^2 + 1$. On the other hand, is it that the objects that I am reviewing do indeed possess something which is there all along and which I can therefore perceive once I alter my focus, a change of attitude that can be taught?

A banal quip that 'beauty is in the eye of the beholder' implies that what you see as beautiful, I may see as ugly. If our conversation stops there, that would be a shame and something philosophical would perhaps be missing. What, may I ask, do you find beautiful in this object that we are regarding? Is there something there – in the object – that I can learn to appreciate or will I just learn to look at the object as if I were looking through your eyes and hence applying your criteria for judging? And so, I may later say, 'Ah, my friend would certainly find this beautiful!' Yet subjectivity in turn demands more: if you say, 'I find this work melancholic', the 'I' can be dropped for a stronger statement, 'This piece is melancholic', which is much more interesting than what you particularly feel: now, we have something to work on – what about the picture makes it melancholic?

Nevertheless, it may indeed be personal associations and that other people argue that the work is a joyous piece, and so the subjective argument could be justified. For example, if I say, 'I find X beautiful', I may be referring to the environmental, cultural, psychological and rational background upon which I make my choice: this means that subjectivity is critical to appreciating of what 'beauty' consists, and should you have shared a sufficiently similar life, read the same books, looked at the paintings, buildings, sculptures and people that I have, you too will agree, broadly speaking. On the other hand, your disagreement on this 'beauty is in the eye of the beholder' theory can be construed as merely a recognition that your historical and thus present context of perceiving beauty is different from mine. Accordingly, intrasubjective agreements could be tested scientifically: do people of similar backgrounds and educational exposures produce similar approbations of beauty? But even if they did, would that mean that the beauty is objective, or merely that the interplay of social forces is quite powerful?

Alternatively, is X beautiful because of some inherent qualities that are objectively recognizable – its form, shape, symmetry, colour, balance, harmony, and so on? It can be claimed that the mind has evolved to recognize certain forms as possessing beauty, in that perceptual recognition of them (analogous to the recognition of space or the passing of time) produces an emotional feeling that other animals do not share. An older tradition deems that the beautiful is an emanation of the divine, the truth or the good. All theories similarly generate the problem of when I encounter beautiful things, will I know it, in the sense of knowing that one is in love, or do I require a modicum of education and an extension of my observational faculties beyond the daily banalities?

> But what if man had eyes to see the true beauty – the divine beauty, I mean, pure and clear and unalloyed, not clogged with the pollutions of mortality and all the colours and vanities of human life – thither looking, and holding converse with the true beauty simple and divine? (Plato, *Symposium*, 211e)

But once we can begin to determine what it is about a work or a view or a person that produces descriptions then we can begin to work harder and the vast field of aesthetics opens up: attitude, value, representation, intention, geometry and symmetry, psychological responses, distance of the viewer, cultural forms of beauty and other topics, which can be applied to music, art, sculpture, architecture and dance. And the beauty therein, like the night, remains beguiling.

Analytical philosophy

This is the name given to an approach to philosophy espoused particularly by twentieth-century Oxford philosophers beginning with Russell and continuing through the work of Wittgenstein and Moore. The thrust is that all that we speak should be analysed to help secure better meanings and hence, hopefully, to resolve philosophical problems.

The motive behind analysing statements and words is naturally clarification, but the analytical philosophers believed that they could uncover the logical structures hidden behind statements and so, by reducing problematic or ambiguous statements to logic, solutions could be revealed. Russell and Whitehead had worked on reducing mathematics to logic and they were optimistic that similar advancements could be made across philosophy. Eventually, their mathematical analysis was seen to depend on non-logical propositions (everything has to begin somewhere!), and similarly enthusiastic attempts to analyse language meaning, while sharpening thought, have not succeeded: philosophy can be particularly enigmatic and not easily reduced.

The goal is to resolve statements as simply as possible and thereby forge a stronger link between what they purportedly mean and the real world referents they picture (the picture theory of language). Deploying logical terms such as 'not', 'all', 'or', 'and' and 'if', and then pursuing their truth-values is the hallmark of this kind of analysis. Propositions are true if their components (if this then that) run together; these components should be reducible to basic facts ('there is a book on the table'); but if a proposition could not fit into the scheme, then it would be consigned to metaphysics, that is, nonsense. Problems involve the truthness of the elementary facts presented – but what determines truth? If it is the definitions used, then the logical analysis does not take us anywhere except in a deductive expansion of the terms – such inferences will be valid, not necessarily true; if facts are said to be pictures of the world, then we need to know how these facts are to be verified ('I left a light on upstairs') or falsified ('All crows are black') – these controversies nonetheless do not demean the strength of the demand that we should all be more rigorous and clear in our speaking and writing.

Animal rights

From the beginnings of human thought, science, culture, song and art, animals have played an important role acting as resources, totems, symbols, diviners, gods incarnate, as well as predators, vermin and family. Their function has tended to be local, reflecting evolved relationships with certain animals, a cultural force that sometimes dominates present philosophical discourse on the animal kingdom, particularly those animals that our literature draws into our imaginations. In a sense, this skews preconceptions of our thinking on animals, so it is useful to remove our thoughts from the particular (the fluffy) to the abstract, removing our locally defined emotions with respect to other animals.

A line is often drawn between our species and the rest of the animal kingdom. To some, reason is a reflection of the divine and thereby sets humanity ontologically (or theologically) apart from other animals: we reason, they don't. For those of the rationalist persuasion, the incredible emergence of reasoning is sufficient to set us apart rather than any recourse to theology. Both camps may present distinct visions of 'the rest of the animal kingdom' as being either wholly or partially subservient to our needs or powers because of its irrationality. However, if rationality is defined as behaviour that secures the interests of the agent then all living entities are rational – so anthropocentric rationalists have to add extra faculties to the concept, such as self-consciousness, imagining the future and language.

Sextus Empiricus presented the case of a reasoning dog pursuing a prey; the dog tried two out of three possible routes for scent and failing there immediately took off down the third. Philosophers have discussed whether the dog reasoned 'if not X nor Y then Z' or whether it merely picked up the scent. It is an empirical question but not one easily answered, since hounds' ability to scent is so much more refined than ours – did the dog merely pick up the scent on the third attempt? Nonetheless, huntsmen have tales of canny hounds (and canny foxes) that strongly indicate the ability to anticipate. But Descartes rejected the dog's rationality in his characterization of all animals as machines, non-thinking and non-feeling (a view that underpins vivisectionism); his is an extraordinary theory but defended on the basis that only humans may be said to possess a soul (an ethereal rational faculty) and one held by many key religions.

Other traditions – cultural and philosophical – prefer to conceive of humanity as a *primus inter pares* (first among equals) at best, or an equal among equals, while others look upon humans as something worse than the rest of the animal kingdom. In this last theory, other animals are compared more favourably to human attributes: some can run faster; others can fly; some are stronger; others can swim deeper; and so on. This popular logic, however, is not quite proper – to compare the faculties of different species on the same grounds is fallacious. It also implies that it is fallacious to reject the status of other animals on the grounds that they cannot speak or reason.

Bentham exploited this logic to seek out a deeper common ground on which to present a new relationship with the animal kingdom: the commonality of suffering. However, even this step, which draws upon the perhaps unique human emotional reaction to needless pain or wanton violence, presents problems if the assumed commonality is indeed uniquely human: predators do not (seem) to worry about the suffering of their prey; nor do they seem to gloat over the injuries of deaths of others, even of their own kind (elephants excepting perhaps).

Animal rights theorists present a range of arguments justifying the expansion of rights beyond the human realm. Some claim that all living creatures deserve the respect that people give each other (sometimes), offering justifications that they deserve not to be hunted, shot at, controlled, managed, or domesticated for pleasure or food. A few such as Peter Singer extend the circle of moral personhood along Buddhist or Jainist lines to include the microscopic realm or to those animals deemed an immediate and clear danger to human life, accepting perhaps the right of people to defend themselves against animal aggressors as against human aggressors.

Partiality towards some species is, however, acceptable – in life, we choose with much partiality whom we fall in love with and to assert that we should fall in love with everybody equally would seem a very weak argument on many grounds. To raise the status of some animals as being more equal than others is a cogent move, but the philosophical problem is what kind of status is being asserted.

Usually, the principle is a moral one. It is immoral or evil to commit harm against persons. 'Person' is the term used to designate one of a moral status, which implies deserving respect, rights or dignity, depending on the preferred language of the philosophy. Defining moral personhood is a difficult process however, for on what grounds should personhood be established, except those that are attributes of our own species? It is difficult not to talk in anything but human language and concepts, something other animals cannot do.

In a popular argument, Kant advised against treating animals cruelly on the grounds that such behaviour is likely to translate into cruel dispositions in the agent – it is, ironically in the case of

Kant – a consequentialist argument, one that looks to the outcomes of the action. Kant is a renowned deontologist, one who looks at doing the right thing rather than considering the consequences. It is a point taken up by Nozick, who argues that in choosing rationally, animals such as cows may prefer utilitarian thinking, for more would live for fewer, over deontological thinking in which fewer would live longer.

Animal rights theories present their own problems for those who reject human rights, but the moral import of animals is not lost on those who support or reject such rights and who even favour domestication, hunting, farming, fishing or pest control. It becomes devilishly difficult to proclaim rights for some (including our own species) over others or to assert that some deserve legal protection and not others: mammals over insects typically, and big or furry things over small spiky things – until Disney produces a new cartoon on the hopes and loves of viruses.

Aquinas, Thomas (1225–1274)

Born to an aristocratic family, Thomas of Aquino, rebelled against family expectations and chose to join the poverty embracing Dominican order. His brothers kidnapped him back for a year and even tempted him with a woman, but Thomas's passions lay elsewhere; once fully ensconced in a scholarly environment at the University of Paris, he grew very corpulent (fatter than Hume it seems) and wrote *Summa Contra Gentiles*, *On Kingship* and the enormous tome the *Summa Theologica*, an apology which needs an apology. In 1272 he removed to Naples to help found a Dominican monastery, dying 2 years later.

Thomas was a truly broad ranging and influential philosopher and theologian, whose writings altered the mainstream thinking of the Catholic Church supplanting those of Augustine. Generally speaking, while Augustine merged Platonic, dualistic philosophy with Christianity (the City of God and the City of the World), Thomas's innovation was to supplement traditional Augustinian Christianity with an Aristotelian logic and conceptual framework that Augustine lacked.

In effect, Thomas produced a powerful division between philosophy and theology, which has left a strong philosophical and cultural impact that retains a grip on minds today when we allow religion and science their separate epistemological spheres. The result was to provide thinkers with a justification of applying reason to the world. Various thinkers had been turning to study the secular realm and the Church offered by no means a unified vision of theology and philosophy, but Thomas presented a way forward for what we now call science in a manner that eventually became the acceptable orthodox and which, incidentally, promoted Aristotle to an unassailable philosophical position that warranted execution should a monk veer away from the doctrine.

Thomas offers a realistic vision of his fellow man: our ability to understand the truths of the universe and the truths of God is limited by our intelligence and by our own desires to pursue intellectual thought. Intelligence is one thing, action another. Knowledge of the world is dependent upon the senses (hence Thomas's philosophy permitted the expansion of empirical investigations that percolated and accumulated over the next few centuries to create the scientific revolution); knowledge of God and His truths are dependent upon revelation though. Moreover, following Aristotle, Thomas emphasizes that we are also rational creatures and that the human mind is capable of much learning, erudition and contemplating God. Where Aristotle claimed the highest and noblest pursuit for man to be contemplation, Thomas easily slipped in 'contemplation of God'.

The human mind is the soul, an immaterial and separable substance temporarily connected to a particular body. Humanity stands above the rest of the animal kingdom in a hierarchy of complexity, and above humans are the incorporeal angels. When man contemplates, he is stretching his potential into the angelic realm, but of course the pure thought said to be characteristic of angels lies frustratingly beyond: just as Plato and Socrates held, our body restrains our soul. Reason mixes the senses and the will (the will to learn), but there is another route to knowledge and that is the path of faith. Faith can illuminate the minds of the intelligent as well as the dull, he argues, but to believe must be a voluntary matter: faith cannot be forced (except in some dire political situations).

Below the angelic level of pure thought, humanity can achieve much knowledge. Our very being reaches out to know, and Thomas agreed with 'The Philosopher', as he called Aristotle, that everything seeks an end: all entities possess a purpose: that is, they do not just have a function, but they are on a path towards an end. The ends to which things act are good, although immaterial entities naturally do not know the ends to which they are fated, so their ends must logically be chosen for them. For a theologian that can only be God. Just as there is an end, there must also be a beginning and the origins of the world lie with God; here Thomas took over Aristotle's concept of the 'prime mover' for a logical adaptation to the Christian creation story: the more we know of this world the more we accept that the primary cause must begin with the unmoved mover and first cause of everything.

Thomas provided five justifications of God's existence. God is the unmoved mover, an Aristotelian idea, that follows the incidence of movement back (Y is moved by X and in turn X by W, etc.) until we either must accept an infinite regression or an unmoved mover. Secondly, a first cause for the universe (and all movement) can only be God, for there cannot be an infinite regression either in time or causation. Thirdly, and imitating the second, there must be an ultimate origin for everything. Fourthly, on a different tact – imperfections exist in the world around us (we are always complaining of something), so these can only exist in comparison with a perfect being. Fifthly, all things both living and non-living possess a purpose and that purpose can only be given to them or make sense if there is a God. Contrary to what the ancient thinkers held, Thomas claimed that God can create the universe out of nothing, a useful argument for theologians, it turns out, against materialists who deny the possibility of something out of nothing. But in each case, Thomas sought to prove what he already accepted as true: the existence of God, which is certainly not going to encourage atheists or sceptics.

Considering the impact and impetus of the Christian doctrine of original sin and man's innate perversity or imperfection (underlined by Augustine), it is unsurprising that Thomas accepted the general doctrine of man's inability to be a pure, moral being: that belongs in an increasing order to the angels and finally only to God himself. Agreeing with Aristotle and Augustine, Thomas argued that happiness cannot be found in pleasure seeking or in material possessions. Nor can it be found, contrary to Aristotle, in philosophical contemplation, for the truths men seek lie beyond the world accessible to human senses. Echoing Socrates, Thomas claimed that 'no one is therefore happy in this life'. Man may thus live a life of virtue in accordance with his nature and to enjoy pleasure and to order his life according to reason, but *true* happiness escapes him – the closest he can get is the beatitude of religious contemplation.

Analogously to the hierarchy of lower to higher corporeal entities politically, man must order his own self and his community. Just as in the man, the mind must order the passions and biological needs, so in society, those of:

> superior intellect are natural rulers while those who are less intelligent but have stronger bodies seem to be made by nature to serve. (Aquinas, 'Summa against the Gentiles', III.81)

Aristotle's aristocratic charge is thus rekindled – but unsurprisingly so. European life was hierarchically ordered according to social status, but what bubbles excitingly in Thomas's argument is his next point that government based solely on violence and passion leads to disorder: cool-headed reasoning should rule men's affairs – here is the philosopher's perennial call to statesmen to order their affairs rationally. But with Thomas, the ecclesiastical charge to save men's souls is added – theologians ought to become philosopher-kings, or at least advise them in the pursuit of the holy life.

Yet Thomas recognized that most of mankind are not capable or willing to pursue political affairs coolly, just as they are not able or willing to give their minds over to the contemplation of God: in the vein of the Athenians, while the masses toil and live the pleasurable life and being incapable of understanding all of the self-evident axioms of God's system (some they will get, others require effort), those who are capable of exercising the mind should devote themselves to religious contemplation and thus rise to a position to teach and instruct the lower minds, and guide the hedonistic populace for its own sake and good. Thereby, resorting to his overriding ontological hierarchy, Thomas argues that just as the body ought to be ruled by one mind, so too should society be so ordered by one rule and ruler – there can only be one Christian people and accordingly all the faithful must agree on their faith. Social life he acknowledged as being pluralistic in that men pursue different secular and hence short-term ends, but because a few men are capable of asserting the minds to seek the higher truths, it is they – the new philosopher-theologian kings of the middle ages, who must guide the general populace to direct their lives according to the right rule of nature and of God – that is, the virtuous life. 'Man needs someone to direct him towards his end' (*On Kingship*, ch. 1). He needs society – man is, following Aristotle, a social animal – but his life needs governance. Thus we return to Plato's assumption that a community needs a skipper, a captain of the social boat, to steer the group in the right direction; accordingly, there must be a way for man to be governed.

Indeed, in the ordering of men, slavery is not an unnatural state of affairs and is acceptable to Thomism. Most philosophers have their idiosyncrasies and contemporary prejudices which can be more or less forgiven (we are not they), however, Thomas's general philosophical vision is at times clouded by his faithful acceptance of his religious order – like Augustine he prostrates, and arguably sacrifices, his mind at the Church altar. Accordingly he limits the possibilities of his thinking: in his ingenious amalgamation of Aristotelian logic to Augustinian Christianity, Thomas certainly produced an exceptional and voluminous defence, but a defence that, while producing some excellent philosophical insights, remains in intention and therefore at heart an apology for the status quo. Yet in his finer points we find the seeds for justifying the intellectual freedom to explore the world that blossomed later in the Renaissance – certainly his most enduring benefit to humanity.

Aristotle (384–322)

Aristotle, incidentally famous as Plato's greatest student and tutor to the teenager Alexander the Great, stands with Plato at the fountainhead of the Western philosophical tradition that flows into Scholastic thinking in the thirteenth century and still maintains its grip and attraction. The father of logic, Aristotle rejected the metaphysical duality characteristic of Plato's philosophy and the immortality of the soul and criticized Plato's Theory of Forms. In contrast to Plato's motivation to raise philosophy to universality, Aristotle argued that each discipline should follow its own rules, leaving philosophy to guide our thinking as we submerge ourselves into particular disciplines, echoes of which we hear in Wittgenstein in the twentieth century.

Educated as the son of the physician to the Macedonian King, Aristotle studied at Plato's Academy for 20 years. On Plato's death, Aristotle travelled and developed a love of biology from which he advanced the notion that all living entities exist for a purpose – they are going somewhere in their actions, and therefore we can study the ends of things (teleology). It was an argument that maintained a grip on scientific thinking down to the nineteenth century and the emergence of Darwin; mainstream biology now rejects a teleological description of life in favour of a haphazard emergence of those most fit to survive and reproduce.

Aristotle returned to Athens to open up a competing University to the Academy, namely the Lyceum and its walk, the Peripatos, which gave his followers the name peripatetics. The Lyceum offered a broader and more scientifically oriented curriculum and encouraged the pursuit of research; however, following Alexander's death in 323, anti-Macedonian feelings in Athens prompted Aristotle to retire to Chalcis where he died.

In contrast to Plato's belief in a world of supernatural Forms or Ideas, which claims that the things around us are poorer reflections of the perfect Forms, Aristotle contended that reality is what we encounter in the things around us; when I see a woman, I perceive her to exist in her own right as an individual entity. There is no superior Form to which she may be said to partake or belong, there is only her, just as there is only this table in front of me, this dog, this cup, that tree. Whereas Plato works from the top down – each move away from the higher group effecting a diminution in the individual's metaphysical status – Aristotle works from the bottom up; the higher groups are, moreover, not entities that exist, they are abstracts – creations of the mind to help us understand what we are observing and their relations with other things.

In perceiving, we categorize – group – things together; and in grouping, we immediately involve logic, and here Aristotle introduced syllogistic arguments (all xs are y; all ys are z; therefore all xs are zs – and variations on the theme); it is not an exhaustive account of logic, but one that certainly gripped logical analysis when Aristotle was ever considered to be *the* authority on all matters philosophical, something, one gets the impression, he would reject given his highly thoughtful and balanced approach to matters so evident when we read him.

Understanding the world begins with observation. Yet that is not to conclude that Aristotle was a simple materialist who demanded that in looking at the things in front of our senses: we aim to understand what we see, and we, as humans, are peculiarly curious about what we look upon. To look is to engage in our first encounter with reality; to think takes us further, namely into the realm of being (ontology). Perceiving the particular can lead our minds to consider the commonalties that may pertain to similar particulars – we aim to group, and to forge higher groupings of things and so our experience of the world leads us to 'what nature knows' and to advance 'from what is better known by is to what is better known by nature'.

Each entity we perceive exists; moreover, it is this existence which attracts deeper concern. In the *Metaphysics*, Aristotle posed a question that he recognized as innately human – to ask after the nature of being, the study of being *qua* being. What is it to be? What is being? Being relates intimately with an entity's essence: essence is what remains when we remove all the accidental qualities of an object – when we remove skin colour, hair colour, height, weight, mood, emotional disposition, and so on, we are left with man *qua* man; and what is man? A rational being. All entities also possess a purpose by virtue of their nature – man's is to follow his happiness; the contrast is with Plato's Forms, which are eternal, unchanging; the biologically minded philosopher could not resist philosophizing upon the obvious birth-growth-maturation-degen-eration-death cycles of living entities; change is necessary, and is innate in a body – a block of metal can become a statue, that is, take on the form of a person; a musician takes on the form of a musical person; each entity and part of an entity has a purpose to fulfil: the heart circulates the blood, and the blood has the purpose of supporting the entity's life. A thing's potentiality defines its final cause. Finality, or where a thing is going (or is potentially going), was an important theme for Aristotle – marble to statues, organs to life processes, human life to happiness, human mind to contemplation.

Humanity's rationality distinguishes us from the animal king-dom, not in the sense that animals are thought to act irrationally, but that their mental abilities are restricted to associations and memories, while the human mind is driven by curiosity and the ability to philosophize. Yet not all humans are equal in that regard, Aristotle observes. The inequality of man underpins Aristotle's thoughts on ethical and political issues: some are born to rule over others, said the son of the physician to the hegemonic Macedonian court. Slavery is understood as a matter of nature – some are born to serve their betters.

> That one should command and another obey is both necessary and expedient. Indeed some things are so divided right from birth, some to rule, some to be ruled. (Aristotle, 'Politics', 1254a)

But what determines social superiority?

Civilization begins when people become political – that is, they belong to a polis: the polis was the Ancient Greek city-state, usually walled, possessing a central acropolis, temple and a form of government decreed by the people. Nature draws man and woman together to form a family, but while the family temporally precedes the formation of clans and then villages, the state, to which a growing community is naturally drawn to form, is logically prior to the existence of the individual – that is, to the civilized individual, whose civil status depends on the existence of a state. Accordingly, the state is a moral entity, evolving logically from the innate tendency of humans to congregate. However, anyone who lives outside of a polis is a savage or outlaw, one implicatively held in great contempt by Aristotle in a view that motivates many an imperialistic jaunt throughout history.

The purpose of the polis is to ensure the best form of life for its citizens; it should secure the rule of law over the rule of men, that is, the polis should be rationally formed, accepting, however, the plurality of human pursuits to be reflected in a range of constitutions (Aristotle collected over 150 constitutions); the constitution ought to prevent tyrants (self-serving politicians) from taking power, and the polis ought to educate the populace sufficiently. Once the proper political framework is in place, one that guarantees the security and peace of the population, then the citizens can turn their attention to the pursuit of the life most befitting a human – the good life.

The life proper to man is to pursue happiness, and that can only come through the advancement of the mind; and the highest activity that a man can achieve is contemplation. Not all can reach the higher echelons of life, for breeding counts – whereas Plato opined that talent emerges with a child's development, Aristotle argues that it is there from the beginning. Nonetheless, potential certainly requires education – it does not emerge of its own accord; this is because the pursuit of the good life requires learning good habits from an early age – it is harder to learn them later, he wisely notes.

Such good habits develop from right behaviour, avoiding excesses, acting properly according to the circumstances, pursuing happiness rather than pleasure, forging true friendships rather than utilitarian ones, love stemming from self-love and extending outward to similarly virtuous people. The virtuous life stands in contrast to other ethical positions' visions of the good life: the deontologist demands that we pursue duties regardless of pleasure; the hedonist says pleasure should be our end; the utilitarian says that our duty should be our neighbour's pleasure: the virtue theorist asks what sort of person will we be if we do X. Who we morally are then turns not so much on one act but on many, for the many acts form our character.

And what of the soul? While Plato believed in the Pythagorean-Orphic immortality of the soul, Aristotle preferred to posit the soul in the body for its lifetime – and that's it. Soul is the form that living matter takes: living matter is certainly differentiable from inorganic, for it is fused with self-regulation – with life – but that animating essence fades with the body's death. Your soul is in charge of your nutrition (held in common with plants), your perception (held in common with animals) and your thinking: which, as a human, you naturally possess the capacity for! Yet if all living entities possess a soul, what is the cause of soul in the first place? Relentlessly does Aristotle push the question: you exist, you are a mind; but whence your mind? It could only have come from another mind – and if we follow the regressions, we cannot but conclude that all minds are caused by the ultimate Mind, or God. The connection to the medieval occidental Christian Church falls into place: Aquinas probably could not believe his luck in discovering a razor sharp logician whose arguments could easily sponsor theological doctrines! Yet Aristotle is not clear on the role of his God: at times he is not a creator, for the universe is for him eternal; sometimes he thinks of God as the initiator, at other times as the unmoved mover, the source of motion in the universe, but unmoving in himself; the source of all thought.

Aristotle's philosophy comes down to us through his pupils' notes and were once locked in a vault for a couple of centuries before being bought by a Roman book collector! But this great philosophy of the ancient world was barely taken up by the Romans – his influence migrated to the Middle East and to the Arabian world, where he influenced generations of Arabic scholars and scientists; he only truly surfaced in the Western canon in the mid-thirteenth century when Latin translations of his works began to circulate; his influence was boosted immeasurably by St Thomas Aquinas, who merged Aristotelian thinking with Catholicism. Although his works lend themselves to scientific inquiry and observation, the Church and its related organs of education raised Aristotle to unquestionable heights: his writings were on par with the Bible and it became heresy in the medieval ages to question him whom Aquinas dubbed 'The Philosopher'.

After much bloodshed, violence and intellectual fighting, scientific inquiry eventually won the battle for ideas over dogma in the seventeenth century and Aristotle's influence waned. Nonetheless, once scholars were free from having to agree with the Aristotelian doctrine as translated and imposed by Latinists they could look freshly upon his works and they discovered that there was still much to enjoy and consider; notably, his ethical and political theories resurged in the nineteenth and twentieth centuries, most recently in a revival of 'virtue theory' in ethics and his work on metaphysics continues to present translators with umpteen challenges. Aristotle still has much to offer the modern reader, despite the partisan mis-reading of his work generated in the Middle Ages.

Augustine (353–430)

Augustine was born in Tagaste in AD 354 (in modern day Algeria) during a time when the Romans still ruled North Africa and he died in 430 in Hippo during a Vandal siege 20 years after Alaric sacked Rome. Like Aquinas, he approached philosophy from the position of a Christian apologist, seeking to defend the orthodoxy from attack. Some philosophers demote his contributions to philosophy because of this; nonetheless, his influence in the history of thought and his impact on Catholic Church doctrine is undeniable. Augustine earned much fame through his letters, books, and his rhetorical skills and he remains an enjoyable thinker to read, presenting at times what seem to us very modern arguments as well as in a clear manner.

The young Augustine initially allied himself with the officially recognized vein of Christianity, although he had dabbled in various sects, most importantly the locally popular Manichean sect, whose philosophy divided the world into two powers, good and evil, which vie for mastery. As a 'born-again' Christian, he later asserted the unified nature of the universe against the Manichean thinking, which became a heresy. With Augustine, we also clearly hear again Plato's voice in a man who sought to justify and explain the nature of the Other World but who ably welded the general, but to his mind incomplete, thrust of Platonic philosophy to the Christian theological inheritance that had evolved in the three centuries since Christ's death. Yet we also detect the extrapolation of Stoical ethics – again merged with Christian thinking and Eastern promise of eternal salvation – into an almost absolute renunciation of this world in favour of retaining a purity to the soul.

For Augustine, Christianity offered the ability to reach a higher religious level – the level of beatitude, that the traditional schools could not. In attacking Pelagius, who asserted that man is born free of sin, Augustine insisted that we are born with original sin and that it is only through grace that we can be reconciled with God. Nonetheless, we each possess the free will to reject God's grace and hence turn our backs on our soul's salvation. This becomes an important argument in Augustine's theory of evil, which rightly still attracts our attention. Evil, he argued, cannot exist in its own right (thus rejecting the Manichean view); instead, evil is dependent on a turning away from God and absolute goodness. All sins are thus man-made and, accordingly, chosen by us. Tainted with the inherent wrongness of Adam and Eve's transgression, born of lust and perennially tempted by lust or the pleasures of the body in this world, the good Christian can keep his virtue by renouncing the lower drives or emotions in favour of an intellectual contemplation of the works of God. Man is born in pain and is born to die what Augustine called the first death: the death of the body; the second death is the soul's turning away from God, which is a much more grievous death than the first. There is no second chance for the aggrieved soul.

Critically, intention plays a vital role in securing goodness: in the *City of God*, Augustine reasoned that if a women were raped, she could remain morally innocent of the act unless her mind permitted some enjoyment: her soul would not be defiled so long as she stayed aloof and unconnected to the deed. This theme repeated in his views on sex – sex should be for procreation only and not for enjoyment. A man, he argues, should be able to perform his conjugal duty without relinquishing his mind to the base pleasure of the act. His comments may seem to us rather ironic, given that he (presumably) enjoyed the company of a mistress in his younger adulthood.

The gravest sin that turns men away from God is thus the force of lust. If the will is to remain pure, it should avoid all lustful temptation, and this, Augustine mused, was Rome's problem. While his thoughts on Rome are equivocal, he declared that Rome's power was dominated by the desire for domination, an evil that vexes and exhausts the human race. Rome's fall, which Augustine was living through, was not something that Christians ought to fret over; hence we can read Augustine as merging Stoical elements with the Scriptures in his desire to relieve the mind of secular, ephemeral worries such as the growth and decline of empires.

Writing during the collapse of the Roman Empire, Augustine patently wanted to present a vision of a new world order in which the theology of Christianity would encompass men's lives and souls. All that had gone before was defective in relation to the new order that could be produced: the fall of Rome as a secular empire could thus be replaced by the Christian empire of men's souls wedded to God's justice. The Romans and their subjects, he exhorted, must find salvation in Christ – that is, after all, all that should matter for the soul. Although he thought the city of Rome would survive the invasions and sackings of the Goths, it is important to recognize that:

> the earthly city will not be everlasting . . . the earthly city is generally divided against itself by litigation, by wars, by battles, by the pursuit of victories that bring death with them or at best are doomed to death. (Augustine, *City of God*, XV.4)

For what is the life of a city compared to the eternal life and hence, whatever policies a city pursues, they are to be put into the context of the infinitesimal brevity of life on earth?

In many respects, Augustine's theology turned Christian minds heavenward, and the ensuing Dark Ages were certainly characterized in intellectual circles as a focus on otherworldliness rather than on the mundane and scientific.

Being

Being what? The English verb is intransitive, so it can uphold 'I am' as a self-sufficient grammatical statement. Shakespeare's *Hamlet* naturally is often referred to: 'To be or not to be, that is the question', but he is just toying with living or not living, which is eminently obvious, but the philosopher can demand more. A stone is, yet it need not be (or have been). I am, and yet I need not be. I may die, yet my molecules will maintain an existence, yet they need not do. These things, including myself, seem contingent, that is, not necessary, but perhaps they demand something necessary for them to be contingent – they need existence, a deeper permanent continuity to their ephemeral combinations.

> The concept of 'Being' is rather the most obscure of all. (Heidegger, *Being and Time*, 'Introduction', 2)

Being plagues some philosophical minds. Some just accept that things are and demand that we then move on to ask what stuff are they made of – are they material or is everything immaterial? How do we know about what exists? To the latter, questioning that 'things are' seems an irrelevant annoyance: they just are, now begin thinking about them. This forms the subject area of ontology, the study of things that are. It is an area that has an enormously wide and subtle influence, for all the sciences deal with things and have to relate them. Ontologically, things can be first divided into kinds such as universals or particulars, concrete things or abstract things. Consider how biology works to group entities into species, genus, family, and so on to grasp what is meant here.

While considering kinds and their relationships seems a commonsensical move, questioning what is the nature of existence

seems either highly appropriate or a completely ludicrous endeavour. But the tradition of analysing being itself is long, beginning
with Parmenides ('nothing can come from nothing') and the
problems he invoked are taken up by Plato and recently gaining
attention in the works of Heidegger and Sartre and other Continental philosophers. For Sartre, there are two types of being, the being
of entities (things-in-themselves) and the being of consciousnesses
(things-for-themselves): human consciousness is essentially a nothingness – *pour-soi est rien.*

The analytical tradition focuses on the language of being: what
is meant, logically or grammatically speaking, by 'is'? In Anselm's
ontological proof of God's existence, being is attributed as an other
description, one that is necessary for the perfect being. Yet is being
a property? That would suggest it be a noun, a thing to be observed
and verified, but modern logicians often denounce such a move as
a result of semantic confusion or explaining how 'is' is used as
attributing certain characteristics: the thing is a strip (instantiation);
it is a thin, silvery strip (quality), it is magnesium (material), it is the
chemistry teacher's (identity). A thing exists in this instance, with
this quality and of this material, and is related to something else in
this regard; for something to exist, it must possess an identity, Quine
adds. That is, we encounter something and can then proceed to
describe it as best as we can.

While Continental and Analytical traditions seem divergent, here
they merely respect the division of being into entities and into
pervasive somethingness that has us puzzled after a few glasses of
wine.

Belief

'Do you believe in global warming?' is a question frequently put to
scientists and thinkers. What, though, is meant by belief?

Plato separates knowledge (knowledge is 'of what is'), ignorance (ignorance is 'of what is not') and belief (belief is of 'what is

and is not'). Platonic belief is a hybrid then, and he allows that belief, like knowledge, can provide good answers, but the proviso is there that one's belief may be mistaken, that is I can believe in things that do not exist. Augustine and Aquinas both saw belief as an act of understanding requiring an intellectual effort, which means that merely invoking belief is not sufficient: ideas and sensory data must be compared before belief can be produced – but it is still not the same as knowledge.

The bridge between knowledge and ignorance remains, with philosophers debating what kind of relationship can be established, if any, between knowing and the world which knowledge and belief are meant to represent. Externalists argue that the mental constructions that we make aim to refer to the external world, so if I pronounce a belief about global warming, it should have some connection to the reality to the phenomenon, a connection that can be verified. I may be proven wrong. Of course, it is difficult for most of us to verify the statistics and theories concerning such a vast and complex issue, so we can instead form a reliable belief. Reliabilism implies that the belief I form is based on what sensory data I can perceive and what conclusions I can draw using my own thinking, plus, we may add, what I can throw in from my comprehension of other people's theories and data. Belief on that argument requires actively thinking about something, as Augustine noted, in contrast to making a leap of faith and believing without any thought at all.

Internalists, however, claim that I do not need to refer my belief to the external world: it is sufficient that it should be justified by my own reflection. This allows my logical processes to be examined as to their validity (i.e. how did I get to my belief?), while others claim that even those processes need not be examinable – that is, to form a belief, I can make up my own epistemic laws. The latter certainly shifts belief into a new untouchable realm of subjectivity: 'I know the world is warming, because I've thought about it.' This may be said without any evidence or logic provided and is philosophically behind many a corny film: 'just believe, man'. This is closely connected to the influential argument of the nineteenth-century philosopher, Alexander Bain, who held that belief is that upon which one is prepared to act: Hume had noted that belief implies an emotional commitment, which is echoed in Bain's thinking, and together their thinking (or beliefs in belief!) provides an explanation of modern issue-based politics and the emotive calls to action: 'I believe the world is warming' implies now, 'I am prepared to do something about it.' The problem here is that belief can be, although not necessarily, far removed from the reality. And what exactly is to be done? What actions ought to be taken? Like the film image of Indiana Jones stepping out onto a chasm only to find a translucent bridge, belief can reflect an underlying reality; consider, in that regard, whether a suicide bomber killing civilians has a misguided sense of belief in means and ends. The externalist will demand that we connect belief not only to the reality of the world but also to the reality of what is effective – a harder task indeed.

Bentham, Jeremy (1748–1832)

Bentham was a political and social reformer whose utilitarian system demanded that all that we do in life and in politics be subject to a cost–benefit analysis: a belief that regularly attracts broadsides.

Born in London and educated in law at Oxford, he rejected a legal career preferring to challenge the prevailing conservative legal tradition in favour of a radical overhaul based on what he adumbrated as utilitarianism. The premise to his thinking is that we are subject to nature's great masters, pleasure and pain, and that we naturally pursue the former and avoid the latter. Conservative thinking placed importance on the role of tradition and implicatively traditional wisdom both in the rule of law and constitutional affairs and in the pursuit of the good life. Rights, according to the earlier legal theorist, Blackstone, were natural and enshrined in the evolved forms of law that were handed down: rights are 'nonsense upon stilts', cried Bentham, who asserted that all rights are dependent upon legislation, that is, they cannot be natural.

All aspects of life could be subjected to a utilitarian calculus of weighing the good against the bad, pleasure against pain, and while many predecessors would acknowledge the role of pleasure in motivating action, they would reject the apparent narrowness of Bentham's psychological assumptions: in equalizing all before him, he rejected any conception of higher goods, famously decreeing that push-pin (a billiards game) is just as good as poetry if it gives the player the same pleasure. Later (less egalitarian) utilitarians preferred to adjust his critique to allow for a greater weighting to be given to 'higher' pursuits, which in turn bridled those who preferred a more down to earth vision of utilitarian calculations. He also turned his 'felicific calculus' to the non-human animal kingdom:

> The question is not, Can they reason?, nor Can they talk? but, Can they suffer? (Bentham, *Introduction to the Principles of Morals and Legislation*)

Bentham's challenges were highly influential in reforming British government and its policies. Bentham was enthused with the idea of re-codifying the law, seeing it as a 'little game that I could play at alone'. Supporters uphold him as the fountainhead of a number of social and political reforms introduced in Britain in the early nineteenth century, but as is so often the case, the history is more complicated. While he preferred to keep government intervention to a minimum of protecting people from other people, followers, including John Stuart Mill, preferred active intervention, following the maxim of the 'greatest good for the greatest number'. Herein much trouble brewed, for what, the philosopher asks, is deemed to be good, and who are to constitute the greatest number? Is it merely a process of adding up people's preferences? But what if they are not commensurate? Then we have non-starter at the gate.

Weirdly, his preserved cadaver remains at University College for meetings.

Berkeley, George (1685–1753)

George Berkeley studied at Trinity College, Dublin and was ordained as an Anglican priest in 1710. He is principally known as a proponent of idealism, the theory that the world external to the senses does not exist.

Initially, in his *New Theory of Vision*, we read Berkeley expanding on Locke's work, examining how we come to know, for instance, the distance of objects as they fall on our senses. He rejected a Cartesian argument that distance is understandable through a geometrical analysis of the positioning of objects (arrayed in a three-dimensional matrix in front of us as it were) in favour of learning the customary connections and hence distances between objects. The Cartesian theory implies that distance is immediately understood, which Berkeley thoroughly rejected – the mind learns distances through experience of relating one object's distance to another's.

For Berkeley, the senses provide immediate access to the world but that vision presents a theory of discrete divisions of objects seen: the tower in the distance is physically shaped differently from the tower that I touch when I reach it – they are for Berkeley different objects. Locke may have balked at this extension of his empiricism, for it rejects his principle of how we learn gradually and by degrees; nonetheless, Berkeley's application forms the basis of the psychology of visual illusions, static depictions that alter with a volitional shift in focus (consider the prints of Escher). That a customary connection forms the relationship between distal objects is comprehensible, but Berkeley's next step in his *Principles of Human Knowledge* extends the implicit scepticism of all sensorial knowledge to the rejection of material objects existing externally to the mind.

Berkeley begins by rejecting the possibility of abstract knowledge on Lockean grounds, but whereas Locke developed a theory of abstracts as emerging from the application of sensory experience to increasing numbers of particulars (after seeing several cats, I produce an abstract of 'cat'), Berkeley insisted that this leap between the percept and the abstract is not possible. Therein he laid the seeds for the twentieth-century logical positivists who argued that all words must be reducible to referable objects. Ideas, Berkeley continued, must therefore remain as referents to particulars (and hence, he implies, Locke's *Essay* should not have expanded beyond Book II); nonetheless, the particular idea (e.g. a circle drawn on a blackboard) can be said to represent any circle one would particularly like to consider (so the mind need not have to name each and every single instance of particular types and thus fall into a debilitating requirement to identify every percept: this piece of grass is called George, this one is Günthe, that one's Belinda . . .). Abstracting though is not necessary for communicating, as all that can be learned about the properties of things – even geometrical entities – can be derived from particular examples.

Berkeley's next argument, which does not necessarily follow from his anti-abstractionism is that 'to be is to be perceived' or *esse est percipi* if you fancy the Latin. Berkeley was a strange example of an empiricist (someone who believes knowledge is gained via the senses), an idealist (the objects of the senses are absolutely mind-dependent) and an immaterialist (there are no material substances). If ideas are objects of knowledge, then there must be a knower – and that knower is mind or spirit. Minds, he accepts, are distinct from ideas (hence his empirical bent), but for something to be, it must be perceived, otherwise it cannot be (i.e. known). Something cannot both exist (independently of the mind) and not be known – that is logically inconsistent, he notes. My immaterial mind comes to know what exists as ideas, so why cannot we say that they come from extramental things, physical things, as common sense would demand? Physical things do not exist, Berkeley insists, but there is a factor that generates these impressions upon our mind, and this can only be God.

This is a reaction to Locke's theory of ideas: Locke assumes the existence of a material substratum, an underlying physicality to the universe of things, that cannot be logically held to exist. First, Locke's secondary qualities (colour, sound, taste, etc.) cannot be said to exist independently of a thing's primary qualities (solidity, extension, figure); if secondary qualities are necessarily dependent on primary qualities (the cat's smell is intrinsically part of the cat object I perceive) it is possible that they both intimately belong to a physical substratum. If such a material substratum exists, then materialism is acceptable and we may proceed accordingly along Lockean grounds. Berkeley however, rejected this existence as illogical: one cannot form an idea of the substratum (which Locke accepted, *Essay* II.xxiii), and so without an idea of the substratum, a Lockean is left trying to justify its existence, which Berkeley claims he cannot:

> But what reason can induce us to believe the existence of bodies without the mind, from what we can perceive, since the very patrons of matter themselves do not pretend, there is any necessary connexion betwixt them and our ideas? (Berkeley, *Principles of Human Knowledge*, § 18)

But his ultimate argument against matter is the thesis that we cannot consider any thought that we possess, and hence any sound, smell, touch, taste or sight, to exist unperceived. Lockeans retort that the action of perceiving necessarily presumes a percept (a thing perceived) and that Berkeley is asking for an impossible logical feat in demanding the Lockean to distinguish between ideas and things perceived; that they are separate entities must therefore be a given.

Berkeley prompted a defence of Locke's philosophy by David Hume but he also influenced the German idealism of Kant and Hegel.

Causation

Science parades various versions of causation: nuclear, chemical, mechanical, electromagnetic and biological. Logically, causation is about how an X causes a Y to happen. If X is said to cause Y, an inference is to suggest either that whenever X happens, Y must follow, or that in the absence of X, Y does not happen at all; which implies that if we find a Y, then an X must have happened. But when? And what is the mechanism between X and Y? It seems that the human mind demands that a mechanism be present, whether it is the 'hand of God' or physical force acting upon Y, but working out the logic becomes devilishly difficult.

Siena plays a note on the piano. What causes the note to form? We chase the thoughts: pressing the key; a flexing of muscle; a motor neuron signal from the brain . . . but then what? She replies that 'I pressed the key', but who is the 'I' – is it the prime mover here, centred, we could say, on the will to do something, perhaps firing neurons may be found in a small part of her brain. Moreover, without energy in the body, we know that she could not have performed her task, so we turn to the food she ate, the markets through which her food was delivered, the earth from which the food was drawn and we may alight upon the Sun blaring away enabling photosynthesis; we may continue our path and return to the Big Bang, some 15×10^9 years ago, and finally say, 'There! There is the cause of Siena pressing the key, for without the Big Bang, the conditions would not exist.'

Yet such a trip, while valid, is hardly philosophically exciting; it provides too simple an answer to the reason why a note was heard: Siena is after all an intermediary between the Big Bang and the note! So we may prefer to dwell on the 'I' and emphasize how it acts to disrupt the physical flow of universal energy to divert it in a new direction: that is what can make us sit up and think harder. Avoiding physical determinism, Kant stresses that our minds necessarily invoke causation – a useful product of evolution we might accept, but which leaves us intimately understanding the universe as predetermined regardless of whether the universe is so predetermined.

Hume, though, rejects the concept completely: cause is merely an association that our minds place on successive events – there is no mechanism, as such, merely the connection between X and Y that we concoct by observing regular correlations between events. We invent cause: when a key is struck, a note is played. But not always – a certain amount of force is necessary. Yet is that not dependent on previous experiences? It may not happen tomorrow.

If our explanation becomes predictive, so much the better for us, but that may not provide a strong scientific argument – it just may happen that each time Ezekiel prays for rain, it rains (he may be good at reading the subtle signs for impending rain!). This encourages some to consider causation in terms of probability, with there being no certainty. Siena, however, may not be content with her note being a probable; she refers back to her willing the key to be pressed and the certainty of a note emanating from the piano as the hammer strikes the string. She prefers, as Mises argued, that in the human realm causation rests with her and goes no further.

Conscience

Raskalnikov in Dostoevsky's *Crime and Punishment* commits the perfect crime, but then is plagued by his conscience. Why? What reason could there be for dwelling on that which is now history and which belongs to another space-time? St Augustine encouraged us to do as we will, so why should we then recall what we have done, dwell on our actions and feel remorse?

> If only fate had granted him remorse, scalding remorse, harrowing the heart and driving sleep away, such remorse as tortured men into dreaming of the rope or deep still water! Oh, he would have welcomed it gladly! Tears and suffering – they, after all, are also life. But he did not feel remorse for his crime. (Dostoyevsky, *Crime and Punishment*, 520)

Joseph Butler described conscience as 'a superior principle of reflection . . . which passes judgment upon himself . . . pronounces some actions to be in themselves just, right, good' (*Five Sermons*, II.8). Raskalnikov cannot help but judge his deed; however, he is unable to unleash upon himself the pent up demand that could permit a catharsis and redemption, because redemption is impossible. For Butler, the content of conscience is universal and embraces justice, veracity, regard to the common good. Yet Locke, writing earlier, was quick to challenge any innate predisposition in conscience to form universally recognizable principles of conduct, an argument picked up by Adam Smith, who explained conscience as a psychologically resident impartial spectator, sitting in judgement of one's acts and formed by one's background: thus approbation and condemnation would pick up parochial flavourings.

The internal discord that is generated in the mind and which produces concurrent emotional distress and which together can produce illness is a peculiar habit indeed. This prompts those who suffer from a bad conscience to ask what it is and wonder about those who do not similarly suffer that they must be lacking a conscience for some reason that keeps them below the humane level. If Butler is right, theologians may claim that God implants a conscience in each of us: inscribed on the walls of our heart are the commandments to do good and avoid evil, so when we sin against them, our conscience is afflicted. It is a cogent theory and one that sustains much religious conviction. Secularists have replaced God with Nature – that Nature implants moral knowledge as disposi- tions that have evolved and emerged in our species over thousands of years.

However, Locke's thesis is rather damning of the objectivity of conscience: 'some men, with the same bent of conscience, prose- cute what others avoid' (*Essay*, I.iii.8). May there, however, be a common disposition to conscientious reflection, regardless of its content? But some appear to be without conscience: those who murder or who call for murder without signs of remorse. It becomes a psychological question concerning the extent of authentic remorselessness, yet if a lack of conscience does exist (absolutely?) then perhaps the absence could be called pathological, a rare illness producing an 'inward deformity' as Shaftesbury puts it – he becomes twisted and sick. Perhaps he is a genetic throwback.

Nonetheless, Locke's theory is also malleable: just because I do not lift a finger for your cause does not mean that I am without conscience for other causes – my lack of interest does not justify my prosecution; whereas, for those who hold conscience to be innate and its content universal, my prosecution would be a matter of course.

Consciousness

When does a living entity become conscious, or, when does inani- mate matter become conscious? And if an entity is held to be con- scious, does that necessarily imply that the entity be self-conscious, or can something be conscious without being conscious of itself, for consciousness generally implies being able to be aware of surroundings?

It can be argued that the incidence of consciousness is a scien- tific question, one invoking a reply to a set of criteria: if this and that, and so on, then consciousness; but the games begin when we try to define the criteria.

Your own consciousness seems a given: you assume that you possess an awareness of a world around you and a world within you – your dreams and memories and so you may accept that you possess a self. But if you are asked to perceive your consciousness in the same manner as we ask you to look at this book, logic seems to fly into a spin – can you be aware of awareness? Perhaps, only through self-awareness of watching your actions from within or through others' reactions to you.

Being conscious of an external world implies a very broad category of living beings, for awareness of the external world can be described of many creatures – even single cells are conscious in that regard, for they respond to the environment and deal with sustenance and invaders analogously to people. To some it may seem untenable to call a cell conscious when its actions are reducible to chemical and physical processes, although vitalists would reject such a move; yet if there is a branch in the great evolutionary tree of life along which 'conscious' entities emerge, it must still be asked what constitutes the tripping over from being merely chemically reactive to being conscious? Is it a unification of processes that begin to possess purpose rather than function, or the introduction of soul – and hence another kettle of fish?

Indubitably, increasingly complicated animals exhibit a growing consciousness of surroundings and of past associations. A horse recognizes its rider, but does a plant recognize the hand that feeds it, even though talking to plants apparently encourages their growth? In death, a body loses the personality that gave it its character – consciousness is seemingly lost for good; implicitly, we accept consciousness as unique and fragile and are thus drawn to other living entities when we are alone in a solidarity with consciousness, but does that mean that all consciousnesses are One, in a mystical sense of a transcendental spirit uniting us all? Logically, that does not have to follow – consciousnesses can still be unique and independent.

Ethically, the philosophy of consciousness treads into some difficult areas. Ethicists may refer to the horizon of self-consciousness as
defining moral personhood: once self-consciousness is attained,
then the entity becomes morally significant – that is, it (dolphins or
the great apes) gains either personhood or quasi-personhood and
according to some thereby they deserve similar moral protection to
that which is given to humans. On the other hand, newborn babies
can hardly be said to be self-conscious, so do they lose our moral
recognition? If a person loses consciousness, do they thereby lose
their usual protection and may be left to die or life-support machines
be switched off?

Recently (2007), a comatose man's consciousness was 'reawak-
ened' by electrical impulses fired into his thalamus, which underlines the materialist vision of the mind or consciousness depending
upon the physical. But when we consider consciousness from the
impartial view that the traditional scientific method demands, we
lose our footing: consciousness remains embedded in a subjective
vision inaccessible to all others – so not only will you never know
what it is to be a bat (Nagel), you'll never know what it is like to
be me.

Continental philosophy

'Continental philosophy' is a broad brush tarring many philosophers
on the European continent with the same intellectual lineage and
attitude. It is a term often used by critics of European thinking
that they see as stemming from Hegel and Marx and firing phenomenology, existentialism, critical theory, structuralism and poststructuralism. While quite disparate, there is perceived to be a
shared suspicion of the analytical tradition that developed in
England under Russell, as well as a shared vision of politics – usually
being highly critical of economics, capitalism, bourgeois institutions
and morality.

Historically, prior to the rise of nationalism in the eighteenth and nineteenth centuries, intellectuals typically were versed in the *lingua franca* of Latin and hence could keep abreast of each others' work. Nationalism acted to demote Latin in favour of the local language, which thereby also acted to isolate (usually temporarily) innovations and thought. After the First World War, the split between the English speaking world and Continental philosophy widened until interest was slowly rekindled in phenomenology and the works of Sartre and Heidegger. Translation naturally ensures that the bridges between the two traditions have not been completely lost, and as with any collective, the geographical stereotyping possesses some loose truths about membership: ideas do not respect political boundaries and so there are analytical Europeans and Continental philosophers around the world. In time, scholars may look upon the division as a temporary philosophical hiatus akin to the loss of the Greek texts after the fall of Rome.

Crime and punishment

'Crime' is a word that connotes a transgression having taken place, but that implies that there is a something to be transgressed and so we must look more closely at what is being referred to.

If someone steals, the presumption is that theft is wrong because there are private property arrangements that forbid or limit what can be done with each other's property. Take the property rights away and theft disappears – if all own everything, then nothing can be stolen. Similarly with life – why is killing deemed wrong? One reason is that an individual's life is unique and must be respected and supported morally and perhaps economically too – but that is a particular philosophy emanating from humanist elements in the major religions and secular philosophies, and, if we are immersed in the assumption culturally, we need to make a concerted effort to shift focus to consider an alternative perspective.

Imagine a world in which a person's life was not held as sacrosanct and inviolable. It's not hard to do – most of the present and of human history is replete with this vision: from slavery to social engineering and war, we look upon people being used, killed, stolen from, defrauded, tortured, regulated, experimented on and cajoled into doing things that they would not willingly do. Arguably, the humanist vision has always been a minority vision in contrast to ideologies justifying the abuse and violation of others. If you are a humanist, such acts are infringements, but of what? A person has a right to life, the humanist argues, but what is a right? Is it something ontological and identifiable, or is it a logically necessary description of a human (i.e. you're human, therefore you have this right), or is it something conditional and state or socially defined? If it is an ontological right, a self-evident concept perhaps, then it is necessarily criminal to attack another person; if on the other hand, it is a conditional right, conditionality implies that the 'right' is in effect a mere privilege. Yet privileges are fragile in that they can be removed either by cultural and social changes or by legislation: thus what was a crime yesterday is not a crime today.

If a crime has been committed the criminal should be punished. But why? When the wrong has already been committed, what good can result from imposing another form of violence against the perpetrator? Why reach back into the past of things-gone to enact a violence today? Many warring communities have engaged in endemic and cyclical warfare because of historical transgressions and we can ask – where does it get them? A typical response is that the criminal must 'pay' for his action, but why? Because he has committed an offence and needs to redress the situation – in violating another's life or property or committing an act deemed socially or by the state to be wrong, a punishment must be imposed.

Currently in Western countries, the exaction is demanded from the state on behalf of the victim, but critics argue that that skews incentives regarding both criminal behaviour and punishment, for the victim remains impoverished financially or physically, while the criminal loses time, money, or even life to a third party, not the one offended; according to libertarian critics such as Rothbard, the right of punishment belongs to the victim (or immediate family or estate) not the state, and the victim may forgive the criminal, demand payment or exact a physical punishment in retribution tempered by proportionality.

But who decides what is proportional in this regard? If values are objective entities that allow us to ascertain the value of a child's life or that of a car, then an adjudicating representative may impose a fine or punishment deemed proportional to the damage inflicted. But if values are subjective entities, this poses intricate problems – sentimental value outstrips the value that another may put on my child's life, for instance. That is often why we are deeply affected by crimes against ourselves rather than against others: if values were objective, we would all become angry at the loss of another's property or life as if it were ours (because it would be ours); but because it is not, we acquiesce with a quiet lament for their suffering.

There is an absurdity in disproportional punishment – taking the life of a criminal for his theft of a chocolate bar, but that does not undermine philosophers asserting a justification for disproportional punishment should it deter the criminal or others with similar intent. If a severe punishment works, then a utilitarian could justify imposing a disproportionate sentence to secure a world with less crime in it.

But can we be sure that punishment actually deters? With respect to capital punishment, Mill noted:

> We partly know who those are whom it has not deterred; but who is there who knows whom it has deterred, or how many human beings it has saved who would have lived to be murderers if that awful association had not been thrown round the idea of murder from their earliest infancy? (Mill, 'Speech', 100)

Mill's argument can be inverted, for it is based on the assumption that deterrence has worked – but no evidence could actually support the theory: murders still take place where capital punishment is permitted. Mill would retort that the numbers would have been higher. Whether deterrence works or not cannot be verified, nor can it really be falsified. Unless there are restrictive safeguards, the utilitarian philosophy is also not averse to punishing the innocent in order to deter further wrong-doing – the Roman army would kill every tenth man should any member break its laws; a mob may be satiated in its desire for blood by an innocent. But those who believe in the sanctity of innocence cannot support such moves – a 10per cent or even 0.0001 per cent rate of sacrifice in society to secure peace and order still represents a 100 per cent violation for the innocent killed.

The existence of capital or corporal punishment may also act to deaden sympathy towards the sanctity of life and may act to increase crime through the dehumanization of others as evinced in capital or corporal punishment. The killing of another, even if justifiable according to retributive and utilitarian principles, is so shameful or disrespectful to humanity that we should, Tolstoy encourages, eschew it completely in favour of non-physical forms of punishment: forgiving, shaming the criminal or re-educating him to live a better life.

Realists (i.e. those who think others' opinions are woolly ideals) reject such ambitions as meaningless, but striking evidence can be uncovered of criminals altering their predatory thinking in various communities, using non-violent approaches to punishment both with children and adults as well as the methods of Monty Roberts and similar teachers applied to animals.

Death

Death is ostensibly the ultimate fate of all living creatures. It is often described as The End, but what is ended? Philosophers differ on what the event implies, the gross problem being a lack of evidence

to support any theory: is it an ultimate end or just part of a process –
a middle, or even the beginning of a new adventure? From a physi-
ological perspective, death is the cessation of bodily functions – they
fail to work and hence fail to sustain the life of the organism, and
so the body's cells break down and begin eating each other. Failure
can be precipitated by a multitude of factors of course from old age
to trauma, but since life is so extraordinary in so many respects, our
thoughts seem at times unwilling to accept that death would be
annihilation of all that we consider alive in ourselves – no matter
how many have died around us and before us, it is weird and disconcerting to imagine one's own dissolution.

Thinking of death brings to the fore our thoughts on life. When
a loved one perishes, our mind concentrates on what has happened
to her, where she may be said to be now, but also on what her life
meant – its value, its connections with us and others, what she has
left in terms of deeds and reputation. If we genuinely face the possibility of death (as going into an accident or engaging in military
action, say), the mind sharpens into a fearful focus or into a resig-
nation to the fates. Some deaths can be 'beautiful', like the man
who free-fell off the World Trade Tower on 9/11; others can be
'heroic' or 'tragic' or even 'authentic' in the sense (as Heidegger
puts it) that we can sincerely and resolutely acknowledge that we
are moving ineluctably towards death (we can ignore that fact).
Survival encourages reflection which can prompt a reorganization
of values, but also a thinking about the nature of life and its
philosophical status.

In viewing a dead person most of us would describe that something is now missing that was there before, an energy or vitality
perhaps, or for others the spirit or the soul which is assumed to
either have 'left' the body or to have diminished with the dimming
of the body's functions. For the materialist, the body and mind are
of the same substance (matter), and the death of the one logically
necessitates the death of the other – of body and mind; for dualists
though, who see the body as material and the mind as immaterial,

the death of the one is not necessarily connected with the death of the other, an inference which usually holds that when the body dies, the mind/spirit/soul persists. Not all dualists agree with the argument, for it is perfectly consistent to claim that the fate of the immaterial mind is somehow connected with the fate of the carrier's body: proving how often requires another mechanism such as an intervening deity who separately ensures the death of the mind with that of the body. More popular, however, has been the claim that the soul is able to survive the death of the body – that it enters an immaterial realm and, in the conjectures of some, is then to be judged according to its deeds or to be recycled into another body.

The growth of Western medicine has shifted thinking on death for many people who have also moved away from theological visions of life and the universe. Atheistic secular philosophy rejects the Other World of angels and God(s) and emphasizes that life is a fortunate but haphazard construction of chemical elements that form together through the useful function of DNA replication to produce cells, tissues, organs, organ systems and the organism that you are. Yet the reductionist tendencies of some medical philosophers are not accepted by others, who, while agreeing with the physical constituency of life also posit a life force that animates the entity – a force that is seemingly so obvious to us the conscious living for the essence of our vitality, which chases life and flees from death. That does not logically imply that the extraordinary force of living material generating a soul that can outlive its physical foundation, for, despite the complexity of sentience, it may merely dwindle with the failing energy captured in the trillions of cells in the body.

An entertaining prospect (for some, that is) is the possibility for the dying to recharge themselves by body swapping: as your physical body begins to deteriorate, the contents of your mind are uploaded into another body (or computer drive) – a donated body or a newly cloned body from your own DNA. Such science fiction provides a wonderful source of testing not just for our imaginations but also for our thoughts concerning the nature of life and death. Could we stomach the absence of death? The youthful mind cries out, 'Yes!' but the older mind reflects upon interminable shopping trips, comedy reruns, friends' marriages and break-ups, and it may begin to look upon death and annihilation as a natural inevitability to be welcomed rather than feared. The idea of saving your memories (and self perhaps) electronically does imply that thoughts not only have a physical basis (neurons) but also are physical – which takes us to the philosophy of mind.

Descartes, René (1596–1650)

René Descartes was brought up by Jesuits; he joined the army, discovered philosophy, left the army, or army and wrote up a series of meditations that changed philosophy's perspective; he died of pneumonia from tutoring the Queen of Sweden philosophy in the early hours of the morning. Let that be a warning to us all.

He is considered the initiating thinker behind modern philosophy. Historians like to have some starting point but we do return to him frequently not just for the issues that he pondered but also to gain a sense of the philosophical adventure upon which he embarked: a sincere attempt to provide epistemological certainty, in other words, to say that he knows that other things exist.

What initially appealed to Descartes's mind was the certainty that mathematics provided, and turning its logical attractiveness to philosophy he sought to haul contemporary philosophy (as he saw it) out of its scholastic morass. Secondly, the rediscovery of the Ancient Greek and Roman texts had encouraged a return to scepticism, and since scepticism may lead to nihilist or solipsist conclusions, which dogmatists of all colours find repugnant or troubling, a reaction ensued which some thinkers sought to deal with by working out a secure foundation upon which to build a philosophical edifice. Ironically in his fervour to reject scepticism, some of his arguments, which push the sceptic's arguments to extremes, have become favourite questions for sceptics, for they believe that Descartes did not produce the edifice to justify systematic philosophizing.

Let us begin with his method of doubting. In a famous sequence of doubting arguments, Descartes, sitting by his fireplace, as I am now, mused upon the sceptical attitude by doubting the validity of his senses: he began to doubt the existence of the room around him drawing his doubts onto the existence of his very body. Empiricists are philosophers who argue for the validity of the senses, but Descartes emphasized that the senses can be mistaken, so they do not provide a reliable guide. Therefore sensory evidence should be rejected if we are to found a cogent base. Descartes's procedure is a useful tact at any time: how do I *know* that the room that I am in, and whose existence that I normally would take for granted, is something that I can actually justify? Is it truly and undeniably self-evident? His motive, remember, was to test the sceptical attitude to its extremes to see what remained, so the possibility of *any* doubt became sufficient to cast knowledge down and to start again.

Indeed as an exercise, forcing a theory into its logical extremities is useful, for often what is implied in a theory easily begins to tend towards its ultimate rendition under different thinkers or times – we relax into our implications. And Descartes was curious as to what would remain of knowledge when the sceptic's theory was extended. Initially, he was content to acknowledge that it would be foolish to doubt the existence of the fire and of his own body, but what, he asked, if he was dreaming? Could the sceptic reply to the conjecture that all life is a dream? It would seem a difficult one to extricate a reply; however, in dreams we encounter representations of things and people, whose origin can only be reality. But this move does not quite resolve the underlying sceptical thrust, for why should our waking 'reality' be a reality as we assume it to be and not some other form of dream? There are many replies at this stage, but pushing the dream further, Descartes continued to ask what if his entire life and all of his thoughts existed in a demon's dream (or in modern parlance, the product of some clever software – that *we* are 'the Sims')? At this point, he realized that the constant element that he encountered throughout his experiment in scepticism was himself – he was imagining and thinking these things through and therefore, because he thinks, he, at least, must exist. This is the origin of philosophy's most famous quotation, 'I think, therefore I am.'

Yet the *cogito* as it is known (Latin for 'I think') is not sufficient, for Descartes realized that if knowledge and existence depended on the thinking 'I', only his world could be at all proven, and he was keen to avoid the solipsist conclusion that would rid the universe of everything except himself – and thereby implicitly put himself into the position of God (not a good step in religiously sensitive times). So he invoked the existence of God as a necessary element to secure the validity of his knowledge of the world. Descartes was able to realize that he himself existed but he was also able to realize that a perfect being must also exist: the fact that he could imagine the existence of such a perfect being was sufficient, for Descartes, to accept that God exists – for only a perfect being could implant in his mind the idea of something much larger (or ideal) than what he himself could imagine. Descartes also employed the ontological argument as a backup: God is perfection, and perfection implies existing, so God must exist. In Descartes's system, the certainty of God's existence was required to underline the validity of thinking, otherwise solipsism triumphs. However, it was Descartes's reasoning that brought him to the arguments for God's existence, so how could he be sure that his reasoning was correct? This produced what is known as the 'Cartesian circle' – a circular argument is one whose terms and conclusions pursue each other, none of them being justified from outside of the circle, which is rather dizzying, particularly for solipsists.

Descartes caught the problem and tried to extricate himself from the cycle by trying to anchor some basic conceptions as being so self-evident (or axiomatic) that their rejection would be foolish. His answer has not satisfied all, although we do meet an expansion of this move in Kant's theory of the mind's categories. Nonetheless, for Descartes, the combined certainty of his own existence and that of God's provided him with an 'intuitive' justification for proceeding epistemologically. Believing that he had provided a cosy pair of premises from which to begin thinking (the *cogito* and God), Descartes now allowed the senses back in to provide evidence of what we encounter: observation of the extramental world is, after all, highly useful for not doing injury to oneself.

In proceeding from the justifiable premises, Descartes argued, scientific procedure is to be unified by one method – the quantitative method. All entities and their relations can be measured and plotted – indeed, Descartes invented coordinate graphs after watching a fly crossing a ceiling while he lay in bed. Quantitative analysis gave science an impetus from which it is still influenced – for good and ill: critics complain that Cartesian reductionism has led to an overuse of mathematical methods and statistical analyses, particularly in the social and medical sciences in which qualitative relationships also play important roles. Accordingly, Descartes is called a rationalist, one who believes that *a priori* reasoning provides the surest method of unfolding knowledge and, for many attracted to rationalism, mathematics provides the best method – its procedure of working from a set of axioms to increasingly complex conclusions should be mimicked by other disciplines. However, it must be noted that like many philosophers, Descartes should not be readily boxed – in much of his writing, a commonsensical emphasis on the senses is evident.

Nevertheless, the aim is to reduce the sciences to follow the mathematic method and the reason for this is based on his argument that all physical entities must possess extension (into the three dimensions) and thus can be mapped geometrically and their relationships, and so on be described mathematically. But since all things possess extension (and thus can be measured and mapped), he could not logically accept the existence of nothingness – of the void. Except in the case of his own mind.

In thinking, Descartes reasoned that his own existence could be separated from his body, which was a useful conclusion for one who also accepts the existence of God and the Catholic doctrine on the immortality of the soul. Despite his free-ranging meditations, one gets the impression of a tainted conclusion, for there is a sudden leap to the immateriality of the soul, something which is highly contestable even on his own premises. The argument generated Descartes's mind/body dualism, which attracted much contemporary and present commentary.

In evaluating his thinking self, Descartes believed it self-evident that it did not possess extension as such, that it is immaterial, yet happily he thought it connected to the physicality of his body. The body exists materially, taking up space, moving through space with its soul intact. But why should it be that the mind is self-evidently immaterial? Intuitively so, he believed. The mind is clearly one and entire, unlike the body, which can lose parts and so be separated; it is, however, distinct from the body and therefore separable from it, an argument which permitted Descartes to return to theological conclusions concerning the immortality of the soul. Yet the underlying difficulties are not hard to envisage: how does my soul not slip out of my body whenever I move? Allow me the Cartesian chat-up line, 'Why don't I just glide out now and join your body?' More pertinently though, how does my immaterial self activate my material body into action?

The duality of mind/body is philosophically juicy and Descartes's thoughts have motivated much discussion and promoted a division of the subject of mind into various camps: interactionists believe that mind and body are distinct yet interact (as Descartes practically did); strict dualists, who assert the division cannot produce any connection, which produces interesting thoughts on how a nervous impulse is thereby registered in the mind; materialists, who reject the mind as immaterial; and idealists, who reject the mind as material.

While Descartes was supportive of anatomical research into the human body and fascinated by Harvey's work on the heart, he was dismissive of other scientific theories which were later to gain intellectual and scientific support. He fell back on scholastic reasoning rather than empirical study. He rejected, for instance, the possibility of a vacuum and the existence of atoms (for God could always divide what we think as indivisible, otherwise we are imposing a constraint on His omnipotence); he argued that the heavens and earth were of the same matter and thus other worlds could not exist (for this matter already is assumed to take up the whole universe, leaving nothing left for other worlds). Such arguments may seem strange to the modern thinker, but while we acknowledge that Descartes as the founder of modern philosophy, we must also remember that he was immersed in the scholastic traditions and explicitly refers to that tradition:

> I have nevertheless made use of no principle which has not been approved by Aristotle and by all the other philosophers of every time. (Descartes, *Principles of Philosophy*, 331)

With that caveat, Descartes's writings remain an essential component of the modern philosophical canon, partly for some of the conundrums he incidentally created, partly for the positive contributions to a systematic theory of philosophy, but assuredly for the style of his *Meditations* – a personal adventure into how his mind deals with knowledge.

Determinism

Determinism is the view that every event has a prior cause. This seemingly simplistic sounding theory creates huge intellectual fallout.

Does it mean that every event that happens, such as a thought, must have some antecedent causal condition to it? That has been read to imply that people cannot possibly have free will: that whatever they do has prior causation and thus that they must be tied to it, and similarly, any physical event that is observed must be understood as having a prior cause or set of causes: the house is ablaze, there must be a cause. Presently, you cannot help reading this. Everything that went before necessitates you in this action, even if you now put the book down.

As often with philosophy, imprecise language can be a barrier to understanding. Determinism must be separated from fatalism, which adds to the logic of causality the complete ineffectiveness of human choice in the series of unfolding events that surround and are thrust upon us; it must also be distinguished from predestination which includes in its formulation of causation another agent such as God who determines what our actions will be. While often contrasted with free will, the nuances are too subtle for them to be so simply opposed, for determinism can admit the play of human choice and allow that choice to enter the great matrix of events as acts.

Dualism

Duality describes an entity or problem that divides into seemingly incompatible realms, for instance mind and body, good and evil, form and content, freedom and determinism, or being and becoming. In each, the one side is said to exist exclusively of the other, which implies that both may pursue an independent existence that proponents may expand on.

Dualism opposes monism (an entertaining dichotomy to think about!), which is the argument that all entities and issues that philosophers concoct are reducible to a single description, such as good and evil are reduced to moral causes, being and becoming to existence, mind and body to mind-body. Monists assert 'Ockham's razor' to remove extraneous arguments: why clutter thought with unnecessary elements? Yet many thinkers reject monism as not serving comprehension: at times it is pertinent to examine an extreme form of an issue in order to gain a grasp of its character and nature – for example, comparing evil with good or removing the mind from the body. Dualists however underline that the separation is ontologically valid in itself and not just for intellectual purposes: mind *is* radically different from the body. The mind thinks, the body does not, it is argued – the mind is immaterial, the body material. But then why should we stop at a duality: are there not some subjects that warrant a pluralistic division?

Consider the mind and body. Dualists such as Plato, Descartes and Leibniz, stress that the mind is an immaterial object, which may or may not live eternally. If it is immaterial, it is not beholden to remain in the same body for any duration – my mind could vacate this body and enjoy a new vehicle, perhaps your body. That this does not happen does not disappoint the dualist: thought, they remind us, is mental and while apparently connected to physical brain states, it is impossible to perceive your thought of a 60-foot elephant running amok in your images of vast savannahs and picnics with T. S. Eliot: prod and poke as they may, neuroscientists cannot uncover the image you have. So if thought is apparently without solidity, where does it occur? In an immaterial mind, the dualist replies, hence the distinction made between mind and body. But how can an immaterial mind affect a material body? This has proved troublesome for dualists, for they either present concessions to the materialist and assert a theory that the mind does interact with the body (interactionists) or they remain steadfastly dualistic but posit the ability to bridge the divide in the hand of God. Others (epiphenomenalists) reject any interaction and merely have the mind as a depository of experiences and incapable of causing bodily movement, which is self-regulating by itself.

Elsewhere, Hegel believed that the inherent momentum that dualities possess will necessarily be overcome – in opposing one another, a synthesis forms from which a new form emerges, all eventually reducing to a single entity – the absolute spirit.

Education

It could be said that philosophy is education and that a philosophy of education is rather oxymoronic: philosophy is the study of wisdom, which is, one would hope, intrinsically educative. Yet there is plainly a set of approaches that emerge from education concerning education's function, purpose, ethos, breadth, duration and assumptions concerning knowledge and its use. These in turn are dependent upon prior philosophical preconceptions.

> The unexamined life is not worth living. (Plato's Socrates, *Apology*, 38a)

Socrates argued that the job of a teacher is to tease knowledge from the pupil's mind, for knowledge is held by the soul, which, between lives knows all that there is to know, but when reborn into a person the body restrains the mind from knowing. This implies that teaching involves generating experiences for the pupil to re-invoke understanding. In contrast, empiricists such as Locke, reject innate ideas in favour of all knowledge being the result of experience. But in itself, this would not seem sufficient, for the mind has to engage to begin thinking about what is perceived – knowing *that* something is, knowing *how* it works, then knowing *what* to do with it.

Politically, education is often restricted by those who would prefer to control an obedient and uncritical population, which is why education has also been seen as a means to empower people politically for various ends. However, once education becomes politicized for whatever purpose, it is difficult to sustain or to justify teaching pupils to be critical, for critical thinking can be levelled at governing and revolutionary processes. To what end are children to be taught? To become obedient servants of the Church or State (Luther), good citizens (Rousseau), virtuous individuals (Locke) or to seek perfection?

Educational principles are also derived from thoughts on human nature. If we assume that abilities are fixed (according to genetic inheritance, say), then education becomes framed; if we assume abilities are flexible, then education becomes flexible and open-ended. Educationalists consider the range of expectations governing a pupil's potential and seek to work with them or encourage adaptation. Sometimes, educationalists have sought to diminish those expectations by demeaning the human potential that they are implicitly aware of: the child is sinful; learning is morally or politically dangerous; curiosity is culturally destabilizing. Otherwise, some hold that education is morally less important than enjoying the hedonistic pleasures of life or that beyond the basics any intellectual thinking becomes useless or dangerous.

Naturally, if we believe education to be the lever by which we raise ourselves to greater heights such implications are troublesome: Aristotle argued that the pursuit of the intellect was the highest form of life that a man could achieve, and that the educated differs from the uneducated as much the living differs from the dead.

Egoism

Egoism entails that the self is either the motivating moral force and is, or should be, the end of moral action; it is distinguishable from *egotism*, a psychological overevaluation of one's importance or affairs (akin to nationalism). That is, egoism is divisible into a positive and normative ethic. The positive ethic conceives egoism as a *factual* description: people are motivated by their own interests and desires and cannot be described otherwise. Whereas the normative egoist ethic proposes that people should be so motivated, regardless of what presently motivates their behaviour.

Some may reject that the individual has any choice claiming that a person's acts are determined by prior events which make choice illusory. Nevertheless, if an element of choice is permitted against the great causal impetus, it follows that a person possesses some control over her next action, and therefore we may inquire as to whether she should choose a self- or other-oriented action. That is, we can ask whether she should pursue her own interests or should she reject self-interest and pursue others' interests, and to what extent is other-regarding acts morally legitimate or applaudable compared to self-regarding acts.

At first glance, psychological egoism does not get far philosophically speaking: it asserts that all our actions are self-oriented and motivated, which, if true, merely describes a fact about the world such as gravity is 9.8 m/s^2. All actions that are described as altruistic or self-sacrificing have their veils removed to show underlying self-oriented behaviour: Josh gave money to the beggar to remove his feelings of guilt; Harriet threw herself into the river to save the drowning boy because she could not conscientiously live with herself afterwards had she not attempted a rescue. Charity and sacrifice may thus be held as selfish acts. Yet even with such a critical or realistic depiction of motivation, grand theories can be wrought: Hobbes, for instance, sought to justify a strong government on the basis that selfish behaviour would need curtailing; Mandeville and more famously Adam Smith argued that self-seeking behaviour actually led to social benefits.

Opponents exploit counterfactual evidence to criticize this theory – surely, a host of evidence supports altruistic or dutiful actions that cannot be said to engage the self-interest of the agent, especially if the agent loses precious values or even dies? But what may

count as counterfactual evidence becomes an intricate issue and
one that is difficult to resolve: how do we know whether at the
moment of supreme sacrifice, a soldier was not thinking of himself
(his reputation for instance, or his desire to meet his maker)? Private
intentions remain private. The problem arises whether any evidence
can actually refute psychological egoism – if no refutation is possible, then it is a closed theory, resting on the status of an assumption: neither verifiable nor falsifiable.

At this point, do we flip a coin to see if we should be psychological egoists or psychological altruists? Is there any chance of
considering either position (and less dualistic alternatives) scientifically? Motivations are difficult to authenticate, so perhaps matters
are confused by considering intimate as well as behavioural evidence: why not just look at what people do? Hume offers six
rebuttals of psychological egoism (which he calls the 'selfish hypothesis'): it opposes moral sentiments that engage in a concern and
motivation for others such as love, friendship, compassion and
gratitude; it attempts to reduce motivation to a single cause, which
is a 'fruitless' task – the 'love of *simplicity* . . . has been the source
of much false reasoning in philosophy'; evidently animals act benev-
olently towards one another, and if it is admitted that animals can
act altruistically, then how can it be denied in humans? Fourthly, the
concepts of benevolence cannot be meaningless – sometimes the
agent obviously does not have a personal interest in the fortune of
another, yet will wish him well. Fifthly, we have prior motivations to
self-interest; we may have, for example, a predisposition towards
vanity, fame or vengeance that transcends any benefit to the
agent. Finally, even if psychological egoism were true, there are a
sufficient number of dispositions to generate a wide possibility of
moral actions, allowing one person to be called vicious and another
humane, and the latter is to be preferred over the former.

When we step beyond a descriptive theory of human nature,
we enter the realm of normative egoism, of what one ought to

do. Normative egoists argue that it is right to pursue one's own interests, for different reasons of course. Rand presents a strong absolutist defence of rational egoism – that the individual possesses a right to her life and morality should reflect what is in her interests *qua* rational being (rather than a whimsical, emotional being, whom she views as the antithesis of a rationally minded egoist). Others argue on consequentialist principles that we should act self-interestedly because in doing so, we do help our fellow men more than if we were trying to help them, such is what economics and history could be said to explain ('the path to hell is paved with good intentions').

Empiricism

The empiricist rejects any possibility of innate knowledge – all knowledge that we gain is based on what we perceive with our sense so what our minds are working with when we make scientific conjectures, create imaginative stories and comprehend what is around us, is gained absolutely from the senses.

Several problems immediately come to the fore: what guarantee is there that when I perceive an object in front of me I possess knowledge of it? Locke argued that the object impresses itself upon my senses and that impression is the basis of the idea that I have of the object, but as Berkeley pointed out, such an argument does not require the existence of independent objects in the universe, merely a universe of ideas – Berkeley, was a unique empiricist who rejected the existence of mind-independent objects but who allowed the thesis that what the mind knows does come from ideas it experiences: the leverage being provided by God. What if we read empiricism in terms of the impression of sound waves from a noise, photons from a light, chemicals from a piece of food upon our nervous system? But how do I begin to formulate knowledge concerning those impressions? Is it when I individuate perceptions and then name them, but what about those impressions that cannot be individuated? Kant, who has empiricist tendencies at times, argued that some aspects of this extramental physical reality (space, time) cannot be experienced as such, they can only be known *a priori*.

This would suggest a retreat to innate ideas, but allowing the mind to formulate conceptions of space and time can be justified if we bring in an evolutionary hypothesis to support the empiricist tradition: although particular forms of knowledge are not given to us (arguments in favour of specific innate ideas fail on empirical grounds, since different people have different theories on what knowledge is innate), the ability to perceive the environment and to understand that it is formed in three dimensions and that our actions take place through time would be a highly successful trait to pass on through reproduction: those incapable of negotiating a three-dimensional world and associating events with time would be highly unlikely to pass selective breeding ('where's my mate?'). If the mind is wired for knowledge, others have argued persuasively for the wiring of the mind for language acquisition and moral behaviour – the possession of conscience, for example. However, Locke's ghost reminds empiricists not to go too far in asserting the existence of structures necessary for knowledge which may lean towards structures learned in society.

Taking in evidence my mind forms a picture, and it is these pictures that become the basis of further merging and unique creation of higher-level thoughts and ideas into concepts. Plato believed that concepts were evidence of another realm – that the concept 'cat' did in fact refer to the Ideal Cat that existed in the other realm; Aristotle rejected his master's inference and preferred to focus on the empirical evidence of many particular entities that we group together in a mental tool, a concept, called 'cat', because each particular cat shares with other cats some qualities in common that can be drawn from them through our investigation. In many respects, this broad investigative procedure underpins modern empiricism – to check and validate facts with the senses and then to group data according to concepts. A good example comes from Linnaeus's biology and the categorization of animals and other living things into genii and species and so on.

This raises the concern as to what extent the empiricist relies on induction – on the gathering of data from the senses – to formulate theories concerning the world. Induction, as Popper has proposed, cannot work alone: we cannot stare at a collection of facts, watching a series of events pass us by or a series of reactions in a test tube or stare at a long list of data unless we possess a working theory as to what we are investigating. But where does that theory come from? Strict empiricists would claim that it can only come from primary evidence itself – it is not innate, such that the build-up of experiences from infancy, merged with learning and the tales of others, encourage the mind to formulate broader ideas (the beginnings of philosophy!) by which to understand the world. Weaker empiricists may allow some innatism to creep in concerning the nature of the theoretical frameworks that we establish.

Economics provides a useful example: statisticians present data from which induction is supposed to be employed to discover theories of human and commercial action. However, these are purely historical matters and no amount of looking at the data will encourage a theory to jump out – deciding what data to look at presupposes some thinking about what is important; correlating this with other data similarly assumes an implicit working hypothesis, and so on. In contrast to inductive theorists, deductive theorists argue that all of economics can be worked out logically from a simple premise – humans desire to improve their conditions (whatever is meant by condition, for that does not necessarily imply material conditions). Particular issues that arise (such as hyperinflation) can attract our attention and encourage us to work out further details, but the evidence that inductionists parade is arguably useless unless understood through theory: a datum can be read from many different

angles and hence be subject to many different theoretical conjectures as to make it inherently misleading.

This multifaceted issue represents an interesting problem for
empiricism across the board – that an individual eats a burger offers
a fact that can be read many different ways, never mind the assassination of J. F. Kennedy. In Dickens's *Hard Times*, Gradgrind insists
on the children learning nothing but facts – an unsubtle mockery of
the empiricist tradition; Nietzsche rejected empiricism with his
quip that there are no facts, only interpretations. But empiricists
would not reject the need for interpretation: interpretations require
facts and facts can only come from experience, and differing interpretations can be anchored by a return to the facts upon which
they are based – this is the basis of Popper's critical rationalism.
In the absence of facts, interpretations run amok – whether this
involves government secrecy or theological mysteries, and for
some historians of ideas, it was in reaction to the ignoring of observational evidence in the West's Middle Ages that the empiricist
tradition grew up.

Environmentalism

Environmentalism asserts the primacy of the environment in human
affairs. As a philosophy, most of its relevance is found in the areas
of political and ethical philosophy, although implications for epistemology and metaphysics can be readily deduced. Environmentalism
seeks a radical overhaul of anthropocentric perspectives in contrast
to humanist theories of being kind to animals or respectful of the
environment for the sake of human dignity or dire consequences:
its politics and ethics demand that the earth comes first.

Beginning with morality, environmentalism inverts the Judaic-
Christian ethos and demands that humanity should behumble itself
before nature not just respectfully towards the planet but also by
disengaging from harming the landscape and animals. That is not
to say that religions or secular ethics have not demanded that we

raise our consciousness concerning the environmental effects of our actions or that all environmentalists necessarily expect that we diminish our moral status below that of other animals, but the logical gist of environmentalism is that the environment ought to come first morally, legally and politically.

Politically, environmentalists differ on how power can be used to establish environmentalist ends. Here they may split along traditional lines between those who believe that political power can and should be used for environmentalist projects and those who do not think that the state is capable or is even a detrimental power that should be eschewed.

Consider a natural disaster. Humanists would expect that people raise funds and offer their time or skills in 'managing' the aftermath of the disaster – to some extent or less. Such interventionists may argue that the power of the state to muster resources should be deployed for protecting and managing the affected environment and/or the people. Anarchists highlight the need to let both the earth and the people sort themselves out, arguing for non-intervention either as a duty or as a consequentialist ethic (that active assistance often undermines the ability for a targeted people to reassert themselves, from a biological, species oriented perspective). The same is true for managing resources: interventionists proclaim the need to use the state to alter economic arrangements through taxes, regulations and prohibitions to curb human economic growth or activity, while the more libertarian criticize the impact that states have on environments and their own ecological footprint as being too large and uniform to recognize local subtleties and requirements. The anarchic elements would prefer that states be unwound and that people be allowed both by governments and large corporations to retreat to a more primitive existence, one that they claim would be closer to how humanity ought to live – that is, more 'naturally'.

Metaphysically, the environmentalist challenges the ontological hierarchy of traditional moralities and political philosophies to stress the overarching value of the universe or of planet earth; in more romantic thinking, earth is 'gaia', a self-organizing entity that becomes godlike (Gaia is the Greek goddess of the earth). Opinions divide as to whether humanity is thought of as an integral part of the holistic vision of earth and life, or whether humanity is thought of as an inimical, evil blight whose existence – or more particularly, whose mind – disturbs what would otherwise be a perfect balance. Such thinking reminds us of the curse of original sin that some theologians believe was imposed upon humanity by the God of *Genesis*: having upset the edenic idyll, man and woman were thus to suffer pain and death; but whereas the legend gives humanity dominance over nature, the environmentalist metaphysic underlines humanity's innate and persistent evil done to nature. Some implications would have earth exacting revenge upon humanity's billions through war and disease, with only a holy few elite environmentalists (of course) surviving to repopulate the earth on a new neo-Palaeolithic philosophy of harmony and balance.

Epistemologically, environmentalists encourage us to reconsider how we think about the world by altering the priority of our perceptions: instead of seeing resources to exploit for our own benefit, we should see the innate value of the landscape – of the rivers, the hills, the mountains and beasts that inhabit our neighbourhood. In economic parlance, the environmentalist is keen that we consider the externalities of our actions and take them into consideration when we plan how we should act.

However, much environmentalist discussion often assumes the validity of objective values, that some landscapes or animals are valuable 'in themselves'. It is a popular move which tends to silence debate, but for the philosopher this is an angle that justifies further examination. If a mountain is deemed objectively valuable, we would initially expect that all people would universally agree to its value, and failing that we would expect there to be logical reasons as to why some people did not see it as intrinsically valuable. Skiers may wish to enjoy its slopes, farmers its vegetation or grazing, climbers the steep sides, photographers the views at dawn from the summit, and so on. Asserting that all of these people are wrong in their use and that the mountain should not be used at all for human purposes prompts us to ask why one group trumps the others' valuations. This is because, for the environmentalist, value comes from nature not from humanity. To those who do not thoroughly despair of humanity, people are allowed their choices but on an equal footing with the rest of the animal kingdom and non-animal entities such as rocks. Some 'deep ecologists' assert that animals and landscapes have 'rights' not to be interfered with, others prefer to maintain the importance of the planet to all of its inhabitants and not get bogged down into justifying the rights of pebbles and peas.

In effect much environmentalism that is paraded in the mainstream media emanates from a broad church, within which philosophical and political arguments rage; courage stems from those less involved in city riots than those who quietly go off to the woods to live.

Epistemology

We pride ourselves on our knowledge – it gives us an ability to understand what is going on around us in the world, in other people, and in ourselves. At times, though, we can also behumble ourselves with ignorance: we cannot know everything, for we have neither the time nor the capacity to learn. Science has disclosed how restricted is our sensorial range, for visibility is just a small part of the overall electromagnetic spectrum and hearing captures only a range of frequencies available. Nonetheless, technicians have been able to bring those hitherto hidden frequencies (i.e. light and sound) to our attention, so that we may explore them further and employ them in science and industry.

Certainty distinguishes from belief – that I *believe* there to be a statue in the garden is a different proposition from that I *know* there is one. Epistemology examines what we mean by knowing, believing and certainty, and then how and if we may ever be said to be certain of some things, and whether that can be said of religious, scientific, psychological, artistic or moral ideas. Is there truth? How could we know it? Can we be certain of our knowledge?

Epistemology raises questions relevant to the sciences but also to our basic modes of understanding. Several broad philosophical traditions have emerged in the quest for certainty – there are those who argue that we can be certain of what we sense and those who claim that we can be certain of what we think. Naturally, there are those who seek to bridge the gap across what they see as an artificial dualism, and those who prefer to draw upon a deity for certainty.

For theists, the evident inadequacies of the human mind and its senses encourages them to turn to God as the guarantor of all that is known and to be known. That may be the case, but how can people profit from God's certainties? Traditionally, adherents have had recourse to revelation: God reveals Himself to the chosen, who then have a duty to inform the rest of the world what He has offered or shown. Sceptics, who may or may not believe in God, remind us that in showing Himself to people, the problem of knowledge has been cast back into the human realm – we now face the problem of dealing with a human being, who, according to the revelation proponents themselves, do not possess the ability to be certain in what they know.

Rationalism proposes that certainty can only be found in the workings of the mind and from the logical connections that can be drawn from propositions. Empiricism retorts that the mind is initially empty and that everything that we know is learned from the operation of the senses encountering and perceiving things in the extramental world. Problems arise for both positions – how can I entertain a proposition of a triangle if I have never perceived a three-sided shape? Or how can I fully trust my senses, when at times I know that they fail me – especially when tired or ill? Pulling the two together suggests that I should validate the evidence of my senses with an application of logical thinking, or my logical thinking should also connect back to the senses to ensure that I am not speaking logical rubbish.

Perhaps the notion of certainty is misplaced and we should err on the side of probability. I can accept that there is a high probability of the existence of the statue in the garden; would I be so certain on a foggy night?

The sceptical tradition is a powerful and useful one in Western philosophy – it has acted to challenge what we know; it does not necessitate epistemic nihilism, however, for constantly seeking better ways of knowing implies that we do not reject knowledge. Accordingly, some philosophers can claim that there are some things about which I can be certain (2 + 2 = 4, the probability of rolling a 6 on a die is 1/6), others that I can only offer probable statements regarding events (blue skies indicate warm weather), and others that I can offer no certainty whatsoever (God exists). Should I turn to statements of probability, I would be faced with having to provide criteria for 0 and 1 – the parameters of knowing something for certain, so what would they be? I am no further forward. Scepticism has been very influential in challenging pseudo-scientific and religious pronouncements and even when we feel that we are certain of an event having happened, it is always worthwhile remembering a Humean arched eyebrow.

Ethics

What ought I to do is a different question from what am I doing, have done, or what I will do. It is a normative proposition rather than a positive description (which can be checked against facts). That is, what am I doing demands a description: I am concocting a lie; what I will be doing similarly invokes a description: I shall lie, but from a description an ought can be derived – should I lie?

The distinction between description and prescription provides one (of many) ways in which to begin thinking ethically. In concocting a lie, I can consider whether lying is intrinsically wrong and can never be ethically justified; or I can consider whether lying is justified by its expected consequences and then divide the results according to what I may get out of it or what others may get out of it; or I may ask myself what kind of character I would be if I choose to lie. In asking these questions, the three main ethical theories of deontology, utilitarianism and virtue theory are invoked.

A deontologist, following the moral philosophy of Kant, proclaims that a lie can never be right – acts are either moral or immoral in themselves – and that it becomes a duty to do the right thing because it is the right thing to do. Kant argues that we should act as we would have done to us (following early Judaic-Christian thinking, well, the ethic is, as C. S. Lewis explained, practically universal), and to think whether the act in question could be universalized such that we must ask would anyone be right to lie. Kant emphatically denies the moral worth of lying. In a famous example, he argues that if a murderer enters your house to discover his next victim, it would be wrong of you to lie about their whereabouts. Far better to be honest, and to hope that the victim has meanwhile escaped! Kantians have long had trouble with this argument and have sought to adjust it according to the extremity of the situation (which would allow an adjustment to the universality clause), while critics have pointed out that Kant's universality is in turn based on the repercussions of an act and therefore we should consider those rather than the act itself.

Consequentialists demand that we think about the results of the lie. What is the lie for? Imagine being on a date and your partner asks if they look good – Kant would demand an honest reply, 'No, you look dreadful', and doleful consequences may ensue; but then again he may reply, your partner may prefer your honesty and thereby you gain their trust. A consequentialist replies, however, that may ruin the entire evening or sour the atmosphere and hence may be an anti-social and an unfriendly gesture; far better to lie and to keep relations smooth and comfortable. A division can be made here between short-term and long-term consequentialism: long-term consequentialists recognize that short-term benefits may not be conducive to longer term benefits, and so may agree with Kant that it is far better, on consequentialist grounds, to be honest now to promote longer term trust and friendship which can produce more rewarding benefits.

Bentham's consequentialism called utilitarianism presents a more rigorous attempt to weigh costs and benefits by seeking to quantify the potential results according to the effects they bring and how many people are affected by it. In many respects Bentham's plan underpins social engineering dreams of increasing 'the greatest happiness for the greatest number'. However, critics present unpalatable situations in which the few gain greater benefits at the cost of the many, or the many over the few; in thinking about lying to a date, the utilitarian should think about the host of repercussions that may ensue directly (a disappointed evening), indirectly (a more trusted friendship) and opportunities foregone (dependent on the reaction!).

Virtue theorists reject the binary representation of ethics of deontology versus consequences. Instead, virtue theorists ask: what kind of person would you be, should you lie? A liar, or a diplomat? Context becomes vital here: think about the situation and what is appropriate – to upset your partner does not seem a virtuous act. Etiquette (which is a refined form of virtue theory) would have you deflect the reply diplomatically: 'You look fine [for the evening]; but I prefer you in the red dress [avoiding the lie].' Your friendliness and trustworthiness and honesty may thus remain intact with a little tact. It is these virtues – forms of character – that virtue theorists are more interested in. Aristotle argued that virtues are formed over a long term, of cultivating good habits by doing good things. Discussion then begins on how that should begin with a great deal of emphasis on ensuring the right kind of education for youth from the beginning. Adam Smith presents a robust virtuous theory that recognizes the social formation of virtues and our comprehension of the morality or immorality of an action by the response of our conscience which acts as an 'impartial spectator' on all that we do. We are forever reminded what we have been taught to do, what expectations of conduct we have learned, and what our contemporaries would think.

Virtue theory aims to avoid the duty bound ethic of Kant – it is my duty to inform you that your dress does not suit – and the vague and open-endedness of consequentialism – I'll lie now so I'll enjoy a snog later, but it too has its problems: virtues may be fickle and sometimes fashionable and are often relative to one's culture, which demean their status in the eyes of those who would prefer a universal ethic binding on all. What would you do? Why?

Evil

Like beauty, evil is a word that when uttered fills the mind with connotations and philosophical implications and a similar analysis of hidden or implied meanings can be made.

The notion of evil is deeply attached to theology and the problem, coined by Leibniz, of *theodicy*: if God created the world and the world was 'good', how can evil exist? One answer throughout the ages has been that evil is committed by those who do not understand that God created a good world, or by those who are taught to understand but then reject the argument: God permitted free will and people turn away from God by their own choosing. Augustine offered an excellent description of this kind of evil: evil is not a self-sustaining, independent entity – an ontological 'evil' – that throws itself against God or goodness; instead, it is a turning away from the goodness and God, and so evil is chosen by man. Evil is thus man-made. This implies, however, that those who turn away can be identified, and perhaps should be, to diminish or to abolish evil from the world by turning back to the path of the right-eous – a policy that humanists who see evil in a different light emphasize as causing much of the intolerance and violence between religions and against those who reject religion.

But if God is omnibenevolent, theologians need to explain how evil can be said to seep into this system. Critics have lamented, for instance, the implication that seemingly evil events such as a natural disaster can be said to be good. Perhaps, a little bit of evil is necessary in God's system, so that we may know good. Similarly, determinists also face the problem of how a person can be said to turn volitionally from God or doing good if all actions are said to be predetermined – does God thus choose some people as agents to commit evil acts for His own purposes to enlighten the rest of us on what should be good action? This would imply that those agents (such as Judas in the New Testament) are mere vehicles and not responsible agents and therefore not to be condemned by fellow humans.

Socrates argued that one does not commit evil knowingly, for to know the good, one cannot but help do the good, a simplistic argu-ment that Aristotle rejected in favour of exploring the weakness of will: I may know what the right thing to do is in a situation but fail to do so because of a lack of will power. Knowledge and will separate, but the connotation remains that evil is done wittingly and hence the agent should be held responsible.

Humanists reject theodicy in preference for understanding evil in terms of ill-effects or bad intentions against humanity. For instance, willingly initiating aggression against another person is to commit an evil act. Since peace is conducive to the healthy growth and adaptation of the individual, war is its antithesis and hence an evil. There is much in this secular theory – first, that the agent has to act willingly, which removes or diminishes the evil act should the agent be acting under coercion or not fully in control of his or her mental state; secondly, that the agent initiates aggression, that is, he or she does not use violence in self-defence, or, perhaps in a pre-emptive attack on one about to commit violence; and thirdly, that the act is against a 'person', which implies of a peculiar moral status that encompasses humanity (and not animals or mountains, say).

In secular ethics, discussion shifts to whether evil can exist independently of cultural norms or whether it does not exist at all; if it does exist independently, can it be said to be a universal phenomenon and if so, how do we know what it is? Moral absolutists defend certain actions or vices as innately evil or immoral, but relativists have often pointed out the lack of universal accord on the particulars as evidence of evil's relativity. Perhaps the turning away from all things human or living forms the beginning of our comprehension of evil.

Existentialism

Existentialism is a relatively modern philosophy emanating from the works of Kierkegaard and the Russian novelist Fyodor Dostoevsky, whose emphasis on the metaphysical burden of individual choice then found fertile soil in the works of Gabriel Marcel, Martin Heidegger and Jean-Paul Sartre, the last also enjoying implementing the philosophy in plays and novels. Some roots to existentialism can be traced back to Stoical, medieval Scholastic thinking and some to the philosophy of Descartes.

Kierkegaard rejected Hegel's conception of consciousness as an entity that could be reconciled in the grand scheme of the Absolute, the ultimate consciousness as it were. Instead for Kierkegaard, consciousness should remain irreconcilably individual and alone. Marcel, who, like Kierkegaard, was a Christian, argued that my life is given (by God), but that at each moment, I could die: so I am always facing death and cannot escape it, so the only psychological escape is the theological path in a belief in the afterlife. For atheist existentialists, that is not an option, and death is the annihilation of one's existence and so death takes on even graver implications.

Choice, for the existentialist, begets an absurdity – here am I about to order a glass of beer, but there is nothing necessary in my next movement, I could after all order the waitress to dance, or I could simply get up and leave singing *La Marseillaise*. Who I am is not predefined by what other philosophers call human nature; so deeper than the absurdity of choice is the premise that 'existence precedes essence'. The past certainly contains my previous choices and actions and all the contingencies that brought me to this point of ordering a beer: these I cannot change; but I am free to choose who I will be in the next moment. We are each free at each moment to choose our nature as defined by my unfurling future.

You are free. Those are powerful words that throw responsibility for choosing actions back to you and to your life – only you can choose, says Sartre. The power in freedom is dizzying for the existentialist, who feels 'thrown into' this world of choices: after all, you did not ask to be born, but here you are having to define your personality through your actions and the burden is wholly yours. This may lead you to dread the world, dread your next action, because you are free like a god to choose. Your existence therefore precedes your essence (personality, definition, nature) – hence the term 'existentialism'. The existentialist inverts the Scholastic doctrine that essence precedes existence, which implies that the world's nature comes before its existence.

In some respects, the existentialist presents a strong libertarian view of the freedom of will (libertarian in this sense implying the theory of free will), and it can be challenged by various retorts that seek to underline the innateness of character or predispositions. For example, that I am slow to anger is an element of my character there from my birth; that I am thoughtful is more a product of my own formation. Sartre would reject the former though – even under torture, he argues, you are free to scream, or not to scream.

Evidentially this is possible; however, Sartre's condemnation of those who try to blame their nature as living inauthentically rather than their own choice in the matter is often taken as too moralistic, especially when people are in trying and extreme conditions: the scream can be authentically chosen after all. The Stoics would have partly agreed – that I cry out in desperation may be a momentary lapse of reason in the face of a wall of water about to descend upon my boat, but I can regain control of my self by controlling my emotions and hence face danger 'stoically'. In contrast to the Stoics, who thought that yours and the worlds' destinies were fixed, the existentialists reject determinism.

In Cartesian mood, the existentialist proceeds to befuddle your experience of your surroundings: the room that you are in could be a different colour, the table could be a giraffe, the lamp a snake, the bed a Ferrari: why they are the things that they are is mere contingency rather than any necessary logical development of the universe. Again, the metaphysics is giddying and playful; in art we see existentialist themes in surrealism, of disturbing landscapes and contorted figures; in plays, we find exaggeration and absurdity, as in Kafka's extraordinary dark novellas.

Fallacies

A fallacy is an error in logic. The key issue in detecting a fallacy is that the conclusion *appears* to be implied in the premises but a more scrupulous consideration unravels a jump in reasoning, a mis-use of language in which ambiguities are played upon, or the inser-tion of new information or other premises to sustain the desired conclusion.

It is for this reason that logical arguments which 'prove' the existence of things such as God completely fail; all they can do is unfold the necessary implications of their premises – change the premises, and you change the conclusion, hence no certainty of external entities can be gained from logical analysis alone. Perhaps, we should reach for Disraeli's famous quip: 'there are lies, damned lies, statistics', and add 'logic'. Nonetheless, because of the nature of language and the philosophical relationships that can be formed between words and things, logicians debate the nature of fallacies, especially once they get beyond the simple mistakes in reasoning.

Popular fallacies:

The many questions fallacy.

Sometimes a question is asked when a prior question is necessary, in other words a question may presume too much. The classical example well worth repeating is, 'Have you stopped beating your wife?' It is a leading question which implies an affirmative to two other questions: (1) 'Are you married?' and (2) 'Have you ever beaten your wife?' These must be asked first, otherwise how is the defendant to reply? Yes? No?

Fallacy of the undistributed middle.

'All environmentalists believe in global warming. Professor Qwerty also believes in global warming, therefore he must be an environmentalist.' The argument presumes another premise that Professor Qwerty is indeed a member of the environmentalist lobby, which we are not told – there may, after all, be other groups that believe in global warming but do not ascribe to environmentalist views.

Post hoc ergo hoc (after this, so because of this).

'The world is warming; increased CO_2 emissions preceded this warming. Therefore increased CO_2 emissions cause global warming.' Not necessarily: just because something happens after an event does not mean that the event caused it. I clapped and Cindy's bra fell off. Nothing to do with me, guv.

Argumentum ad baculum (argument by appealing to the cudgel).

'You will agree with what I say, or there will be hell to pay.' Usually offered in a more subtle way ranging from regulatory commands to foreign policy machinations ('You're either with us or with the terrorists', – George W. Bush). Contentiously, this may not be a proper fallacy as some may argue that force can indeed be construed as producing validity, but that premise would thus require stating explicitly.

Argumentum ad hominem (argument to the man).

The politician's favourite ploy: 'Adolf Hitler was evil, so his vegetarianism is evil.' This comes in a variety of flavours in which parties, countries, races or religions 'must be wrong' because they are deemed to be wrong on other matters. But the fact of who is asserting the proposition has nothing to do with the proposition itself.

Argumentum ad verucundiam (argument to respect).

This we encounter in endorsed advertising or when well-regarded people are asked to give an opinion in a debate. The mere fact that David Beckham wears such and such glasses, says, according to the advert, that they are cool, good, high quality, and so on; or Mikhail Pletnev endorsing Steinway pianos for those sporting a different aesthetic. Or a professor may be drawn into conferring weight to support an argument as 'an expert'. In each case, a level of expertise and/or respect is assumed to transfer easily to another field. This is not to say that the endorser is not unqualified to speak on other matters, but that what is proposed or argued should stand by itself, separate from personality or fame.

Argumentum ad ignorantium (argument to ignorance).

If a proposition has not been proved true, we assert that its conclusion must be false. 'Global warming has not yet been proven, so it must be false!' No, it has not yet been proven nor has it been falsified. The argument attempts to skip the reference to reality and hence the possibility of verification by scientifically gathered data.

On the other hand, consider: 'if a proposition has not been proved false, its conclusion must be true.' Why should that follow? 'Creationism has yet to be proved false, so it must be true.' It may be true, but it may also be false; the lack of falsification does not render something true, as Popper outlined: all it says is that we have a working hypothesis that we must rigorously keep on testing in case it does turn out to be false.

Argumentum ad populum (argument to the majority).

This is a common fallacy committed by every survey on people's opinions, which these days proliferate online. 'Only 16% of Americans believe the Official Report into 9/11' (New York/CBS News poll, 2006). Neither the 84 per cent of sceptics or the 16 per cent of believers are guarantors of the truth: the truth is something independent of what people believe, even if a 100 per cent believed in X or agreed with Y.

Argumentum ad misericordiam (argument to pity).

Daily, advertisements exhort to give money to some poor wretch who needs water, education or housing. But whether the poor should be given charity is however a separable moral issue from merely engaging my instinct to sympathize with others. A closer analysis may uncover political corruption and war that have impoverished these people and that charity is only ensuring the continuance of war by subsidizing its effects. In a less charged example, children often implore their parents, 'Please, mummy, please!' It is an argument designed to be won through engaging the parent's emotion – a wonderful fallacy.

Feminism

Any –ism suggests an ideological body of thought relating to its stem, but the word 'feminism' presents such a vast collection of ideas and policies that it is almost redundant except as a mild introduction to a philosophy seeking to accentuate the female relative to the male. Logically, that can either imply asserting an equality of women with men from a present inequality, asserting the supremacy of women regardless of their present status, or even raising women's base status to one higher but still retaining a sense of inequality beneath that of men.

Popular feminism in the West has tended to encourage the first ploy of demanding equality of the sexes, whereas radical feminists have preferred to see an inversion of patriarchy into matriarchy, while feminists working in traditionally strict patriarchies have worked for raising women's status from a low level.

What feminists have tended to claim is that the inequality of the sexes as measured by economic, political, legal and moral status is not natural but a cultural contrivance designed by males to maintain their hegemony over women. Each claim should be assessed in turn, as should the initial proposition that male power is a contrivance; similarly, like Marx's view that 'hitherto the history of all societies has been one of class struggle' the feminist claim refers to an implied universality, which does not reflect all societies' experience of gender relations. Focusing on the West, there are differences in the levels and nuances of relations, while a general description of patriarchy is historically acceptable.

Some philosophers have seen the eminence of men in the sciences and arts and male dominance in politics to be evidence for patriarchy's naturalness and hence evidence of men's superiority. This is fallacious though, for the possession of power is no guarantee of a person's natural aptitude never mind right to power, and the *de facto* general exclusion of women from certain disciplines is no logical argument in favour of man's superiority. Women were (and still are to some extent) systematically excluded from entering many professions either through explicit prohibition or through an endemic cultural undermining of women's confidence or education: therefore, they could not compete on an even keel with men who were granted the education and the privileges denied to women.

Lively debate flourishes within feminism concerning the nature and extent of gender differences. That there are two sexes is given, but 'gender' implies characteristic roles for women and men. Those who believe that gender differences are contrivances therefore argue that such differences should be removed – but that unfurls into what constitutes 'difference': should we wear the same clothing, or does that reflect our sex rather than our gender? Or should the two sexes be brought up identically and given the same expectations? The latter is more popular, but here feminists have debated whether equality can ever be attained and whether certain aspects of female psychology or innate dispositions do indeed emerge despite equalization programmes, and if so, what implications do they have for gender? Even if there are natural tendencies to differ that does not in turn necessitate the dominance of one sex over the other, just as one person's greater abilities in all things necessitate another's subservience. Ricardo explained that mutual benefits from trade, or what we may extend to include interaction, may still be had even if one party is evidently superior in all talents than another – it is a useful principle in assessing feminist political and economic arguments, one that transcends much of the debate, for it focuses on mutuality and the benefits from cooperation over conflict.

Talents are dispersed unevenly over the population within both sexes, and while we may admit that some gender roles accentuate some talents over others, the stereotyping involved is not sufficient to prove logical necessity. For example, woman = maternal, loving, caring; patently there are women who have given birth who are none of these. There are women who enjoy fighting and men who enjoy peace and quiet. At the root of gender conceptions lie collective descriptions, which may pass anthropologically in terms of loose descriptions to enable our thinking to gain some insights, but ultimately the individual must be encountered. Experience tends to uphold the multifarious nature of individuals and diminishes the justification of gender collectivization.

In cultures where explicit political and legal barriers manifestly exist to freeing woman from subservience, debate may pursue the course of revolution or the course of gradualism. Revolutionaries tend to describe the present inequality as emanating from artificial power structures which, once overthrown, will permit women to live freely among men. Gradualists, who tend to be more conservative in their approach to politics, warn against unleashing violence in the name of change, for it is likely to rebound; instead, deeper cultural changes ought to be effected that challenge long-held expectations of women *vis à vis* men, whereas a revolution is likely only to disturb the surface but not the depths of people's thinking. Evidence is as foggy as defining feminism – one could argue that women's empowerment in the United Kingdom evolved slowly (albeit from a relatively good position compared to some cultures), but then Chinese women have seemingly enjoyed an immense lift up in expectations and access to life's riches because of Mao's revolutionary communist policies. The cost though is still to be reckoned.

Positive discrimination lies between the two and seeks to rectify gender imbalances as seen in employment statistics; however, for some feminists, these present new contrivances that act to embed certain classes of women in power over other classes (or races). Libertarian feminists despair of using the government to socially engineer women's lives and the intervention into voluntary, albeit prejudicial decisions, though those frustrated with a history of subtle and not so subtle oppression do not mind employing such programmes in order to effect a quick change on utilitarian grounds and for the dignity of the present generation and its positive effects as role models for future women.

Beyond the mainstream feminist movement, whose breadth of debate is sufficient in itself to warrant much more thought and discourse, are the radical feminists who would invert patriarchy into matriarchy. Highly critical of men, they see the world's ills stemming from male power and abuse of cultural and political supremacy. The world would be better if run wholly by women and men became subservient to women, either because men are incapable of ensuring peace and environmentally friendly acts, or because after 3,000 years of patriarchy, it is now 'women's turn'. Some prefer to turn their backs on men in all relations including sexual, arguing that lesbianism is more peaceful or a necessary political step in liberating woman from man. Reproduction of the species could be sustained by keeping a few chosen men and their sperm on tap.

Such political visions of feminist utopias rarely appeal beyond the fringe but fringes are exciting as well as entertaining to regard – often those working on the 'outside' become the 'mainstream' or can influence the orthodoxy in unexpected ways. On the other hand, permitting the fringes prompts us to understand the mainstream better, from which all can benefit.

Free will

Are you free to choose, to originate your thoughts and desires, and hence the ends towards which you act? You may not be free to act as such (you may be tied to a chair) but within your mind, are you free from all antecedent conditions that would otherwise determine what you thought and what intentions, dreams or goals you have? That is what the discussion of the free will provokes – is the mind free to will its own ends, or is it subject to or determined by other structures or external influences?

Determinism poses a challenge: every event or action has a cause – that is, the will cannot be free in the sense that is meant above, for what is thought of, dreamed, desired, feared, and so on, is caused by prior events, usually but not necessarily held to be physical events. This seems acceptable, but the libertarian (not of the political variety) retorts that determinism would imply an infinite regression of events reaching back into eternity (or round a circle perhaps), and that any positing of a prime mover or initiator of this flux would imply a contradiction and an arbitrary assertion – such as all events began with God and/or the Big Bang. So why not ditch the closed nature of determinism and permit a more reasonable termination of cause in the will of a sentient individual? That is, allow an indeterminism that recognizes the freedom of the mind or a compatibilist theory that permits determinism in the extramental physical realm and an indeterminism in the mental realm?

Similar to the topic of determinism the choice of concepts can skew debate, which has prompted some to dismiss the problem as semantic and hence non-philosophical; Wittgenstein thought that the subject should go the way of witches and phlogistons, that is, it should not be part of the philosophical paradigm. That seems, for a problem that has beset human thinking for thousands of years, rather rash. If we trace an action back to an individual and push our thinking further we often bump into the individual's will and may justly claim that Sarah bought her friend a present because she is Sarah and is self-determining and hence free of any coercive, historical or supernatural influences. She is a free agent in that regard and any attempt to find ulterior causes is to negate her nature as a sentient, self-determining being. To claim she is self-determining because she is self-determining suggests that freedom of will should be held axiomatically, which is not highly attractive to those who want to know why she chose to do as she did. The libertarian retorts that the axiom is sufficient: while theology can claim the primacy of God as the prime mover of the universe, libertarianism demands that the individual be acknowledged as the prime mover of her actions.

The freedom to form a will cannot, according to some such as Sartre, be found as a physicist would wish to discover. The individual consciousness is free precisely because it is a nothingness, and so could not be determined except by the self acting upon itself for itself. When the self acts in the belief that it is indeed determined so to act, then Sartre is entertainingly lambastic: people who believe that their actions are determined are bastards. Certainly to the point, but what does that mean? That they deny their humanity and consciousness and hence the freedom of their will.

But am I so free to choose my next step? If we accept that people are consciously free, that does not mean that choice is distinguishable from determinism – what I choose next is indeed determined by what ideas I possess about choice, value, means and ends. It is merely my will that chooses among the many possibilities running through my mind and some of those possibilities may be determined by prior structures either inherited genetically (a highly dubious move) or subconsciously. Freud's psychoanalytical approach challenges the entirety of human will explaining that gross elements of it are subject to subconscious rather than conscious motives.

Nonetheless, shifting internal responsibility for a decision does not refute the libertarian argument, for it merely allows for the recognition of a variety of psychological reasons for why Sarah chose to buy a present. That she did, remains philosophically intriguing.

God

The word 'God' has had and continues to have vast potential psychological and sociological effects, believers living according to religious precepts, offering prayers, money, time and even their lives in sacrifice to their God. Indeed, regardless whether God exists or not, the actual word 'God' has riven minds, peoples and cultures for thousands of years: the word has left atheists shuddering at the immorality, violence and hypocritical actions committed in the name of 'God' but has given believers life, hope, joy, presence and security.

How does a philosopher begin thinking about God? Sceptics may proceed analytically examining what is implied in the word, others with great respect and awe, while believers may begin with their personal or cultural experience of God – all can produce complicated systems, seemingly self-sufficient and immune to criticism. But the philosopher must not baulk at what is apparently held as axiomatic. Invoking God should not stop analysis: people may hide behind the word to halt all trespass by those who wish to pry more. Historically, we can detect struggles in sceptics' writings, who perceived God somewhat differently from their compatriots or who wished to distance themselves from religion. At times, they have had to weave a fine balance between their own reasoning and parochial authoritarian strictures on freethinking. But freethinking is the *sine qua non* of the philosopher – she must have unconditional authority and freedom to roam intellectually. While the onus once was, culturally and politically speaking, on the atheist to prove his or her case that God does not exist, today, notably in the West, the onus has shifted: that is not true in all parts of the world, nor in all parts of the West. The vision of the atheist is, historically, the most provocative and provocation is a useful jolt to the alluring temptation of the familiar, although philosophically speaking beginning with the atheist's position can hardly be called provocative: philosophers demand that we justify the perceived existence of a cat on a mat, never mind that of an omnipresent God.

The obvious opening is 'does God exist'? That is, is there an entity, which is often described as omnipotent, omniscient, omnipresent, sometimes all-loving, sometimes a revengeful destroyer? Theologians have tended to divide on God's existence by evidential proof or proof through rational argument; alternatively, deists argue that God started the universe but then sat back to let the laws of creation produce what they do, so evidential proof may not be forthcoming.

The empirical argument for God attempts to validate his existence through what we perceive: saying 'I know God exists' is to imply that I have my very own evidence of His existence, that He has revealed Himself to me. Some people claim to have seen or heard

God: epistemologically, what is being asserted by the one to whom God revealed Himself is that He became distinguishable from all other things, just as the clock facing me is distinguishable from the mantelpiece.

Accepting revelation implies that there is an ontological or metaphysical division into the physical entities that make impressions upon our mind and the ethereal divine realm, implying that ne'er the twain shall meet in ordinary life. Those to whom God decides to reveal His presence can be described as being drawn from one realm to another by His powers (or He coming through to secular). Yet it is not a wholly satisfactory argument, depending, as it does, on two incongruous routes to knowledge – the secular and the divine, one available to us, the other not.

Furthermore, empiricists, such as Hume, will argue that the testimony of other people – and hence their revelations – should always be suspect: stress and imagination can promote altered states of conscious creating their own versions of extramental reality which are not believed when other concepts are alluded to: 'I saw Elvis Presley' or 'I was abducted by aliens' or 'God told me to found a monastery'.

Lack of evidence may prompt a shift to the primacy of belief: 'believe in God!' Kierkegaard, for instance, encouraged us to just make a leap of faith. Nonetheless, an emotional belief ('I believe p because I *feel* it to be true') is no guarantee of truth: it may be true that you believe p (God exists), but reference to a belief is a separable issue from reference to an objective entity.

The senses can be downplayed in favour of other paths of asserting that a God exists. The great theistic apologists have sought to discover alternative means for 'proving' God's existence. If God cannot be found in the vast array of entities immediately perceived by us, can He be said to exist behind them as their prime mover? Paley argued that just as we recognize that a watch has a designer, so too can we recognize that the world must have a designer. This 'argument from design' is a popular move but, Hume noted, a fallacy: the analogy fails because we do not possess any knowledge of how the universe was made, so we cannot assume that God made it or that such a grand designer exists. There are many versions of the argument from design including probabilistic arguments: life is so highly improbable it must warrant a maker, therefore God exists. But probability is itself a contrivance: we are only working on what we believe to be the improbabilities of life emerging *ex nihili* rather than the actual probabilities, for we do not have access to the universal data.

Other theologians turn to logic to prove God's existence, seeking to deploy proofs analogous to mathematical proofs that are necessarily true. St Anselm's famous ontological argument demands that God exists, because, since there is nothing greater can be thought of as God and since existence is a necessary condition of being perfect (i.e. non-existence would be an imperfection!), then God must exist.

But the ontological argument seeks refuge in definitions rather than substantiating God's existence: God is defined as the perfect being and that His existence is a necessary corollary of his definition. This is analogous to proving that the internal angles of an Euclidean (two-dimensional) triangle must add up to 180 degrees. A closed definition, no matter how complete, clever or awe-inspiring, it does not equate to an external, visible entity. Further work has to be done.

So where does a theologian find intellectual solace if empirical or rational arguments for God's existence are found wanting (often by other theologians as well)? Either he or she retreats to the primacy of personal belief over objectivity or to the axiom that God exists, but adds that human observational skills and reasoning are both inadequate to fathom God anyway, so a leap of faith must be made. Human reasoning or human experience may be woefully inadequate for knowing or explaining God – and that can, in a strange way, provide much solace and humility for the religious mind.

Hedonism

Hedonism is an ethical ideal about the pursuit of the good, and the good is defined by hedonists as the pursuit of pleasure. Pleasure is essentially the titillation of physical processes, although some will add that pleasure can be gained from mental processes too.

Eat, drink, and be merry, for tomorrow we may die. (Imhotep)

For the hedonist, two great powers and hence motives of human action prevail on all that we do – pleasure and pain. The attractiveness of hedonism is that it apparently nails the good onto something substantial that can be felt by people: it is not some ethereal notion that one must dolefully subject one's life to in the hope that in death all will be revealed; nor is it the pursuit of a slippery notion such as happiness. Such is the caricature of Aristippus' philosophy, so mimicked and mocked down the ages that pleasure can only mean the gratification of sensual delights. Today, it still receives much attention in discussions on variations of Robert Nozick's experience machine: if you could plug yourself into the most complicated device that can adapt to ensure a flow of pleasurable sensations, would you do it? Should you do it?

Drawing from biological theories, modern hedonists underline the preserving nature of the pain–pleasure principle: if our actions are torn from adhering to this basic principle, then we are likely at least to live a life of misery and at worst one full of accident and injury – culminating of course in our death: so we avoid pain.

Nature has placed mankind under the governance of two sovereign masters, *pain* and *pleasure*. (Bentham, *An Introduction,* 11*)*

While the nervous system reacts vigorously to immediate pain and tempts us to sweet and pleasurable pursuits, it is nonetheless evident that as the social animals Aristotle ably described us, we must curb such grosser or more basic pursuits. Defecating in the street may provide instantaneous relief, but we have learned to direct our needs privately, partly so as not to give offence but mainly, and probably originally, so as not to undermine public hygiene, from which all benefit. Social cohesion and the accruing benefits result from reining in the basic instincts – and even the cynic Diogenes' exhibition to have sex in public failed, seemingly going against a deep-seated, cultural, biological or psychological inhibition. But while we may acknowledge the rationale behind simple inhibitions and prohibitions that have been developed or which have evolved to promote a basal level of interpersonal hygiene, it becomes harder to justify purely cultural – and hence relative – taboos as being universal, never mind fashionable dos and don'ts of etiquette. Rousseau echoed Diogenes' scepticism of the moral worth of much contrived etiquette, but reasoned that pleasure can either be passive or active – the first is purely biological or chemical, whereas the second, involving direction and intention is volitional and thereby moral.

It is a useful distinction, for it demands that we think harder about what we mean by pleasurable pursuits. To sit and be pleasured physically can hardly endure, for all that we do is subject to the law of diminishing marginal returns: the first hour of being pleasured is delightful, the second, very fine indeed, the third, lovely, the fourth hour, okay, the fifth hour, can I do something else? This suggests that the hedonist must order or prioritize that which may bring the best pleasures. The hedonist can accept that some pain or pleasure foregone is justifiable to reap higher rewards in the future.

Bentham sought a framework to quantify pleasures according to their intensity, duration, certainty, propinquity (nearness), fecundity (how fruitful they are of producing other pleasurable effects) and purity. He also adds extent, that is, to how many others this pleasure then passes, which, when we think of a joke is readily understandable. Sidgwick expanded on this, but when Bentham believed that pleasures and pains can be quantified, he tripped into an awful logical mess from which, some may argue, the world has never really recovered.

Sensory pleasures can be distinguished from attitudinal pleasures, which are philosophically more interesting as they invoke taking pleasure in something: a conversation, news of a sporting triumph, a painting; the two necessarily entwine, but only the latter have the chance of maturing or of being educated and reformed. I drink a glass of good wine, it is all the more pleasurable because it is toast to my best friend on the occasion of his wedding. Therein, we find a new lease of life for hedonism, which begins to raise its philosophical credentials when we commence discussions on what attitudes lean towards better pleasures than others, and perhaps here some may return to Socrates' comment that pleasure without knowledge is worthless.

Hegel, Georg Wilhelm Friedrich (1770–1831)

Georg (no 'e') Wilhelm Friedrich Hegel, born in Stuttgart, matured during the consolidation of Romanticism and German idealism and grew into idealism's most influential proponent and one of philosophy's most capable and subtle thinkers – indubitably hard to read but one certainly worth the sometimes intense effort required.

Hegel mainly taught privately and at Jena University before attaining professorships in Heidelberg and Berlin. The American and then the French Revolutions blew up in his youth, and while at Jena, Napoleon invaded; in the French Revolution he – like many young idealistic intellectuals – saw a 'glorious sunrise' but later, like other figures of the period, was to renounce his earlier enthusiasm as the revolt for liberty turned nasty and finally into Napoleon's empire.

The complicated nature of Hegel's style of philosophy does not make it easy to approach his works, which makes it difficult to know where to begin – critics present different starting points as being the easiest (often reflecting their own passions), so all I can say is dive in where *you* feel most comfortable: if you are interested in political philosophy, begin with Hegel's thoughts on master–slave relationships and then move to his comments upon the logical and political nature of the state; otherwise, if you are interested in epistemology, begin with the introduction to the *Phenomenology* and pursue his argument thereon in. Secondary sources at hand are invaluable – it is easy to lose one's way with his awkward style that is replete with strange turns of phrase and an overabundance of prepositions. There are *things-in-themselves* and *things-for-themselves*, and one often imagines *things-up-themselves*.

From a range of possible entry points that philosophers begin examining Hegel, I am going to start with his epistemological reaction to Kant's conception of an object as a 'thing-it-itself', which implies that the object is essentially unknowable or beyond our ability to grasp its essence; for Kant, we come to know the world through the workings of our mind – when we begin to know or to learn about the world, we necessarily employ our minds, which seems trivial, but our minds are conditioned to see the world through certain categories such as space and time and substance. Our mental structures thereby formulate how we envisage the world and we are hence trapped by them – accordingly, knowledge of things is limited. So where does that leave sense experience?

The German Idealists – Reinhold, Fichte, Schelling, Hegel – sought to resolve the apparent duality of Kant's arguments on knowing things sensed by underscoring the mental nature of knowledge by creating philosophical systems promoting the withering away of any remnant dualisms into a single overarching form. Dualisms are experienced but through a process they fall away to be replaced by an emerging organic whole: the collisions of opposing conceptions (mind-body, form-substance, etc.) are merely required steps that promote a higher realization, which philosophy can explain. Idealists divided on what people could generally understand of this, but Hegel was firmly of the opinion that philosophy's explanations should be universally understandable and not the domain of a professional philosophical elite – nevertheless, his explanations are not thoroughly lucid as one would hope from one seeking to enlighten fellow humanity on the real nature of the world.

If we follow Hegel's explanation of gaining knowledge, we may begin to understand both his entire system and how it is formed as well as the works of many later philosophers writing in the Hegelian vein – Marx, Heidegger, Sartre, and so on.

The overriding purpose is to remove the apparent duality that we face in encountering the world: I perceive a thing. First, let us focus on the perceiving side of the equation: my perception is intimately conscious and belongs to the workings of my mind reaching out through the senses to the extramental world to relate to the object in view. My mind engages with the object – it immediately invokes categories and thoughts of universality, for that is the nature of the mind: that is, if I espy a cat, the very word 'cat' invokes a universal notion that this particular cat belongs to, and so I am imposing my belief system on this particular cat, framing and judging it, as it were, in what is a preconceived schemata of knowing cats *qua* 'cat'. This implies that there can be no pure perception of the thing-itself, for perception cannot be passive, and neither can our sensory encounter be formulated in a way that describes the real nature of the thing seen: every attempt at describing the object returns to the mind's own apparatus of describing objects – a circular justification that the empiricist tradition cannot escape from (should Hegel's argument be cogent, that is). Locke advocated that conceptualizing particulars lead to a loosening of the mind's connection to reality, but Hegel is saying that that grip is untenable even in perception.

Hegel's point here is that the validity of empiricism's claim to know something by virtue of perceiving it is flawed: perception implies a conscious action and consciousness produces only self-referential standards by which to judge its perception – justification can only come from within the system as it were, just as science is bedevilled by the fact that we exist inside the universe and cannot escape it to look properly upon its nature.

Yet Hegel seeks to avoid the solipsist claim that only the mind can know the world, but if what exists is known through the mind and the mind belongs to my particular consciousness, then surely his theory collapses into solipsism? Not at all – Hegel demands that we then consider the thing perceived.

In turn the object cannot stand unknowable – it is very much a part of the mind's vision for it is encountered by the mind. Insofar as it is extramental, the object's essence or internal nature is apparently beyond our immediate comprehension and our sensorial information of the object is necessarily infiltrated with conscious categories; but the object itself also reaches out to consciousness – to our senses and mental cognitive apparatus we could say. It needs mind just as mind needs objects. The object exhibits its characteristics, which our mind groups together, but these innate characteristics ensure that the object exists in its own right and hence (and this is where Hegel gets somewhat strange to the uninitiated) *negates* all other things: it exists for itself too but it also negates itself. But negation does not imply a reduction to a zero for Hegel, instead (as two negatives make a plus) it is a force for change, in which the subject and the object come together to merge into a new subject–object form: both are hence really one and not two. This clever move does not go unchallenged of course, for it depends on a lot of subtle leaps that are either acceptable or unacceptable to some extent or other.

In a nutshell, Hegel argued that an entity includes the necessity of its opposite and vice versa, so that both are two sides of the same coin, both pointing back at each other as Hegel saw it, but a coin that in turn represents a higher form of reality, which Hegel terms Absolute Spirit.

The merging of the dualities is a process which is both logical and historical for Hegel; his thinking is neatly summarized by readers as the formation of a thesis, the application of its opposing antithe-sis, and then both merge into a new synthesis. Triadic or syllogistic reasoning pervades Hegel's thinking, which implies that there has to be an initiating duality to forge the synthesis. We can question whether simple reality is dualistic – why not three or more basic ele-ments (e.g. the 12 dimensions proposed by some string theorists)? Division is the 'source of the need of philosophy', Hegel intoned and this division creates its own momentum as well as the logical descriptions of opposing entities negating themselves and so rising to a higher level.

In personal relations, when two subjects meet (I and you), one of us seeks to master the other and the loser becomes philosophi-cally slave-like. Hegel's master–slave thesis, very poetically written, has become enormously influential throughout the humanities (albeit often filtered through Marx's influences) encouraging gen-der, race and class analyses of literature, films, poetry, art, as well as infusing anthropological descriptions. Analogous to the initial subject–object dualism, the subject–subject duality leads to an inequality, which is then transcended when both subjects (you and I) recognize that each possesses independent consciousness and rational mind. Initial alienation from each other turns into a univer-sality, and similarly, my will and your will are given over to a univer-sal will that necessarily is rational and which acts to order our interactions – hence law. Socially, family opposes society, but both are superseded by the State, a move that Hegel pursues both logi-cally (following an Aristotelian reading of the emergence the State) and historically. In turn, States encounter one another as opposites and, like the master–slave relationship, must seek hegemony or dominance over one another: war is accordingly rational for Hegel, but interestingly he does not follow through this nationalistic rea-soning by asserting the synthesizing of nations into one World Government.

Construing the annihilation of dualistic thinking as indicating the existence of another level of reality gives credence to Hegel as a

theological thinker as well as a philosopher grappling with epistemological and metaphysical problems. God is indeed Absolute
Spirit, which infuses everything and unifies every apparent dualism.
Beginning with Being, its opposite is Not-Being, but both sides
logically imply the other – for example, consider Being without any
entity attached to it, it becomes Not-Being – so again a transcend-
ence is made, this time to Becoming. Because dualities engage in
processes, the result is end-oriented, that is, they lean towards
becoming something, but, critically, all must be rational in Hegel's
exegesis, and rationality guides us to understanding that all the
dualities gradually ascend in triplets to Absolute Spirit.

Absolute Spirit is objectified through nature – that is, it works
through the objective and subjective worlds we encounter (things
and minds): Absolute Spirit is the ultimate reality, but for Hegel
being an idealist, this Spirit is self-conscious – it is Mind, and, critically, this Spirit, or the fundamental nature of the universe and all it
contains, is rational. We may glimpse or begin to understand its
nature through art, religion and philosophy, but it also works through
us as we proceed through history, which unfurls rationally towards
its end, namely Absolute Spirit. Marx was to accept Hegel's general
arguments but reject the idealistic nature of the world in favour of
a materialistic one, hence the Marxian end to which we are all proceeding, is the Communist Revolution. Hegelians can often be
identified by their allegiance to 'end of history' ideals, although it is
not clear whether Hegel posits an end historically as it were of the
universe or merely a logical end – the latter implying that we in the
world will keep on forming new relations, reaching heights or logical culminations of our cultures, before proceeding on new, anti-
thetical lines, until a new synthesis forms in a continuous series.

Hegel's philosophy has been caricatured, distorted, interpreted
along different lines, vilified and praised. It is difficult to maintain a
strict sense of introductory fairness with his writings, but what
should be emphasized is that his works become enjoyable to those,
like myself, who often gave him a wide berth, and that, above all,

he championed philosophy as the means by which we understand how everything around us – all the apparent disparities both intellectual and physical – can be reconciled. I do not think it would be amiss to say that Hegel described and encouraged philosophy's apotheosis.

Heidegger, Martin (1889–1976)

Heidegger is held to be the fountainhead of philosophical existentialism although his writings and thought stretch beyond simplistic labels. There exists phases in his thought from his influential *Being and Time* (1927) to later writings on language, technology and poetry; nonetheless, he often returned to the philosophy of Being – the ultimate philosophical inquiry.

Controversially, Heidegger allied himself to Nazism as Rector of Freiburg in 1933, a move which may have reflected his belief in the purity of the German language and hence its closeness to original thought and its modes, but a move which can also only be described as political naivety at its worst for such a wide and deep thinker. Not that all other philosophers are pure and holy and have never allied themselves with empires, political parties, revolutionaries and spurious campaigns.

In *Being and Time*, Heidegger sought to disclose the phenomenon of Being, which he argued had been ignored by much of philosophy since the Greeks and revived by Hegel. This, he believed, was a reflection of modern alienation from Being – man has lost touch with the world that our primitive ancestors enjoyed, but to rediscover Being requires a heightened sense of one's own consciousness of one's *Dasein*, he termed it, employing a word vaguely implying 'being-there' or 'that-it-is' (from *dass* sein). Where? In the world: we each possess a consciousness grasping out into the world of things, only a conscious entity can reach out to consider being; so *Dasein* also refers to man.

Through *Dasein*, Heidegger sought to refresh ontology: we are concrete individuals rather than ideas but we gain knowledge of the things around us through our relationship with them, underpinned by Being; however, our particular perception of the world is open to misapprehension particularly through the language we use. *Dasein* is the questioner and in thinking we relate Being to our essence; Being brings forth language for us to use:

> Language is the house of Being. In its home man dwells. (Heidegger, *Basic Writings*, 217)

Accordingly, Heidegger highlighted the role of etymology and ur-languages (German and Greek) that he believed are relatively untainted in their meanings from the primordial conception of Being.

Dasein (being-there-man, say) is in the world – intimately connected to the things around and so no duality can arise between his being and things or between the knowledge of things and their relations (science) and our basic experiences and moods towards the world. *Dasein* is also unique in the world in that it is (or can be) concerned with its being. My *Dasein* is inseparable from yours – I do not have to learn or realize this, I am with you always. In existing, *Dasein* also knows that it will perish, so it is a 'being-towards-death' and in death it is released from its tenuous collective nature and is individuated: only in death are you truly alone in the world. But where was Heidegger when he joined the Nazis?

History

In August 1914 a Serbian nationalist assassinated the Austrian Archduke Franz Ferdinand in Sarajevo and a chain of events ensued leading to the downfall of three major empires and the deaths of fifteen million people. A historian can follow the facts through and judge their relationship to other choices right down to the present day, but a philosopher seeks more and wants justifications for the academic exercise. Was the assassination a historical necessity, was it pure chance, or something in between? If you think about your own birth and relate it back to the actions of your ancestors who were affected by the First World War (and few in the world born in the past century were not), does it make sense to say that Gavrilo Princip's shots caused your birth decades later? Can we talk meaningfully about such causality in history?

History is the study of the past – of human events and their consequences. The philosophy of history which historians necessarily invoke is a vast area of thinking involving: the role of action and intention; the relevancy of physical and environmental events; changes in culture and ideas; the meanings of abstracts such as 'the First World War'; whether the reality of what happened can truly be reflected in written accounts; and when selecting what to write about, what should govern a historian's tale; should historical events possess any meaning beyond that which it held for the past; can a past event be said to hold or frame the choices of present generations; what kind of meaning does an historical event possess – would it be mere knowledge (a collection of facts), or should it imply our reverence (our celebration or worship of our ancestors' feats), or could it refer to a deeper principle of human nature or the direction in which events are all ineluctably moving towards. These and other thoughts suffuse the philosophy of history.

> History is the only laboratory we have in which to test the consequences of thought. (Etienne Gilson, attributed)

Gibbon argued that only from the study of human history can we predict into the future; Vico sought to establish principles of human action based on what we could determine of human nature as evinced in history and Herder claimed that human character is historically determined – that is, each era is quintessentially different and should be studied for its own laws and principles. Hegel and notably Marx, sought to find laws of history from an overview of history that may be said in turn to determine events as they happen. But historicism has been criticized by Popper, who argues that the future is open-ended, that is, that our next step will possess a host of indeterminable and serendipitous implications, such as your birth so many years ago.

Hobbes, Thomas (1588–1679)

Thomas Hobbes, born in Wiltshire, England, lived for almost a century through an impressively most trying and revolutionary time in English and British history which saw the unification of the Crowns of England and Scotland, the Puritan Revolt against the Crown in the 1640s, the 12 years of a Republican Commonwealth under the Protectorate of Oliver Cromwell, and the eventual Restoration of the Monarchy in 1660. He was a private tutor to the Cavendish family and taught the future King Charles II while in exile in Paris: it is said that the King kept a portrait of his teacher in his private closet. Make of that what you will.

What is rewarding in reading Hobbes is that he is not so easily boxed as one might gather from cursory summaries of his work in text books like this one. There is a wonderful depth and subtlety to his thinking, a product no doubt in part resulting from the tumultuous time in which he lived, but also in his pursuit of unhindered contemplation using the exacting method he borrows from geometry – of deduction from self-evident maxims.

Hobbes described his birth in 1588 as being induced by his mother's fear prompted by the threat of Spanish invasion, which he charges with creating his pusillanimous character and perhaps his philosophical underlining of fear in politics. His philosophical career began in earnest, aged 40, when he worked through Euclid's principles, and the deductive method permeates his works. He believed that you could deduce all manner of principles – moral, scientific, mathematical, political, epistemological, and so on. However, if you are a deductionist, you do require a basis from which to begin your reasoning. Hobbes reasoned from materialism arguing that the world is entirely material and thus has no room for the immaterial, not that the immaterial would take up much room, but philosophically he rejected the possibility of a spiritual or ethereal realm ontologically opposite to the things that chew manuscripts. Not only is everything material, but everything is also in motion: they have to move to be perceived.

In the human realm, Hobbes used what is called a 'state of nature' concept to exhibit what life might be like for the stateless. From anarchy, he believed, people would be driven by self-preservation and the fear of death to band together to form a state. Without government, we would chase the same values and inevitably end in conflict – the 'warre of all against all' (Hobbes, *De Cive,* 9). He was not the first philosopher to be concerned about anarchy and various philosophers through the ages have conjured up different pictures of what a stateless society would be like. Some have been particularly taken by it but most have rejected it as a fearful state: Aristotle called those who live without government uncivilized, lawless folk. However, one aspect of anarchy that Hobbes maintained is the inalienable right to preserve yourself: even if you have been found guilty of a heinous crime (such as not paying your TV licence in the United Kingdom) and are about to be jailed, then you have every right to try to escape.

From his basic premises describing human nature, three principles follow: to seek peace, defend yourself with all means, and to obey contracts entered into. This last principle becomes the governing reason by which to form a state: the state is formed by engaging into a contract with one's fellows to obey the resulting social contract and the resulting sovereignty. Excepting a convicted person's right to flee from state justice, the citizens ought to give over their powers absolutely to the government, for it is only by delegating their subjective values and hence their reason for conflict to an objectively motivated institution.

The reasons for giving up rights absolutely are twofold. First, Hobbes did not hold much faith in the ability of most men to reason (he holds the traditional aristocratic disdain of everyone else: people are too self-serving and myopic) and secondly, and following from the first, he believed that political (or religious or moral) pluralism is the initial cause of men's misery as evident in the state of nature – or rather in the closest we come to witnessing such a state in civil warfare. The anarchy of civil war is therefore something to be avoided practically at all costs, hence that incredibly divisive force religion should be thoroughly subservient to the state, otherwise nonconformists (like Cromwell's crew) are likely to prove disruptive.

The laws of the government, Hobbes asserted, are to be binding in conscience, and the law is to be protected and enforced by the institutions of power the State can wield. Hobbes argued that legislation, the product of the state, should incorporate natural law – but his theory is often taken to assume that it does not or that Hobbesian justice is wholly positivist, an assumption generated by a category error in what is meant by law here. Legislation is a product in effect of the agreement to give up all matters and instruments to the controlling hand of the state; law may include legislation but may also include moral or natural law, and Hobbes certainly acknowledged the prevalence of the laws of nature which none can change.

Nonetheless, the Hobbesian state, as well as being the fountainhead of all ensuing civil laws and morality, should be the only source of (civil) justice, and such justice effectively can only exist when it is enforced by the instruments of the state:

> And covenants, without the sword, are but Words, and of no strength to scare a man at all. (Hobbes, *Leviathan*, II.17)

Reputation means nothing then. But the monarch or presiding sovereign power is obviously a minority who could be deposed quite easily, so what, asked Hobbes, is the ultimate source of his power? It is a mastery over men's minds that emanates from the concentration of all power in the monarchy, to which is added the power of the sword – the threat of secular punishment.

We give up our powers to government to secure our peace, Hobbes held, but that is not the end of the story, for should the government fail in its primary duty to secure the peace, then it may justly be overthrown in favour of one that will secure peace. However, rebellious thinking and political pluralism are to be eschewed for the sake of peace: too often, such fomenting revolution just leads to slaughter and destruction. We could appropriately imagine that Hobbes's system implies the creation of a totalitarian state, but we would be wrong: Hobbes was not a weak thinker who believed that given enough power peace would flower. Individuals, in forming the social contract, only give up those rights that their fellow men simultaneously give up; accordingly, the resulting Leviathan may be a minimalist institution if people give up few rights to exercise their liberty. He recognized also that the State's use of brute force alone against opponents is counter-productive:

> Suppression of doctrine does but unite and exasperate, that is increase both the malice and the power of them that have already believed them. (Hobbes, *Behemoth*, 62)

Too much power in the state would be self-defeating: what is crucial is winning the cooperation of the subject; hence, for that reason, the sovereign cannot make laws arbitrarily. Again this is a politically profound expansion of his theory, for it not only establishes a theoretical limit to the powers the sovereign may develop, but it similarly implies a veiled criticism of Charles I, who promoted discontent by his failure to read the political situation. On the other hand, since Hobbes submitted that there should not be any independent law making bodies, the fact that Charles's disputes were with Parliament could be read as evidence of the problems that do arise in a pluralist constitution.

Laws, Hobbes further advised, require general acceptability and precedence; otherwise, the monarch would be acting impoliticly. While Hobbes propounded the theory of legal positivism – the theory that the law emanates from the proper law-making authorities, his theory does not entail that the sovereign may act arbitrarily, for such behaviour would more than not cause dissent and division, which remain the ultimate roots of civil war.

However, the attainment and sustenance of power by a sovereign is not a given, the Leviathan must therefore cajole people into thinking that it has more power than it has, and through a self-fulfilling prophecy, it will gain that power. Having gained power, the purpose of the state is to ensure peace both from civil rebellion and from external aggression. These are not its only purposes though, for it must also exhibit frugality, liberality and fortitude. The pursuit of peace is not a basic instinctual passion that Hobbes is sometimes read as implying – the fear of death is such a passion indeed, but the transcending of that brutal state of nature involves rational consideration and forethought: reason leads men away from the natural state of internecine war.

Hobbes placed great stress on the role of reason in human affairs, and hence the importance of the sovereign ensuring a good education for the population. Ideas can obviously lead men astray, but when they are firmly grounded in self-evident propositions – for such was the motivation for expanding the method of Euclidean geometry into the political realm – then sound and valid conclusions must follow. Such is the theory; its elaboration in Hobbes's own work is another matter, but the vision is original and attractive: he was not averse to ensuring that his own *Leviathan* be standard political reading material.

Today his political ideas are a popular description of the anarchy that reigns in an international world that possesses no powerful sovereign body. Many writers use Hobbesian theory as an explanatory device, notably in the realist model of politics, and hence have explained violence and war in terms of a presiding state of nature. He is often linked with Machiavelli on that account, but again I would advise a closer reading of the philosopher to enjoy much more subtle thinking.

Hume, David (1711–1776)

David Hume achieved literary fame in the eighteenth century, penning a best-selling and highly enjoyable *History of England* and a series of essays; his philosophical work, while not gaining immediate attention (he lamented that his *Treatise* 'fell dead-born from the press'), gradually attracted the luminaries and wits of the age. He was even lumbered with Jean-Jacques Rousseau for a while, but by then the quirky chap was suffering from persecution disorders. Hume was overlooked for a chair in philosophy at the University of Edinburgh because of his intellectual leanings and possibly because he asked for some of the more salubrious 'philosophical' works of the period ('something a little more in the philosophical line' being a euphemism for pornographic literature). Hume also missed out on a marriage to a French lass, perhaps because, in the words of Diderot, he'd come to look like an overly well-nourished monk. Hume's mind was sharp though and several critics believe that he is the best philosopher produced by Britain. He is generally defined as an empiricist and a sceptic and politically of the 'Whig' persuasion, but as with all philosophers, throw away the preconceptions and see what you make of him yourself.

Hume's philosophy began with his *A Treatise of Human Nature* and the vision of producing a more coherent philosophy and application of philosophy to the various sciences and humanities by clarifying human nature. If we can understand human nature, then we can understand how we should be approaching subject material and therefore where our limits lie. It is a reasonable plea, and indeed this, Hume believed, is where Locke and his followers had left philosophy, for their method of insisting on observation could be then assessed as to what our observational skills and range really were. So study the mind as we study natural phenomenon – through experiments and observing the effects that arise from different situations and circumstances. It sounds like an introduction to psychology, which of course it can also be, but Hume's motive was broader, for he wished to apply what can be learned from philosophy to all sciences.

But he recognized a division between the natural sciences (which rely on repeatable experiments) and the moral or human oriented sciences. Imagine we wish to test the boiling temperature of iron – we take a sample and heat it and take a reading; we repeat the experiment and encourage others to repeat it until all errors can be ignored and other variables taken out to gain a universally accepted figure. Now try this in a moral situation: a soldier enters a house and kills a wounded enemy soldier. He is pulled up for breaching war conventions. Put him back in that situation though and can we say that he would act in the same manner? Hume indicated that the circumstances – including the soldier's own immediate experience, emotions and thinking – would be different as to render the scientific method of the natural sciences useless.

On understanding, Hume maintained that we perceive the world and that these perceptions or impressions are held in our minds as ideas. He sought to improve Locke's theory of knowledge by distinguishing between impressions and ideas, for, with Berkeley whom he rated highly, he argued that Locke confuses by his overuse of the word 'idea' for both. That said, Hume then proceeded with his own examination of how the mind works.

I perceive the wind blowing on my face, a cold and sharp blast from the north. That is an impression, for it impresses itself upon my senses this instance. Later I am in the cosiness of my warm living room and I recall the idea of the wind and the impression that it had upon me; necessarily, Hume claimed, the idea is a weaker version of the original impression. Likewise, any pain or pleasure I have experienced, I cannot recall to my mind as sharply as the original impressions. This is not to say that an idea cannot attain the power of an impression, for the division is not discrete but continuous with the weaker impressions being overlapped by the stronger ideas: 'Impressions and ideas differ only in their strength and vivacity' (*Treatise*, I.I.vii).

Most importantly, ideas can only come from original impressions. Although the human mind may be predisposed to learning, what it learns originates in the impressions gained from the outside world, but also from the passions and emotions which impress upon us. Imagine trying to explain to another what rum tastes like, or what having a baby is like: only experience can relate the impression – words become useless, floundering in metaphors and analogies. Occasionally, the mind can gain an idea of an object previously not experienced and that is when there are a set of gradations – in colours for instance – and I can manipulate my mind's eye to envisage the new colour. Otherwise, most of the things that I can concoct in my head are the result of previous impressions. As Locke noted, this is when problems arise, for in conjoining different ideas I may produce any number of fictions. Ideas (based on impressions) tend to fall together because of our mind's wont to note resemblance, contiguity, and the relationship between cause and effect operating on objects and things.

Hume presented his most outstanding claim on the nature of cause and effect, which philosophers (and scientists included) believed to be self-evident: if there is an effect, there must be a prior cause. Hume saw it otherwise – from his empiricist perspective, all he can justify is seeing two objects in close relationship with one another – say a ball rolling towards another ball; and while he may see one hitting the other and the second rolling away, we are not justified in claiming that we have seen cause and effect. Even if we were to repeat the experiment over and over again, cause and effect do not jump out and impress themselves upon our minds;

what we call the cause and effect relationship existing between the two balls is merely a habit of mind, a sequence of memories grouped together that match one ball hitting the other when rolled towards it. This implies that we must be thoroughly sceptical of anything that smacks of cause and effect relationships – just because there is an effect, does not mean that there is a cause, he notes, and just because something has always happened in connection with something else, does not mean that it will happen the next time – their perceived relationship may be merely contingent rather than necessary. All of this relates to how we observe things: cause and effect cannot be observed, but our minds do relate things that happen often or always to fall together. We are not justified in pointing to 'cause and effect' for it exists mentally, and we are apt to err.

One other powerful and influential argument that Hume presented in his *Treatise* is the theory that reason is the slave of the passions. Morality, he proposed, has nothing to do with reason, that is with rational, cool, logical discourse explaining how we ought to act. Morals influence action and feelings, and so they cannot be derived from reason – reason is 'utterly impotent'. Our liking or disliking of any object, person or event is governed by the pain or pleasure that it may create: our reason and experiences may relate to us what feelings we have when Aunt Freda arrives or when we lie back in the dentist's chair or when we think of England. Another passion may act to overwhelm the initial one and we may still enjoy Freda's visit (after all, she brings gifts), the solution to the aching tooth, or the pleasures of England past; if my emotions produce an indifference, I do not do anything, but if I do act, it is because I am moved accordingly.

So I am moved to act – but surely, some acts are unreasonable? Hume agreed – if my passions are motivated by things that do not exist, for instance – my fear of a purple-caped, gothic vampire descending the stairs; or when the means that I contrive to pursue the ends that I am motivated to chase are not appropriate.

The former is risible, yet can we truly say that fellow humanity has not shed itself of believing in things that do not exist? Fear and superstition still motivate much political thinking, as Hume was aware of and which he draws out well in his *History*; consider the emotions surrounding global warming, or Al-Qaeda – two concepts that guarantee demands for political action despite controversial evidence. In his day, Hume was highly critical of religion and its superstitions, leaning towards atheism in his writings but avoiding a public avowal. The latter is highly dependent upon understanding the relationship between ends and means, and despite Hume's scepticism concerning the existence of a cause and effect impression, he certainly acknowledges that some acts are conducive to securing ends over others. As students we all have to learn that some study habits are less conducive to learning than others – particularly those involving highly attractive distractions.

Idealism

In turning thought to the nature of the world, some thinkers have argued that thought is all that there is: what appears to be material and physically substantial is in fact only ideas in the mind.

This absolute form of idealism is the stuff of our dreams and nightmares. Hegel presented a complicated form of absolute idealism in which everything that exists partakes of everything else and rises through a necessary series of convergences to the absolute spirit. Hegel's is just one theory of idealism – a metaphysical idealism.

Metaphysical idealism opposes materialism, the view that everything you see possesses a physical substratum to which everything can be reduced – mind, body, even God. How can a philosophy reject what most of us take for granted each day that we get out of bed and encounter the physicality of the floor? An idealist asks what is the fundamental nature of the world encountered and claims it to be mental; idealists may point to the elusiveness of aspects of quantum physics, which seem to indicate that the ultimate substratum of the universe is immaterial, in the sense that subatomic particles can be viewed as waves of energy rather than miniscule ball bearings. Yet the forces involved still act to repel and attract entities, and even if these entities could be reduced to energy waves (strings perhaps), that would not reject the materialist thesis. Nor would it dismiss the idealist thesis, for even then, the idealist shifts to the metaphysical high ground to proclaim that everything is mental anyway – that I perceive my wife implies that there is an idea of 'my wife' walking about, and that I imagine that she too possesses a mind and can gauge where I am and what I am doing also implying that I possess a mind; so if the two of us are forms of consciousness, we face a logical junction: are our consciousnesses unique and independent, existing apart from one another, or are they in turn reflective of a single, greater mind, perhaps what religion calls God?

If all is mental, then various conclusions can be drawn concerning the nature of human relations and relations with the planet: there will be no effects on each other or the world except those we possess in our minds. This seems to make all of our sciences mere exercises in thought, of no relevance to anything except the dream game, nor would attacking another person – if we are all members of the same immaterial existence, an annihilation of another would be analogous to deleting the persona of an internet game: of no moral significance.

Epistemological idealism on the other hand begins, in the modern era, with Locke's insistence that in encountering the external world, objects impress themselves upon us and form ideas in our minds. Berkeley cleverly retorted that indeed ideas are certainly in the mind but what guarantee is there of the existence of things external to the mind? All we can know are ideas – by definition. Looking at an object, a piano, I behold an idea in my mind, that I give a name, but both name and mental object are ideas. What produces the idea – how can it be the thrusting of photons into my mind, for they merely dissipate in my nerves, yet I still retain an idea: the source is within, not without for the idealist. For Berkeley, the external world was certainly to be experienced (he was an empiricist), but this caused a problem of perceiving (mentally) causation: when I stub my toe, how can an idealist explain the causation of pain? Only, for Berkeley, by invoking God, who acts as the great intermediary between the idea of a stone and the idea of my pain.

If there is no God to intermediate, then this form of idealism slips swiftly into solipsism – the theory that since I can only be sure of my own existence, I cannot speak about your existence, for you are a figment of my mind, a pleasant idea I possess that someone maybe somewhere reading this book – it is only my idea, so I am stuck in a world of my own making and with no connection to the external world, for there is none: that is why Berkeley bypassed solipsism to secure a multiplicity of minds in the world via God. But having recourse to a more difficult thesis is often not attractive to philosophers – can we explain the ideal nature knowledge without falling into solipsism and without having to run to God? A materialist explains that knowledge is gained through the senses, by perceiving objects external to my mind, which impress themselves upon my mental tools and hence form knowledge; materialism demands that all is reducible to these material impressions, but the idealist is not confident about the connections between the external world and the mind, for how does an impression create knowledge? If I find a trigger point on your trapezius, you will certainly know that there is an impression, but what constitutes the knowledge? Idealists may then claim that what I perceive is a representation of what exists; this weaker form is proposed by Kant: representations differ from the things-in-themselves, which are unknowable to the human mind, so we are left with dealing with phenomena (appearances). This weakened form can permit a materialist thesis, so the logic and descriptions become refined and entwined at this point, after all, if I am working on a trigger point, you will certainly 'know' that something other than a representation is happening and to say that this pain-release is purely mental is to confuse the 'knowing that' with the 'that'.

Modern idealists work through language to argue that what we know of the world is a linguistic construction, often augmented by 'social construction', as language is a social tool. That is, the world that I produce in my mind is framed by the language that I speak and the culture from which I emanate. Again the problem here is confusing how I know things and what are the strengths and limits of ordinary (or symbolic language for that matter) and that there are things: my world-view may indeed be framed by the words and concepts and hence the intellectual and emotional implications that they have for my understanding and action, but we do not create the world as such, we inhabit it, we are thrown into it as Sartre says.

Intuition

'I knew that', replies a pupil to some new knowledge. A flippant reply we may think, but one going back to Socrates, who asserted that we have the ability to access knowledge that is held deep within our souls – it's just that our body often gets in the way of learning. In this sense, we could say that we learn intuitively – grasping that which is already there and achieving that 'ah-hah' experience, the immediate apprehension commonly complemented by a good feeling.

Sounds a fine theory, but Socrates presumed that our souls, which are eternal, know everything in the ideal world but when they return to earth, they conveniently forget everything – until prompted. Intuition is the grasping of what was once known. The Socratic theory runs through much thinking – religious and secular, for it assumes that we are capable of intuiting knowledge with or without experience or reasoned thought and therefore such intuition can encompass mystical insights and revelations – knowledge gained from the other world(s). There are various plays on this kind of intuition including the early Christian one that only angels and

God can intuit – men and women must reason – and the transcendentalist view that God is immanent in each individual and that the highest form of knowledge is personal intuition of truths.

If the otherworld view of philosophy is rejected then intuition falls back into our laps as a means of knowing about this world and ourselves. Expectedly, thinkers divide: sensualists like Locke claim that intuition is the grasping of a relationship between experiences (or 'ideas' as he calls them); he was reacting against Descartes's view that intuition is mental and logical and does not require experience. Kant sought to merge the two epistemologies, arguing that the mind is structured in such a way as to impose on reality concepts of understanding (such as time and space, without which we could not think), but that we then proceed sensorially to discover things. Intuition becomes useless in that regard, for it acts to sidestep the mental structures of the mind.

> Intuition is that kind of *intellectual sympathy* by which one is transported into the interior of an object to coincide with what is unique and consequently ineffable about it. (Bergson, *Introduction to Metaphysics*, 1)

Others preferred to take up the subjectivity of knowledge: only I can perceive the world, so my intuitive processes involve looking at objects and understanding what they are in themselves as a vision of the essence, as they present themselves to me – such is the phenomenologist theory of Husserl. Bergson preferred to reject any intellectual apparatus though and saw intuition as a form of instinct or primal knowledge.

When we apply intuition to life, mathematicians argue that if a proposition is irreducible and is immediately clear, it is held to be intuitively correct, a position originally held by Aristotle, who claimed that intuition was needed to grasp the fundamental nature of axioms or premises upon which theories are built, for often they cannot in turn be verified. In morality, Moore claims that certain acts are immediately intuited as moral or immoral: both would claim that the reply now becomes not so much 'I knew that' but 'I grasp that it cannot be any other way.'

Justice

The concept of justice fires political rebellion, war and social movements seeking a more just state of affairs. It is naturally a very loaded topic.

Consider a just and ideal state of affairs as being that which all people in a community would agree upon, which sounds fine, but we would have to know what would constitute the community's criteria. They may involve property rights, access to each other's wives, harsh punishments for those lower in the social order, festivities for all paid out of the common budget, an equal division of wealth, an unequal division of wealth, a recognition of certain gods or sacred places, a requirement for toleration, a prohibition of innovation – that is, the particulars can be parochial and illiberal. This is important to recognize, for liberal claims for justice typically imply toleration and rights to freedom and sometimes to a basic standard of living too.

Rawls argued that the liberal description of justice would be what people would converge on were they to argue for principles of justice from what he termed an 'original position'. He invokes a contract theory of society and asks what sort of life would people wish to lead were their own individual attributes and position in the social order be masked from them – in other words, in debating and deciding upon a just society, you could be at the top or at the bottom, wealthy or poor, and since each of us is similarly ignorant, he argued that we would agree upon a generally liberal framework of tolerance and rights as well as a modicum of welfare provision by the government to ensure the worst off are not absolutely impoverished.

The advantage of Rawls's original position is that it seeks to avoid parochial and individual prejudices, because you as a debating representative say, do not know who or what you are, so you are forced in a manner to consider yourself different. Therein lies the first problem that critics raised. Just as many have argued against social contract theory as being unrealistic – there never were genuinely democratic instances of constitutional formation, so Rawls was criticized for forming an interesting but make-believe scenario in which individuality and culture are dismissed. One has the impression of disembodied selves debating, which has echoes of Cartesian dualism, but for opponents is therefore infeasible. Opponents counter that political debate takes place through people who bring their lives and experiences to the table as well as their own cultural expectations, and they necessarily do impact upon debate, in the sense that they cannot be ignored, but also that the local expectations and norms, even if inimical to a liberal, should not be ignored. Imposing a Rawlsian solution on other peoples may not be so acceptable to peoples who are far removed from the liberalism that Rawls envisages people will theoretically converge on. In some respects, this line of criticism may be levied against American or Western political intervention (which Rawls's theory permits), asserting the primacy of democracy and parliamentary forms of government as being a universal political mode.

Rather than beginning from a Platonic ethereal state of make-believe characters, conservatives stress the need for justice to evolve and adapt to particular conditions. While this seemingly permits a relativism to flourish (what is just in one culture may not be just elsewhere), it also can claim that common structures do underlie disparate cultures and the differences in particulars are merely like the different fashions for clothing around the world: all people wear clothing. And so they have rituals about birth, sex, love and death. But how would that relate to justice? The conservative must claim that justice reflects what is due to people according to their station in their particular culture, that is all; notions of international justice are thus looked upon cynically or sceptically at best.

Rights theorists begin from another angle: each individual is said to possess rights and these rights are inviolable. Accordingly, justice relates to the protection of these rights. Should anyone aggress against them, they ought to be punished in proportion to the crime committed, for justice requires a proper redress. Philosophical trouble is in store for delineating these rights: Rawls's presents an imaginative scenario that can certainly bring our attention to self-serving 'rights' (which are better termed 'privileges'); Robert Nozick merely assumes them; natural rights theorists such as Murray Rothbard believe that they stem from human nature; rationalists claim their origin from our ability to reason, and so on.

Arguments concerning the origins or justification of rights may vary widely, but is there a common consensus on what these rights are meant to be? That depends on how a right is defined: if it is something that is to be upheld against some kind of action on the part of others, then it can be a murky concept indeed, unless the language used is strictly precise. I have a preference for the term 'core rights' which denotes universalizable and non-contradictory rights: a right could not be a right to someone else's income, time or life, for instance, for that generates an immediate contradiction; this also implies that a right should belong to all equally. Such rights may be few and present enormous problems, but a clear benchmark, like Rawls's for liberals, is often highly beneficial to expand one's own philosophy of rights as well as from which to examine others'.

Kant, Immanuel (1724–1804)

Immanuel Kant was born into one of the West's most fervent philosophical time-periods: Newtonian science, Voltaire's rationalist criticism, Lockean empiricism, Berkeleyan idealism and Cartesian scepticism were abroad and firing conversation, pamphlets and revolts. Kant's life overlaps with that of his near contemporary, Jean-Jacques Rousseau, outliving him to witness the great upheavals of the *ancien regime*, the French Revolution and the birth of the American Nation. He died as Napoleon was expanding his empire across Europe. Nevertheless, the life of Immanuel Kant is like the procession of the eye of the hurricane, an unnatural calm surrounded by a grand maelstrom. Kant was an exceedingly methodical man and thinker who sought to address the scepticism, doubts and optimism of his age, and to provide a coherent explanation of philosophy's range and limits as well as how it may be applied to life's practical problems.

Born in 1724 to a saddler and his wife, he was brought up in Pietism, a reformed Lutheran theology; he studied at Könisberg University, graduated, tutored privately for a while before returning to further his studies and an eventual private lectureship, a *Privatdozent*, whose salary was connected to the number of pupils taught: an eternally tempting policy to foist upon our universities! Initially his lectures were wide ranging and leaned towards physics, geometry, anthropology and mineralogy; philosophically, his immediate intellectual source had been Leibniz and Wolff, but after reading David Hume he was 'awoken from his intellectual slumber' and sought to make sense of philosophy and to rescue metaphysics from scepticism: the result was the first critique: *The Critique of Pure Reason*.

Against rationalism, Kant argued that the mind's ability to understand is limited, while against empiricism, he held that objects cannot be known fully, for the mind imposes its own structures on what is perceived. Consider the horse that I am looking at through my window: for Plato, the horse would be a physical instantiation of the Ideal horse, which exists in another dimension in the realm of pure Forms or Ideas. The empiricists throughout the centuries have rejected the existence of other realms from which knowledge emanates (although they may individually accept the existence of God);

in the seventeenth and eighteenth centuries, the empiricist argument asserted the passivity of the mind in knowing what was being perceived. According to Locke, I passively receive impressions of the horse into my mind, from which I form ideas. To reconcile the conundrum of how I attain an impression, Berkeley rejected matter and proposed an idealist solution. Kant had much to sort out.

He initially divides the origin of knowledge into that which is known *a priori* and that which is known synthetically (or, empirically). Then, once our minds are engaged, some knowledge can be said to be analytic, that is, it follows from what is known. If I say the horse has four legs and is a herbivore, I am drawing on what is already implicit in the definition of horse. However, if I say that the horse is chestnut, I am presenting a contingent fact that needs verification: being chestnut or being 15hh is not part of the definition and so is 'synthetic' knowledge. But Kant demands that we push our thinking further: there are certain aspects of what I am perceiving that cannot be proven through perception – I cannot conceive of the horse existing in zero dimensions, for instance, so knowledge of space must be a separate kind of knowledge. Nor can I conceive of the horse not existing through time, so this too must be similarly a different kind of knowledge. Kant called these kinds of knowledge '*a priori* synthetic'. They are essential to observation and are inherent in how the mind observes things. Our mind places categories of space and time upon the object, as well as other categories that cannot be empirically validated: reality, existence, necessity, substance, property, mind, matter, states, facts and events. Knowledge is caused by a twofold process of first sensing something and secondly imposing on it the mind's categories, so the external world must conform to the mind and its categories, but this implies, for Kant, that we can only know the appearance of things, not how things are in themselves.

Thus I am now assured that I see the horse as existing in space and time, but I cannot know what he is in himself: that is, how he is without space, time, existence, reality, and so on – in effect, what his Platonic Ideal is, we could say, or what Kant terms its *noumena*.

Despite not being able to know it, it is the thing-in-itself that I perceive. This limitation of not knowing the thing-in-itself encouraged Hegel to advance the idealistic elements to Kant's philosophy to find a solution.

In the second critique the *Critique of Practical Reason*, Kant expanded upon the foundations provided in the first critique to show how his philosophy may work in practice, notably in morality, which was developed in his *Metaphysics of Morals*. We are free to err, otherwise we would not know what a virtuous act is. Kant argues that we possess a moral law that can be known, a law that 'move[s] the mind with increasing admiration and law'. Rather than pursuing an emotive account of morality as one would expect, he insisted that morality is rational and universal. Whether my action is moral or not depends on whether it can be universalized – if it can, then it becomes my duty to do the right thing. This is the ethical theory of deontology and it has been enormously influential in producing debate and setting a standard by which things are judged: its counterpart is utilitarianism, which asserts that the goodness of an act depends on its consequences rather than any notion of it being the right thing to do (regardless of consequences).

In each situation necessitating a moral act, Kant demanded that you ask yourself, 'can you also will that your maxim [in this action that you are contemplating] become a universal law'? If so, it becomes categorically imperative that you do it; and that this ignores the consequences produces interesting repercussions that Kant was all too keen to support. He provided a few famous examples on what we ought to do: imagine being thoroughly depressed, life's turned into a hell and death appears a tempting option. The right action would be to ignore your personal feelings and to preserve your life as a moral duty. Or imagine that a murderous man pursues his victim to your house and demands that you tell him where the victim is. Kant proclaimed that honesty is the best and dutiful action, so you must tell him (and hope, he adds, that the poor victim has made his escape good). It is better for a man to die than to neglect your duty to the moral law. Few Kantians have followed him on this score, preferring to offer adjusted deontological arguments such as saying to the murderer, 'You have no right to that information', or keeping silent, or presenting a hierarchy of duties in which sustaining another's life takes precedence over being honest.

Moral worth comes from doing something without any emotional attachment. The resulting order is rational and universalizable, which reflected the greater order that Kant had in mind: rationality is critical in being a free, autonomous person. Reason is the means by which we become free and such autonomy indicates that each of us an end-in-him or herself, that is, a being deserving respect. Accordingly, you must never treat another as a means to your own ends. This is Kant's 'kingdom of ends', a world in which rational people consent mutually and equally with one another and do not act to exploit each other.

In the third critique, the *Critique of Judgement*, Kant favoured an objectivist foundation for aesthetic judgement. If I look at a painting, a Venus, for example, I may think that she is sexually attractive and that I would not mind having a raunchy affair with her: but such a judgement would be very crass for the representation is stimulating a personal and private inclination (which constitutes the basis of pornography). Nonetheless, my reaction to the painting is subjective Kant admits, so how can he then turn it into possessing an objective status? Initially in Kant's logic, we may find the Venus 'pleasant', which is subjective but which deals with base feelings common with animals; the painting is a representation and so my base reaction is irrelevant – I cannot make love to the image. Instead, I raise my thinking to consider the painting's beauty and I pass an aesthetic judgement on it, and in so doing I pronounce what can be universalized: 'this painting is beautiful'. Such a judgement requires me to abandon any private inclinations towards the subject matter and to consider the painting in a purely contemplative manner and determine it beautiful on the belief that other reasoning people would also understand it to be beautiful. Taste or private reaction is purely subjective, but by claiming that 'this painting of Venus is beautiful' I am making an objective claim. I am not hiding the evaluation of the painting behind what is today so often employed, 'I feel that this is beautiful.' Kant would ask us to dismiss our feelings to present the more positive assertion: then it can be examined.

In that respect, Kant's theory of an objective aesthetic echoes his moral law. Each must be universalizable; but, what if they are not? Optimistically perhaps, he argues that if we insist on our friends contemplating the painting rather than merely reacting to it ('I don't like it'), then, if the object is indeed beautiful, it will gain their agreement not intellectually but by evoking a similar subjective response in our audience. There are four 'moments' that satisfy our aesthetic judgement: quality, quantity, relation and modality. The Venus must be judged beautiful in a disinterested, contemplative manner; it must please universally if it is indeed beautiful; that a purposiveness can be recognized in the painting, not in the sense that the purpose of the painting is sexual stimulation, for instance, but in the sense of feeling a finality or purpose to the representation reflecting the harmony of the mind – which echoes Kant's metaphysical vision that Nature is formed in such a way as to be understandable to our minds, as if it were created with purposes by an Intelligent Designer (but without there having to be one); finally, presupposing that others will share the same feeling implies that we all possess that ability – it is not a logical ability as such, but a 'common sense': if I did not assume that my audience possesses this sense, my aesthetic judgements would be irrelevancies. The last is not something that can be proven, just as the unity of nature cannot be empirically proven must be held as a 'special a priori concept'.

The last 23 years of Kant's life were intensively productive and he has left an influential imprint on philosophy since, giving much impetus both positively and critically to the German idealism that flourished in his contemporaries and after his death in 1804.

Kierkegaard, Søren Aabye (1813–1855)

The man who is credited with starting existentialism is Søren Aabye Kierkegaard. Kierkegaard is nominally a theologian rather than a philosopher *per se*; nonetheless, his writings are philosophical enough and have enjoyed a wide philosophical influence to warrant our attention.

Kierkegaard was brought up by a father who believed that his family was cursed because of his blaspheming God when he was younger: five of Søren's brothers and sisters died while young; however, Martin Kierkegaard made sufficient money to retire to a life of study and reading, which his son was also able to do later. Søren enjoyed his youth but broke off an engagement to Regina Olsen following an epiphany to pursue his thinking and writing. In some respects his writings follow this maturation from a pleasure seeking, short-sighted youth to a man of duty to becoming a man of God. They are not written chronologically in the form of an ascent from the puerile to the godly; instead, Kierkegaard wrote from a variety of different viewpoints employing pseudonyms and replying to his pseudonymous writings through different texts – novels, letters, prefaces, reviews, commentaries, each relishing the existentialist dilemmas and multifarious perspectives that an anguished mind can create. And when one philosophical track tempts us to grasp Kierkegaard's direction, he acted to undermine it, emphasising the poverty of an individual's ability to transcend his limitations of body and reason to become truly godly. Following the Lutheran doctrine, a person cannot attain grace by himself – that power lies with God, so all that we do to raise our souls, intellect, emotions and bodies to the highest that religion can offer is truly in vain. Nonetheless, what we can do is raise our thoughts beyond the immediacy, draw away from the crowd and consider the depths that human and religious paradoxes present.

As a student, Kierkegaard heard Schelling's critical lectures on Hegel and, while enjoying Hegel, insofar as he understood him (which is always a relief to hear from any philosopher!), Kierkegaard rejected several aspects of Hegel's thinking, particularly Hegel's grandiose system which, for Kierkegaard, ignored existence in favour of an idealistic universe. For Kierkegaard, existence meant realizing yourself through your choices: the individual separating himself from sensuous pleasures (which he calls the aesthetic life), then from the crowd and from the commonality of universal ethics (which he calls the ethical life), to face God alone. Kierkegaard was thus committed to free will and an individualism that accentuates the removal of the self from the community; this of course puts you in relief, situated against a background of the world, others, ethical systems, and even religion and God.

Kierkegaard's focus was on the import of choosing to renounce one way of life in favour of another, higher way: from the aesthetic life to the ethical life to the theological life. Each choice is beset by what he calls an either/or decision: either I remain in my old ways or I move up an ethical gear, I cannot have both, as Hegel's dialectical system would imply. The choice to ascend from one form of life to another is identified by linking phases (*confina*). For the hedonist aesthete whose love is erotic and sensual, and for whom ethics is relative, boredom is inevitable, and boredom instigates melancholy and despair (which exemplified Kierkegaard's life) – the aesthete, personified in the literary character of Don Juan is ultimately unhappy; melancholy becomes the springboard into the higher life of ethical living, getting married and taking on responsibilities, and loving others according to the Christian ethic of *agape* (brotherly rather than erotic love). Kierkegaard preferred to skip this step; one always wonders about poor Regina – perhaps she ended up better off than being married to a melancholic theologian sorting himself out with his God. Anyway, Don Juan becomes Socrates, whose tragedy is ultimately to renounce his life in favour of universal morality. The next *confinium* which besets the ethical life is irony. Kierkegaard wrote his Master's dissertation on irony and following his defence of the dissertation he ended his engagement; how ironic, Regina must have thought. Irony, Kierkegaard held, acts to distance your self from events while simultaneously reflecting back on yourself; the resulting sense of unattachment presents a new leap to be made – towards God.

Only the individual can choose his life and values and the ascent to a higher ethical status also implies a further removal of the self from others. In hedonistic youth, pleasure is gained from others and with others, but the ethics of duty as found in the contracts such as marriage that the adult makes, imposes on one a higher sense of individuality. But such an ethical existence is then transcended through one's falling into irony by the religious ethic; here, an Hegelian synthesis of erotic love and *agape* is effected – through sensual and brotherly love, the individual is directed upwards to God. But not sufficiently so; Kierkegaard only gave God the power to offer you grace in your religious mind-set. And at each stage, the individual must choose willingly to move and make a 'leap of faith'.

Language

For philosophers such as Wittgenstein, language is the heart of philosophical problems – the vagueness of words and their lackadaisical employment generate sincerely debated issues, which if only studied properly would evaporate. Nonetheless, Wittgenstein's thesis has not removed philosophical problems concerning the nature of self, mind, body, substance, and so on, although we can admit to insisting upon a clearer prose when examining the contentious. Similarly, moves to reduce propositions and arguments to symbolic logic, while firing much excitement have failed to clear the philosophical decks.

For Wittgenstein, language is a game whose rules we learn in our societies. The game teaches us what is permissible and impermissible in language, but there are many kinds of game and philosophers create problems when they transfer the rules and meanings from one game into another game. Accordingly, the language that we use generates our view of the world (just as playing tennis provides us a means by which to understand and enjoy tennis), for it is through words and their ostensible meanings that we understand things. Not all words have to refer to things outside of us, the later Wittgenstein argued, for what do such words as 'hello' and 'cheers!' refer to? They are part of the game of understanding each other, we could say, and so stand independently of any referents.

In this tradition, philosophy is approached by way of the words being used, offering us enlightenment through clarification. Accordingly, such philosophers are interested in 'meaning', 'truth', 'use', 'reference', and so on, demanding that we take seriously the words we employ. It is a regular demand of such philosophers to ask of a student, 'But what is meant by X?' The implication is that a better position may be generated should the student define his terms – or perhaps the problem would evaporate with a better use of language; but then we are encouraged to reflect upon such words as 'meaning' and 'use' – the two can separate in everyday use, which also provokes interest, sometimes meaning chasing use, sometimes use chasing meaning.

Are meanings important? The implication is that they refer to something, yet in referring a host of problems arise. 'Dog' refers to the object over there, so when I pronounce a word, am I necessarily making a reference to something – and does that thing have to possess a material existence for the word to make sense? This was the logical positivist take on language, but it soon fails, as Wittgenstein noted, for not all words possess physical and identifiable status: I am in pain, but you cannot see my pain, nor can I alienate it from myself and show you it like I can my tongue. Yet does that mean that I am the creator of some or all meanings? If I am, then my world is unique and privileged. Wittgenstein rejected such a move in declaring that in order to pronounce upon the privacy of the mind, I am necessarily engaging in a social game.

It becomes evident that thoughts on language connect well with thoughts on the philosophy of mind. If the mind is deemed separable from the body, what status does that give the language by which we communicate – is it a representative part of the immaterial world made good through the spoken word (the kind of thesis that Platonists propose), or if the mind is a distinguishable but inseparable aspect of the body, are the words we pronounce merely signs of the material world we inhabit and which therefore would be subject to strict analysis for meaning and reference? From mind, language turns to the ontological status of words and to metaphysical visions and epistemological justifications.

Sometimes words are taken to be incarnations of powers, which seems to hark back to mystical beliefs or to works of fantasy, yet philosophy does not completely reject the potentiality of words. Scholastic philosophers of the word divided on whether words – particularly universals – were real in that they invoked the universal mentioned, which was the 'realist' position of Duns Scotus, or whether they were just contrived utterances with no real meaning, which was the 'nominalist' meaning of William of Ockham. The realist position implies that a word possesses a necessary connection to its Platonic universal form, and so may be said to evoke the other entity. A sceptic may wonder whether such a position can be tenable in the modern scientific world, but that is to forget that words come with the games' rules that Wittgenstein indicated and carry with them a host of cultural significances. To say, 'You are beautiful', provokes a host of implications and expectations that allude to the words' powers – the powers built upon psychological, social, intrapersonal meanings, and it is often these awkward notions which so patently affect our lives that philosophers of language either rejoice in or despair over.

Leibniz, Gottfried Wilhelm (1646–1716)

Gottfried Wilhelm Leibniz turned his prodigious talents to numerous disciplines – philosophy, history, language and geology. In mathematics, he invented calculus (independently of Newton, but published his ideas first) and we use his notation today; after showing a calculating machine to London's Royal Society in 1673, he was made a Fellow. He was by profession a lawyer and acted as a councillor, diplomat and historian to the Court of Hanover. He only published one book in his lifetime, *Theodicy*, but his published articles and correspondence were enormous and highly influential.

One of his early aims was to reduce logic to a system of symbols by which relationships could be analysed; such formal logic, he hoped, could also be extended to other subjects to clarify their content, a view that excited Oxford philosophers, notably Bertrand Russell, in the twentieth century. Indeed, sorting out the world's messes became a theme for Leibniz: he attempted to unite Catholics with Protestants and after that failed to unite Lutherans and Calvinists; he also envisioned a united Europe, with the princes of the union coming together to settle their disputes. After the horrendous wars of the seventeenth century, several thinkers sought to rekindle a new *pax romana* as it were (including the Abbé Saint-Pierre, whom Rousseau rebutted), and, in so doing, sowed some of the political seeds of what eventually became the European Union. Louis XIV of France, busy planning his wars, was none too interested, nor was Peter the Great of Russia, who was also busily expanding his empire. The man never tired of trying to bring harmony to one and all: in his last year, he was trying to unite Chinese Confucians with Catholicism!

Critics disagree on what actually forms Leibniz's philosophy, as it was so wide ranging and difficult to cohere, but here we shall concentrate on two popular notions – the idea that everything is resoluble into simple substances called monads and the idea that God has fashioned the world so that it is the best possible of all worlds.

In his *Theodicy*, he deals with evil. That evil or horrendous events happen in the world is always a logical thorn for those who believe that God is omnibenevolent: an evil deed contradicts the proposition, and we must either reject God's omnibenevolence or reject the description of evil things as evil. Leibniz opts for the former: God is morally perfect, so too must his universe be. For any event to happen there must be a sufficient reason for it to happen – that is, it could not be otherwise, and since the universe depends on God, and God could create any possible universe that he wishes, it follows that every event in it is supported by God having a sufficient reason for it happening. That is, God must have chosen the world to have this characteristic, and so, given God's moral perfection, this must be the best of all possible worlds.

Voltaire famously lampooned Leibniz's dictum in *Candide*, propounded by Dr Pangloss; following the Lisbon earthquake, Pangloss is hanged and Candide whipped, the latter quips, 'If this is the best possible of worlds, what then are the others?' Leibniz's argument may seem indecent to those embroiled in horrendous events (and according to Russell it was a mere sap to the Queen of Prussia), but his logic cannot have it any other way: God is omnibenevolent, God fashions the world, *ergo*, the world is good. Think of it the other way around, if Leibniz's God permitted evil, he would not have acted rationally in creating the universe, for to be rational, he must create the best world possible, the best that is among many (infinite) alternative worlds. God has free choice in what he creates, but as soon as he chooses to create a world, he must choose the best. However, that does not mean that what is evil is in fact good: it is just that in this world, the evil that does exist is much less than what may exist in a less than best alternative.

The theory connects loosely with Leibniz's monads (nothing rude). For Leibniz, there is no such thing as extension – bodies do not really exist in the manner that we putatively perceive them; what does exist are souls – indivisible entities – the monads, which are immaterial (spaceless) but self-sufficient, which means that they cannot act upon one another. 'Monads have no windows', is a famous Leibnizian phrase. There are an infinite number of monads – all dependent upon God's existence to be sure, but each in turn separate and distinct, in effect possessing a soul. Why there should be an infinite number is to avoid the possibility of the universe containing nothing somewhere – that is, a vacuum, which affrighted many intellectuals. Replete with monads, then, when we look upon a stone we should imagine a host of monads:

> Each portion of matter may be conceived as a garden full of plants, as a pond full of fish. (Leibniz, *Monadology*, 67)

Although Leibniz rejects the atomic theory of the Greeks (this was before Dalton et al.), as atoms were defined as indivisible physical particles, his monads possess similar characteristics in that he seeks to explain the ultimate nature of the universe with them. But the ultimate parts for Leibniz cannot be material – they are in each and every example unique and immaterial. Moreover, each monad possesses a soul, and your soul – that which you identify yourself with – happens to be a merely dominant monad among the trillions of cells. Conveniently perhaps for his religiously minded audience, monads do not die, so the eternity of the soul is promised.

Every monad is a tiny universe in itself; each mind (a higher monad capable of memory) is a little god, all related to God himself. But as Russell argues, these theories were for the public, Leibniz the private philosopher pursued other lines of thought that hung on logic and removed God, but that a dichotomy exists between his public and private minds is interesting not just psychologically but also philosophically, for what does that say of a person's philosophy or times that they must hide their ideas?

Locke, John (1632–1704)

Like Hobbes, his near contemporary, Locke was born in interesting and tumultuous times, his life spanning the Civil Wars, Cromwell's republic, the Restoration of the Monarchy and the Glorious Revolution of 1685. His abilities and diligence took him from being the son of a rural gentleman to the adviser to one of the Restoration's most powerful politicians and finally to a respected philosopher and educationalist. From conservative roots, Locke gradually became quite a radical thinker arguing for the primacy of individual and property rights, minimal government and religious toleration. In the realm of epistemology, Locke ushered in a robust justification of empiricism and a rejection of innate ideas.

Locke shifted from being a conservative establishmentarian to a radical liberal (later called Whigs in British politics), after meeting Anthony Ashley-Cooper, or Shaftesbury. He oversaw an operation to drain Shaftesbury's bile duct and thereby from all accounts saved the politician's life. Locke was also an amateur medical doctor who worked alongside the seventeenth-century's foremost medic, Thomas Sydenham.

While Shaftesbury formed the first English political party, Locke pursued a deeper justification of individual rights. In his *Two Treatises*, Locke argued that we each possess an inalienable right in our bodies: we are said to own our bodies as a matter of moral and political principle, for if you do not own yourself, who else does? Implicatively, philosophers who reject the individual's ownership of his body tend to argue for broad interventions into people's lives. Locke wished to reject that and by positing self-ownership as his cornerstone, he provided libertarian thinkers and anarchists with a powerful justification for minimal or no government. Locke's logic proceeded to justify private property, for if we mix our labour with unowned resources, they become ours by virtue of our labour. It is absurd to declare ownership of a continent or a planet, by merely setting foot on it, but when you work upon a piece of land, the product is rightfully yours: to say otherwise is to accept that you work for others who may come along and ungraciously take from you your production.

The individual owns himself and his work is his to do with as he wills. Any other who acts to aggress against him through violence

or theft effectively declares war against him and the victim is justified in defending himself at all costs.

> 'Tis the unjust use of force then, that puts a Man into the state of
> War . . . (Locke, *Second Treatise*, §177)

Should a thief be successful, the loss of property would in effect
reduce the victim to a slave, which is the most evil state for man to
live in. In initiating aggression (violence, theft or fraud), the attacker
loses all of his rights and he may justly be killed or enslaved by the
victim. (Locke did not argue against the slavery of West Africans,
for Locke was fully aware of the slave trade: he naively or politically
accepted that the slaves were justly enslaved for having themselves
waged aggressive war on their captors!) Nevertheless, the defender
has no right to extend his just war against the attacker's family: it is
only justifiable to attack the particular perpetrator.

In many respects, it can be asked why people would want a
government, for Locke is often intellectually on anarchy's edge;
however, he asserts several reasons for why people would justify
forming a governmental compact to relieve themselves of the anarchy of the state of nature. He answers because that state of nature
is full of uncertainty and that people are exposed to aggression; the
state of nature also lacks established, known and settled laws, a
known and indifferent judge, and the power to give a judge execution of the law. For anarchists, these are not insurmountable problems and arguably are red herrings, but for Locke they form a
sufficient reason to establish a government. Once set up, the people ought to agree to democracy or majority rule: government can
only be justified through the consent of the people.

Toleration, consent and the right to rebel against those governments that infringe the basic rights of the people become the main-
stays of liberal philosophy down to the twentieth century (now
called libertarian). Whereas Locke initially agreed that religion ought

not to be the province of individuals, seeing plurality as the source of friction and war, he later rejected the principle in favour of religious toleration. Each man ought to pursue his own version of religion without any interference by the state: he was not the only thinker calling for religious freedom (after all the nonconformist groups that had spun off the Anglican Church), but his eloquence and justifications enabled the liberal ideas to reach to greater audiences, as they still do.

In his influential *Thoughts on Education*, Locke outlined an application of educational ideals to the tuition of pupils. Schools tend to discourage learning and also produce ill-mannered pupils, so ideally, education should remain within the home, supplanted by tutors if necessary, but it should not be oppressive, regimental or boring. Children should only be sent to school as a last resort, but if brought up properly from the beginning, the child should be respectful of his parents, and be a gentleman or of good standing and conversant with all ranks of society.

Prior to his fame for his writings on education (he kept his political writings anonymous until his death bed for fear of state persecution), he had penned *An Essay Concerning Human Understanding*, presenting a justification of empiricism and of the scientific method. Descartes's meditations had turned him onto philosophy; he rejected some of Descartes's arguments but not the general thrust that knowledge could be explained and certainty be defended. While Descartes declared that certainty stemmed from his mind (I think, therefore I am) and the existence of God, Locke preferred to start with the senses. The senses are often the butt of many a non-empirical philosopher, who asserts that 'the senses may be fooled' which is all well and true, but where else does one start learning about what exists out there, beyond one's mind?

Locke begins with the newborn child whose mind is like a clay tablet (or *tabula rasa* as it was translated by his French translator and friend, Pierre Coste). How could a child be said to know anything and how could be said to get to know anything except through the senses? Taking various propositions that philosophers have proposed as indicating evidence of innate knowledge, Locke rejects each in turn, typically on grounds of non-universality: any counterfactual evidence is enough to dismiss innate knowledge. For instance, not all people believe in God nor do all people possess the same morality or propositions. Against Descartes, he argues that the employment of reason to detect universally known propositions is a non-starter: surely, these things that we are all supposed to know should be just known?

Once innatism is rejected, we must fall back upon the individual as the sole begetter and owner of knowledge, which sets the groundwork for Locke's individualistic and sceptical philosophy in which he underscores the need to observe with one's own eyes and to think with one's own mind. In contrast, innatism lends itself to accepting what others believe is (or should be) innate in the human mind, which paves the way, he asserts, for authoritarianism and blind obedience, and these are two moral and political tendencies that Locke wishes to curtail.

Any ideas that a person possesses can only come through the senses, but once in my mind, I can begin grouping them together to form concepts through words. Words refer to ideas (things perceived by the mind) and concepts refer to groups of things conveniently subsumed under a single heading: horse for innumerable instances of horses. It is here that philosophers can get carried away with their thinking, Locke warns, for if the words cannot be resolved back down into things that we can perceive and identify, then they become meaningless. A century and a half later, these arguments were extended by the positivists, who claimed that for a proposition to make sense it must be collapsible into identifiable and verifiable terms. Locke may have been aware of this implication, but he was also a Christian who would not dismiss religion as the later positivists would on grounds of non-verifiability or plain nonsense: instead, children should be inculcated in a belief in God from a very early age, perhaps so they may not mature into atheists (Locke believed that children are born atheists).

Images perceived (and held as ideas in the mind) are divisible into primary and secondary qualities: primary qualities are a physical thing's solidity, extension, figure and mobility; its secondary qualities are its taste, colour and sounds. Both imprint on the senses but may be distinguished – that is, I can identify a piano of certain dimensions and shape, note that it is not moving (from my perspective) and then add that it also happens to have a smell and is of dark wood and tastes of polish. These qualities impress themselves upon my mind, I cannot help that – my senses take in the information. Nonetheless, I can alter my focus on the outside world sharpening it or dulling it, I may be distracted: this is when the mind comes into play, for while I am for all intents and purposes passive in my reception of the external world's signals, I am not passive when it comes to using my mind, and it is that which I may alter focus of. I may be aware sensorially of a strange smell, but I do not raise my mind's awareness to study the smell and to compare it with known smells (e.g. slurry on the local farms). As soon as I am thinking though, I am fully cognizant and hence responsible for what I think, however, once my mind releases its hold on the perceptual reality from which it gains its impressions, it is highly capable of becoming muddle-headed, throwing concepts and words around with no anchor to them. I am thus prone to making very strange propositions ('dragons eat unicorns'). Epistemologically that explains the need to revert back to things seen: a healthy move for all thinkers, especially those disposed to flights of intellectual fancy, Locke would advise.

His epistemological theories link well with his theory of education: a child should learn particulars and references and learn how to connect abstracts to the underlying things that they represent, but also to his political theories. The individual should trust his own judgement, not that of an authority's or a priest's and his right to intellectual primacy reflects the importance of political and ethical rights to lead his own life.

Logic

Logic is the study of correct reasoning – of ensuring that what we think is tied together consistently through implication, deduction or induction. Logic examines deductive and implicative arguments to assess their internal validity (internal in the sense that they are closed and can stand independently of reality) and inductive arguments to assess their scope and application to reality. Logic is thus the set of rules by which we argue.

Logic does not produce truths, and herein many mistakes are made – all that logic can do is to progress from premises to conclusions, and if the steps made are properly deduced from those premises, then the conclusion must follow. This is regardless of our desires for the conclusion not to follow, or our knowledge of things outside of the premises. For instance, consider that, 'The Battle of Fulford took place before the Battle of Hastings, and the Battle of Stamford Bridge took place after the Battle of Fulford.' A valid conclusion is that Stamford Bridge did not take place before Fulford. But it is invalid to conclude that Stamford Bridge took place before the Battle of Hastings, even if it did in history – it could have taken place yesterday for all we know *from the information given*.

While most logical reasoning takes place informally when we follow the gist of an argument, formal logic seeks to reduce logical arguments to a series of symbols the use of which acts to remove the ambiguities that may be found in social languages. There is room for both, for it would be difficult to express your reasoning as to why you should choose a career in immunology in symbolic logic.

The importance of logic is that it helps to sharpen our thinking and writing; its use extends into everything we do. Some try to reject logic though, which is an entertaining proposition, for (logically), they imply either that deductive arguments do not hold (but there are insurmountable difficulties in explaining how), or that induction cannot prove anything. There is much more leniency with the latter for indeed every single assertion in an inductive argument can be tested empirically or rejected on the grounds that one's senses are faulty. Consider the reply to the argument '5 + 2 = 7': 'only if you say so'. My saying so has nothing to do with the logical validity of the proposition – each element can be examined and securely followed and no other result can be forthcoming. Rejecting deductive logic is different from rejecting advanced arguments which can be tripped up by some fallacy or logical leap, for all they require is tidying up; it is different again from rejecting inductive reasoning, which does pose separate issues most fascinatingly evinced in scientific and criminal cases in which a series of events have to be tied together (logically) and which also have to be substantiated by evidence. For example, Dr Emoto has argued that ice crystal formation is affected by the music played near the ice crystals, as well as by the scientist's emotional intentions towards the ice. This can be tested – but what if the results do show that indeed certain kinds of music help to form certain kinds of ice crystals and that saying, 'I love you' to the water does indeed help it to form objectively different crystals than saying, 'I despise you'? Sometimes a result is gained independently and repeatedly, yet no coherent explanation is forthcoming – the phenomenon lies beyond our present understanding perhaps, or a synthesis of present information is required that has not yet been done.

For some people, the human mind is not capable of properly reasoning through an argument, especially inductive ones. The quip 'if you say so' is disconcerting in some respects, but what does it imply? That your logic is different from mine? Perhaps so, for your world and the language by which you view the world is necessarily, even if only subtly different from mine. But if we begin to assess the validity of any independent argument, assumedly we would begin to follow some agreed upon rules, for example, 10 > 5 > 2, and thus 2 < 10, and so on, which would remove some of the subjectivity implied in the criticism. What could we conclude of someone who denied such elementary inferences? That there exists another logic, which is possible, but this would imply that they could teach us those rules, or that they are being illogical. Would that matter beyond infuriating others? Arguably, it would not do them any good in trying to cross the road, for the philosophical position that I find most attractive is that logic engages in helping us to understand ourselves and the world more, clearing out the nonsense and helping us to see if our beliefs are compatible with one another. If we do that, we should be able to live better lives.

Love

We've all asked what love is and wondered and worried whether we would recognize it should we encounter it. This implies that love has a nature, something that can be perceived and perhaps examined coolly, but of course some retort loudly that love has no nature, it just is and whatever it is, you either possess it or you don't, but you'll know when you do. This rather mystical reply may seem infuriating but that doesn't mean philosophy or clear thinking is rejected: if love is an experience, it can be seen purely as a subjective one, which only those who have experienced love can smile warmly and say, 'Yes, I've felt love', which remain alien words to those who haven't!

There are three initial theories of love's nature as described by the ideas of *eros*, *philia* and *agape*.

Eros refers to a passionate, intense desire for something, often a sexual desire, hence the modern notion of erotic. If erotic love stems from primal feelings, is it reducible to our selfish genes provoking us to discriminate between other DNA carriers for potential reproduction? A rather clinical way of looking at love indeed, but which fails somewhat when trying to explain the love of childless couples or homosexuals. What is it in the other that we find desirous? Is the attractiveness purely subjective, or does the desired other possess a universally definable beauty, which transcends cultural and personal norms? Plato thought so – the gorgeous person is said to partake in a beauty that is ideal or otherworldly, possessing a glimmer of what the ultimate beauty would look like. Platonic love invokes a sense of worship and of loving the other even if it is not reciprocated; it seeks to supersede physicality in favour of intellectual appreciation and worship. So when someone describes their relationship as Platonic they may mean that there's no sex and/or it's a mutually appreciative relationship, or that the other does not know of the unrequited erotic attachment!

Aristotle prefers to ground love in friendship and the raising of another's value to higher than anyone else's. Philia suggests reciprocity in friendship, appreciation and loyalty and as it rises to the pitch of love, it becomes exclusive and discriminatory, non-utilitarian in that the beloved is loved for her own sake: true friendship is necessarily between similarly virtuous and rational people, while the resulting love constitutes an excess of feeling, which suggests an erotic element of course, but proper love requires a solid psychological basis – it cannot be the base desire of the ogler or of those who seek company to feel secure: to love, you must first love yourself. Without an egoistic basis, one cannot extend sympathy and affection to others. Such self-love is not hedonistic, for Aristotle, it is instead a reflection of his pursuit of the noble and virtuous, which culminates in the pursuit of the reflective life, the highest form of life a man can lead. Do Aristotelian lovers merely gaze into each other's eyes though, discuss philosophy, or do they snog? One suspects that the Aristotelian would permit a range of expressions that incorporate physical and romantic love as well as the joy felt in one's beloved's company.

In contrast to Aristotle's discriminating love, a religious version of love, agape, begins with the paternal love of God for man and dutiful love of man for God, and extends to become the universal form of love preached by peace-lovers and Christians. 'Love the Lord your God with all your heart, and with all your soul, and with all your might' (Deut. 6.5) and love 'thy neighbour as thyself' (Lev. 19.18). Agape has elements of both eros and philia: the love of

God requires an absolute devotion reminiscent of Plato's love of Beauty involving an erotic passion, awe and desire, but which transcends earthly cares and obstacles. The universalism of agape requires a duty to extend love to others equally, even to 'love thy enemies' (Mt. 5.44–45). Such love transcends any perfectionist or aristocratic notions that some are (or should be) more lovable than others. But loving impartially invokes serious ethical concerns, especially if the neighbour ostensibly does not warrant love (or why should one discriminate between who is taken to the altar?). What is it about your neighbour you should love: their humanity or their conduct? Kant and Kierkegaard would demand we treat our neighbour with a dignity that all humans deserve, but is that regardless of their conduct and treatment of you or others? A powerful clause in the Christian notion of love is that one should forgive: love begins with a forgiveness of the other's crimes and misdemeanours, a reverse psychological tool to draw the wayward back into the realm of humaneness and hence into the privilege of being loved. Others would claim that the concept of universal love, of loving all equally, is not only impracticable, but logically empty –

> One cannot be a friend to many people in the sense of having friendship of the perfect type with them, just as one cannot be in love with many people at once (for love is a sort of excess of feeling, and it is the nature of such only to be felt towards one person). (Aristotle, *Nichomachean Ethics*, VIII.6)

So the words, 'I love you' breach a philosophical dam: I love you regardless of your conduct, you're intrinsically lovable, and don't mind me if you don't love me in return, I see you as the best friend I could ever have; my love is eternal, temporary, genetic, whimsical, physical, emotional, cultural, brotherly, filial, political, subservient, erotic, fantastical, needy, utilitarian, and so on. But then we surely must turn our thoughts to the lover – the self.

Marxism

Marxism is one of the most influential philosophical systems in world history. Aristotelianism is probably the second most influential, were someone to do a reckoning of adherents, texts, political espousers and academic apologists, its remit extending from Greece, across Arabia, and into South America with the Jesuits; but Marxism has, in just over a century, been exported from Germany and England to all countries. Russia and China were immersed in communist revolutions and although both countries have pulled back from Marxism in the past two decades, the cultural and political impacts have been enormous. In South and Middle America and parts of South East Asia, Marxist guerrillas and proponents still carry the red flag (while English dons may wear red socks). The effects have not just been political – Marxist philosophy spread into history, literature, anthropology, art, music, and even (temporarily) the sciences. So, what is this immensely influential philosophy that has fired revolution and change and left an impressive mark on the face of the world's political systems?

Marx studied under Hegel, who impressed upon him the inevitable movement of history, progressing towards a better life but rejected Hegel's idealism in favour of a dialectical materialism: material entities (notably economic forces) oppose and then merge to forge higher social levels. And by describing the opposing forces as classes, Marx was able to exploit a politically and culturally charged history attacking class and status, notably emanating from humanistic thinking and the age of enlightenment. The question as to why people should be judged differently according to their social status and occupation motivates humanist thinkers to reject artificial constraints to personal development or prejudicial legal and political systems that thwart whole classes of people such as the peasantry. Marx supplanted onto that a sense of injustice from the economic theory that he learned from reading Smith and Ricardo, who had renewed the labour theory of value while many thinkers were shifting towards a subjective theory of value. Smith argued that the value of a product was worth exactly what labour had been spent on producing it.

Understanding the labour theory of value is vital for understanding an important element of Marxism; although the philosophy does not need the labour theory of value, it has coloured its political aspects. According to Marx (reading Smith and Ricardo), a labouring worker creates exchange value in the goods that he produce, but the non-labouring capitalist takes a percentage from him for his own profit. This implies that the capitalist is exploiting his workers, who have no choice but to work for capitalists because they own only their labour, while capitalists own machinery and factories. It presents a simple duality by which to agitate the working class to rise up and seize the means of production and thereby capture the whole value. Behind its characterization was the notion that exchange value was objective and formed by labour; the objective theory of value is opposed by the subjective theory of value, which asserts that all value emanates from individual prioritization of choices and goods. The economist Böhm-Bawerk pointed out the difficulties with Marx's theory: imagine an artist working for hundreds of hours on a painting yet it is to no-one's taste: does that mean he is being exploited for his work and that he should be compensated (and by whom?) for his diligent effort? Others such as Ludwig Mises noted the problem of straddling classes – does a worker who buys tools become a capitalist (and thereby a class traitor in the eyes of adherents), and what of the factory owner who works with his hands? There are many problems, perhaps insurmountable, for the Marxist theory of value. Arguably, Marxism can shed the theory and still retain much sense; but understandably, supporters may not wish to renounce such a famous element of their doctrine, as the tentative explanation of why workers may feel oppression is certainly a fiery and easily assimilated one.

The other pillar on which Marxism rests is a historicist vision, adapted from Hegel's conception of history, in which the future is already determined by the nature of socio-economic evolution and in which communism will necessarily be victorious. Marx argued that the 'history of all hitherto existing societies is the history of class struggle.' As we move through history, the number of conflicting classes reduces from many in the Roman times through to three in the pre-industrial era (landowners, bourgeoisie and peasants) to two in the industrial era (workers and capitalists). In each case, the numbers of masters opposing the oppressed reduces; the next logical step is the overthrow of the masters and the victory of the proletariats. In examining history, Marx argued, these steps towards a diminished class system could be detected: in Marx's eyes, these movements constituted scientific evidence for his hypothesis but in sceptics' eyes, he only saw what he wanted to see exaggerating that which supported his ideas and ignoring that which opposed them. According to one prediction, the poor would get poorer and more numerous until a critical mass of numbers was reached and the capitalists would be overthrown. This evidently did not happen and the only communist revolutions that took place could easily be explained with alternative theories of opportunistic power grabbing.

Nonetheless, there are two strands to this historicism, both evident in Marx's writings. First, this future is strictly determined in that no matter what you or I do to help or hinder it, the revolution will happen, so we can sit back and wait for it to occur without lifting a finger. Secondly, and much more appealing to Marxist proponents, the revolution can be brought forward through agitation and raising the consciousness of the proletariat that they only have their chains to lose. The former tends to attract academics while the latter attracts union leaders and idealistic students. The division rent Marxism in two during his lifetime, leaving Karl supposedly spluttering on his death bed, 'Je ne suis pas marxiste' – but of what kind, we do not know.

Materialism

A materialist believes that the entirety of the world is material or physical in nature; that is, there are no spirits or immaterial entities except in the realm of our imagination, and even that realm is physical. It is a metaphysical theory concerning the ultimate nature of the universe. Dualists exert the separation between the immaterial or ideal world of forms or invisible forces and the realm of matter or physicality. As idealists reject the materiality of the world, so materialists reject the immateriality of the world, both rejecting the possibility of the two forms of the world being able to co-exist.

Early materialists sought to explain the world in terms of physical appearances resolving the world into four elements (earth, wind, fire, water) or five in Chinese thinking (adding wood). All animate and inanimate entities were said to be formed by either a combination of these basal elements or by one in particular. Historically, the basic element description of the universe was accepted by dualists who also posited an immaterial realm for the soul and God to inhabit, a theory that proto-scientists, keen to understand more about the workings of the world, generally accepted so as not to fall foul of theological authorities. Since gold, silver and mercury in particular appeared to be as non-reducible as fire, seventeenth-century theorists accepted the extension of the number of elements against the ancient orthodoxy, a view substantiated by the dissolution of other well-known compounds such as air into oxygen and nitrogen.

Nonetheless, the chemical explanation of the universe as justifying the materialist vision was simultaneously undermined by the explanation of invisible forces of physics. Newton's theory of gravity permitted the exertion of pull on a distant object; Faraday's work on electricity exploited electromagnetic attraction, again working over distances; more recently particle physicists have demonstrated the Pauli exclusion principle that an electron can either be up or down, and even if removed by a substantial distance, effecting a spin inversion forces the other electron to simultaneously adjust with no apparent physical link existing between the two. Finally, is space-time physical? Einstein's theory suggests that space-time can be warped both by mass and velocity, yet what is being warped? When we imagine a spatial matrix in which bodies exist through time,

Einstein's theory asserted that a body will warp its immediate environment causing gravitational fluctuations. The immateriality of space-time is affected by physical bodies – which would return us to the materialist thesis, if bodies are indeed material.

Idealist theorists prefer to assert the immateriality of the world, an argument readily but only apparently rejected by Dr Samuel Johnson's famous kicking of a stone: but quantum physics has related back to what the Chinese have spoken of as Wu Li, which explains the workings of the universe in terms of living energy – that energy is non-physical but presents physicality. Electrons, for example, are so miniscule as to remove themselves, in the eyes of some from physicality – being intensely wrapped up forms of energy. Physicists debate the ontological status of the miniscule: sometimes orthodoxies emerge, other times the orthodoxies shift under the force of new explanations. Behind the arguments, the philosopher detects the visions of idealists, dualists and materialists seeking to reduce complexity to their particular conception.

Materialists generally come under fire for accepting or implying atheism, a charge that was levelled, for example, against Thomas Hobbes; however, theologians do not have to accept that God is spirit, although most tend to do so. If the universe be physical and it follows that God is physical, it becomes theoretically possible for God to be detected – which raises epistemological issues as to where to look and what to look for of course, which is why most theologians prefer to posit an immaterial and therefore non-empirically identifiable deity.

Mathematics

Think of a number, any number will do. What is it? Yes, but what is it? Does your number exist independently of you and so it is something that I can see, or is your number a mental construction helping you to keep tally of the items that surround us – or is your number a purely mental construction that does not have to relate to the world at all?

Realists, who take their cue from Plato, argue that numbers do exist as independent objects. Consider the sum $3 + 3 = 6$; logically, the answer must be valid at all times and in all places. Does that therefore imply that the numbers must possess some special status? For their status and the validity of the operation does not depend on our understanding or even acknowledging them to be valid. Such an argument can be applied of all logical statements, such as $A > B > C$, so $A > C$, which does lead realists to claim that indeed logical statements reflect a superior or eternal reality. Such philosophical thinking acted to impede mathematical reasoning. Zero, for instance, plagued early Western thinkers who believed it to be the devil's number, for how could 'nothing' exist: exist – indeed, the properties of zero are strange: multiply it by any number and it just disappears – one million times zero is still zero. Zero and infinity were rejected by some of the greatest philosophers, including in modern times Hobbes and Descartes, who could not fathom the reality of something supposedly non-existent – accordingly, they also rejected the possibility of the vacuum.

The Aristotelian position rejects Plato's realism in favour of a reductionist account of mathematics. A number exists as a collection of things (coins, sheep in the field), but you abstract from the particulars to form the abstract, just as a geometer abstracts from the sketches of circles in the sand to work mathematically on abstract circles whose circumferences do not wobble. That is, our numbers and shapes refer to real numbers and shapes (real in the sense of observable rather than Plato's 'real' as implying independently existing without physicality). We encounter the argument again in the empiricism of Locke and Mill, who also noted how the child learns to count from perceptual things. This may explain basic counting and operations, so I can add $12 + 13$ by deploying 25 coins or sticks to prove my case; but how do I then explain that I can multiply $6^7 \times 6^6$ and be certain of my answer? Is there a tentative logical connection between the physicality of things that I can get my hands on to work with and the non-physicality of things that I cannot directly perceive (or wish to count out!)?

Supporters tend to agree with the rationalists who believe that all the relevant details of mathematics are innate and apodictally knowable. For instance, Kant preferred to see numbers as self-evident entities, which the mind just knows, but this leans towards a subjectivity that is not attractive to those who see numbers as possessing universal status. The certainty attached to mathematical operations is interesting logically speaking, for $\sqrt{144} = 12$, so are the numbers and their operations purely logical constructions then? This is what Frege and then Russell sought to claim; they tried to tie maths to a logical foundation, but not all have agreed that they succeeded, for in presenting some basic premises to begin the logical enterprise non-logical ideas are required. Formalists such as Hilbert argue that not all mathematical statements can be proven, but they are nonetheless useful, so rather than worrying whether there is a real foundation or whether concepts such as the infinitesimal in calculus are real, mathematicians should just work with the symbols and their formal relations. However, Gödel pointed out that the validity of formalism cannot be guaranteed within its own system, which once again undermined the attempt to nail the philosophy of mathematics onto the mathematical door.

Metaphysics

Derived from a book that followed Aristotle's *Physics* (meta meaning 'after'), the term metaphysics has come to imply the study of the whole of reality rather than the specifics dealt with in the individual sciences, or in another sense metaphysics deals with the possibility and nature of fundamental reality.

Beginning metaphysics is not easy, for taking up one strand produces a host of implications leading into a specific school.

> Every metaphysical question always encompasses the whole range
> of metaphysical problems. (Heidegger, 'What is Metaphysics?' 93)

For instance, if the world of phenomena is taken as an illusion, it must be hiding something else behind it, or there is an alternative substratum which philosophical analysis may be able to reveal. Alternatively, the common sense position that I encounter is a physical reality: the things I see are really real. But at what point do the things I perceive become 'really real'? Is it when my body bumps into them such as when I place my hand on the table? At the molecular level there is no physical encounter taking place, only an interaction of some molecular structures by another, and if we could see the interaction between my hand and the table, we would see a mass of swiftly moving molecular structures repelling and attracting in a fluid, dynamic combination, and what constitutes the skin's structure would disappear into a complexity of atomic storms: only when we pull back out of the atomic realm do entities become discernible. In other words, our senses have evolved to perceive a particular form of reality that has given our ancestors an edge in surviving (at least for now), but then again, is that reality 'really real'. Beneath the subatomic level (beyond quarks, say), the conjectures of scientists become increasingly familiar to philosophers: is the world just energy, and is energy captured in hypothesized multidimensional strings? No evidence except mathematical conjectures rule here, reminding some physicists that they are now on uncertain scientific ground.

Even if we retain a common sense view of the world, it is not easy to dismiss metaphysical speculations. While we may reject the notion of a suprasensible world, we can still accept that we can think about entities existing beyond those of immediate experience such as causation, substance, being, mind, body, self, time and even space. Kant may prefer to argue that these are necessary categories of the human mind and hence we cannot help but know through these concepts, whereas others such as Hegel, present a philosophy replete with metaphysical ideas that one sometimes wonders what has happened to the familiar 'real' world. Accordingly, some philosophers are sceptical of metaphysics. In modern philosophy, David Hume championed scepticism with his claim that the works of metaphysics should be committed to the flames.

Consider the question that a physicist may pose: 'What is the melting point of mercury?' For a metaphysicist, a prior question must be asked and an answer assumed, namely concerning the universe's nature in which the experiment is to take place: is the universe independent of the minds seeking knowledge, or is it dependent upon how our minds work and how we humans perceive? Is the universe stable with understandable laws, or is it a spontaneously evolving and unpredictable universe in which scientific laws are temporary illusions or fictions? Are there many things in this world, or are the many mere reflections of one ultimate substratum? Do the things that we study similarly possess minds as we do, or can we establish, for certain, a division between the living and non-living world – between matter and spirit?

Once we begin such questions, we are faced with critical issues: can such questions actually be answered such that they will be logically or empirically acceptable (or both)? Not all philosophers accept the metaphysical trail claiming that the goals proposed are ethereal and imaginative or mistakes of language's ambiguities. Others may accept that metaphysical truths do exist, but that our minds are incapable of dealing with the knowledge or methods required to access the truths, which is an argument sometimes deployed by those who believe in God – His nature is beyond human capacity to experience or to reason about, so we must just believe.

'But in what?' demands the critic: if a suprasensible reality is argued to exist, it cannot exist just because I can deploy the term 'suprasensible', just as my use of the word 'unicorn' does not necessitate the existence of such a being. Such scepticism can then be turned on other metaphysical topics such as the self, being, time, reality, mind, and so on. Trying to establish the meaning of the term by referring to an ulterior reality poses innumerable problems in the eyes of sceptics. Wittgenstein and positivists such as A. J. Ayer prefer to reject metaphysics as a problem generated by loose language – if a word does not have an evident referent in the same way that 'dog' = 'that dog there' (and with all the understood rules concerning the relationship between the three words and the referents of 'that' and 'there'), then it should be rejected as a mere noise, for example, 'God told his angels to disperse among the Heavens', should be read as 'Blah told his blah to disperse among the blah.' Similarly, Quine rejects metaphysics arguing that the physical facts are the facts. Hume's is a poignant rejoinder and keeps metaphysicians on their toes, but even if we may speak clearer and strictly employ terms with referents, a metaphysician may reply that the words and referents themselves denote a common framework in which minds, words, and signs all work either between ourselves, which says something about communication, and often between what is said and what is referred to, and that the task of metaphysics is to seek to understand that framework.

Mill, John Stuart (1806–1873)

John Stuart Mill provides us with an enduring and accessible account of a utilitarian philosophy that underpins much of the modern liberal ethos characterizing present political practice. A precocious child, Mill was taught by his father and godfather, Jeremy Bentham, learning Greek at the age of 3, Latin at 8, and before the age of 10 he was reading Plato's dialogues; his reading was phenomenal – history, travel, the classics of literature and poetry. Unsurprisingly, his childhood was sacrificed to his father's pedagogy and all toys and games were frowned upon. The austere, puritanical mood such stifling atmosphere created (he studied at his father's desk as he wrote) leaves a lasting impression which emerges in his criticism of ostentation and idleness in later writings; moreover, the strict educational regime eventually took its toll in a mental depression at the age of 19.

> [My] father, in all his teaching, demanded of me not only the utmost that I could do, but much that I could by no possibility have done. (Mill, *Autobiography*, 7)

From such an extraordinary education, Mill developed a wonderful penmanship and lucidity of prose that sometimes belie a confusion of thought or an appreciation of all positions, depending on your take. Following his breakdown, Mill apparently rejected his father's democratic, utilitarian, *laissez-faire* thinking and scepticism of power; but, despite some dillydallying, as biographers have noted, as the years went by, Mill gradually reverted back to the general gist that his father inculcated on him.

Mill gained intellectual and popular fame through the publication of what became a nineteenth-century equivalent of a bestseller: his *System of Logic*, a treatise written over 13 years or so. In it, he espoused a strict Lockean empiricism and psychological associationism seeking to marry both to a scientific foundation for the social sciences that would mimic Newton's style; he accordingly attacked intuitionist or apodictic epistemology and the Aristotelian syllogism. Intuitionism implies that the mind holds the key to understanding the world, rather than the senses and the accumulation of experiences; he appropriately rejected Kant's philosophy which seeks to ground human knowledge on the mind's categories of understanding and he also concluded that the syllogistic form of logic can neither provide certainty: indeed, there is no certainty, only experience of similar happenings.

Mill also reasoned that all propositions are resoluble into perceived events – knowledge is purely inductive, so each time we find that $2 + 2 = 4$ we renew our faith in what is an habitual assumption. This echoes Humean thinking and is an area of Mill's thought that logicians beginning with Frege have swiftly dealt critical blows although others, such as Kripke, have risen to defend him. When we multiply 10^9 by 10^8 to get 10^{17}, Mill's principle would imply that I have experienced or counted 10^9, and so on, as actual objects, otherwise I am making a deductive leap, which his logic could not accommodate. In language, propositions can be divided into 'real' ones that reflect the existence of objects perceived and 'verbal' ones that merely define the words we employ. Verbal propositions are thereby empty of content and do not add to the stock of human knowledge: knowledge can only grow through perceiving and developing generalizations based on induction.

Mill aimed to strengthen his philosophy by merging induction with naturalism, the theory that we ought to proceed in examining and making generalizations upon our knowledge in the same manner as the natural sciences do. Critically though, empiricism can be severed from naturalism, for knowledge in other subject areas (psychology, for instance) may have to be dealt with different procedures and tests – it is characteristic of Mill's philosophical endeavour to maintain the connection between the two, so his comments on physics may swiftly follow similar thinking on social or political issues.

With such a strict empiricist ethos, Mill rejected any possibility of deductive truth as found in the traditional syllogisms such as 'all men are mortal, Socrates is a man, therefore Socrates is mortal', on the grounds that the major premise (all men are mortal) is actually an inductive hypothesis based on the experience that we have of men dying – arguably, there could be an immortal somewhere (just as there could be that proverbial white crow). What the earlier Scholastics had held, that the syllogism proves a particular from a universal, Mill inverted: from the particular fact, a universal may follow – we know that particular men, including Socrates, die and the assertion 'all men are mortal' is simply a reminder of what we draw from our experiences of men. As knowledge becomes increasingly complicated, we make generalizations and their strength depends on the evidence backing them up – stronger and truer laws of nature will thus emerge from comparing generalizations and building on them until laws of nature, from which no exceptions have been experienced, are gleaned. Unsurprisingly, Mill welcomed Darwin's inductive theory on the origin of the species – it echoed his epistemological programme of building up from particulars to theories and laws.

Considering cause, Mill proposed that all events have prior causes and it behoves us to consider all of an event's causes – that is, antecedent causes C_1, C_2, C_3, . . ., C_n, all may cause E to happen, which while seemingly correct does render studying causes and effects an experience for eternity; he nevertheless acknowledged that we become habitually interested in those causes that have more sway or relevance than others. More importantly, his logic of causation has some unnerving consequences for volitional acts – surely, everything that you do has prior causes, leaving you to become mere flotsam on an impersonal sea of causation? He indeed wrote that:

> The metaphysical theory of free-will, as held by philosophers . . . was invented because the supposed alternative of admitting human actions to be *necessary* was deemed inconsistent with every one's instinctive consciousness, as well as humiliating to the pride, and even degrading to the moral nature, of man. (Mill, *A System of Logic*, 547)

Your mind and its contents are the result of your experiences and perceptions, in that you are passive, and so your actions are similarly necessary by what has gone before in your mind. Thus psychological associations formed in your mind enter the causal array prompting an action – but what of your will to change? If it is there, it is there because a desire to change has arisen (prompted by antecedent reasons) and so you are free to alter your character, he argued, or rather that you possess the power to do so because the power for change has arisen in your psyche. Behind your psyche lie the circumstances of your particular context, and these may aid or diminish your pursuits in life.

Mill adhered to his father's associationist theory (that your mind's ideas associate in a manner similar to the way in which consecutive events may be described by the physical sciences) and expanded on the importance of getting environmental conditions right for others to ensure both their moral and political potential. Emphatically, if early education can be got right then people will advance, but if the foundations are not conducive to learning and to higher associations then people will necessarily flounder. Mill's theory has varying implications here – while he paid lip-service to a minimal state libertarian political philosophy, he argues that children's education is too important to be left to the whims of ill-educated parents and so it must become a legal obligation to educate them (he was, however, against state sponsored schools); when considering women, Mill proposed that the differences between the genders are similarly circumstantial – if the laws are changed to permit equality, then women's and men's talents should converge.

> All women are brought up from the very earliest years in the belief that their ideal of character is the very opposite to that of men; not self-will, and government by self-control, but submission, and yielding to the control over others. (Mill, 'The Subjection of Women', in *On Liberty*, 487)

Once freed from debilitating conditions that diminish human potential, people should be free to pursue their own lives, so long as they do not commit harm against others. This is Mill's eruditely penned message in his *On Liberty*. The child and other people whose mentality is not sufficient – idiots and the 'barbarian' races (with whom he had no contact) – deserve governmental protection of a minimal kind, but there the limits on action should halt. If a woman is about to commit an act injurious to herself, we may well recommend that she thinks twice, but we have no right to stop her 'for her own protection'. Too often, the patronizing principle has led to economic and political stagnation, Mill warned, and so should be eschewed.

However, a distinctly patronizing philosophy seeps out of his own liberal proposals – the barbaric races need to be controlled and educated and hence to be brought up to become civilized. In this he was highly influenced by his father's *History of India*, in which James Mill's utilitarian philosophy was merged with a vaguely historicist vision of civilization development: if a country's morals were lacking (and evidently they were in the case of widows having to 'join' their husbands on their funeral pyres) then the entire society was condemned as being below the par that England could ascribe to: so regardless of other traditions intellectual or aesthetic, India ought to be subject to civilizing control just like children.

Politically though, for civilized people enjoying a good education, life would become universally good – indeed too good in a way: we would all become the same. Should liberalism succeed in its extension of the benefits of capitalism and the freedoms of thought, speech, religion, movement and association, then all will rise in their station to become equally middle class or *bourgeois*. So we need a few eccentrics to stir things up now and again, Mill recommended. Progress – moral or scientific – typically stems from the individual who breaks from the crowd with heterodox views. In a vision that many present thinkers relate to, the ubiquity of mass culture and homogeneity of thought and lifestyle threatens the individualist who remains change's hope: the unorthodox or intellectually gifted should not rise to take over the state and hence control people, but they should lead people by example and by teaching to experiment beyond the norms of everyday life. Indeed, Mill, the child prodigy, wrote particularly sensitively on the importance and fate of the individual. The mimicry that characterizes modern life – a life of new popular conventions and customs that drive most to wear the same clothes and think the same vacuous thoughts – toll the bell of stagnation for Mill. (Look around you,

how is our society doing through Millian eyes?) But true to his associationist principles, the genius or innovator is like a flower: if placed
in a bed of detrimental soil and weeds then he or she is not likely to
flourish. That conditions must be improved for the successful main-
tenance of individualism is an inescapable implication, yet one that
lends itself to Mill's utopian thinking of the educated leading the
uneducated as they did in Victorian schools and as he did with his
younger siblings. A dim echo of Mill was recently heard in Tony
Blair's 1996 platform: 'education, education, education'.

Mill's representative government should be elected by those
capable of intelligently commenting and voting on policy (the
boundaries of which should be kept to a minimum anyway), thus
excluding the illiterate, and those of higher mental achievements
(such as himself) should be given more votes; voting should no
longer be secret though, for the educated must lead by example
and public voting be therefore promoted; finally, MPs should be
free from political manifestos, for again, the superior intellect (of
which he is again our example, successfully standing for election in
1865) should give the MP the ability and right to judge more judi-
ciously than his voters of lesser intelligence.

Throughout Mill's clearly written prose we experience the vision
of man keen to ensure the defence of civilization and of the higher
values that civil culture can offer – education and forming better
social conditions are necessary to that ambition as is a strict adher-
ence to naturalist empiricism to undermine the dangerous dogmas
and prejudices of intuitionism. Philosophy mattered to Mill for it
reaches out into all disciplines and parts of our lives – such was the
radicalism that he inherited.

Mind

When a thought takes place, where does it take place? When an
object is perceived, where is it perceived? When an action takes

place, whence did it initiate? The answer is usually considered to be 'in the mind', but inquisitive philosophers demand what is meant by that and it is not a pursuit that may be likened to grasping at clouds, for how we view the mind has a broad and influential impact on a variety of subjects and life.

The philosophy of the mind asks what is the nature of the human mind and what, if any, is its relationship to the body and to the extramental world and whether my mind is unique and distinct, or inseparable from others' minds.

For a materialist, there is no difference between the material world and the mind. That is, the mind with all of its thoughts, images, associations, reasoning and memory, is the brain and the brain is the mind. To the other monist (someone who perceives the world as possessing one kind of nature), the immaterialist, the mind is nothing different from the immaterial world, for all is mind – one universal mind, to which yours and mine intimately partake and without individual distinction. 'My thought' is indistinct from 'your thought', which seems intrinsically difficult to sustain, but a supporting analogy would be that my radio could tune into the same radio station as yours, so why reject the possibility that our thoughts could similarly tap into universal thought? Hegel believed that the universe is a living spirit, which has been read by mystics and philosophers alike to explain the distinction between animate and inanimate matter: life is driven by a guiding force, so my mind and yours are only apparent distinct realms for they share a common denominator that inextricably links all living (or perhaps only sentient) beings.

Opposing monists are dualists, who claim that the universe divides into two kinds of substance – material and immaterial; dualists accordingly see the mind as immaterial, which helps to explain the apparent lack of dimensions that thought has, and the real world as material, which helps to explain the apparent physicality of the extramental world – the world that our senses encounter.

The dualist position seems to explain a lot. It may, for instance, be asked of a materialist, 'Where is the thought of green?' And even if a brain scan can identify that certain behaviour or sensations cause a specific part of the brain and its associated neurons to fire, it still does not follow that green is visible to anyone but the thinker of green. Imagine being able to enter a brain, magnified to the size of a mill, Leibniz wrote in 1714, 'we should not see anything which would explain a perception' (*Monadology*, 17).

'Where am I except in thought?' the dualist proceeds. Here an obvious problem arises that was pointed out to Descartes by Elizabeth of Bohemia: how does the immaterial mind cause a material body to act? Even with today's understanding of anatomy, an awkward gap arises when we consider what activates the motor neurons that fire muscular movement: the signal from a brain lobe may be followed to the raising of the arm, but what began the signal? The self, the mind, the soul, the psyche are all proffered answers, but how does this immaterial entity effect upon a material entity? Descartes mumbled a reply about the pituitary gland, which leaves critics unimpressed, for the gap between material and immaterial still pertains regardless of where the bridge is supposed to be – for the immaterial bridge must stretch into materiality at some point: but where is this 'Ghost in the Machine', asked Gilbert Ryle?

Epiphenomenalists avoid the causality issue by proposing that the mind is a depository of acts, a kind of smoke, which receives inputs but which cannot act upon the physical body. We seem to feel pain, but really this is just the body reacting to a dangerous stimulus and activating a sympathetic response; the mind is separable from the physical action. This leaves the body tied to the flows of physical life, being tossed upon its waves as it were, but the mind sitting angel-like, recording events but not initiating action.

Two recent theories seeking to bypass the mind–body duality of Descartes are logical behaviourism and functionalism. Logical behaviourism reduces the mental to the behavioural, so when

I think, I am behaving, which entails publicly visible actions; all psychological language must be reducible to statements about behaviour, otherwise it is nonsense. This strict view of the mental invokes immediate retort: I may be thinking, but of what? Who can tell? Or I may look as if I am thinking (as in focused, concentrated thought) but I'm merely daydreaming.

Functionalism similarly tends to depend upon a materialist premise, but asks not what is the mind but what is the mind for? Being in a mental state is being in a functional state, according to this theory: functionalists accept causes of mental states, explain that mental states can influence each other, and that they cause behaviour. The division between mental and material worlds is a logical, categorical mistake, argue functionalists, a mere mental contrivance that causes a lot of intellectual problems and ramifications: if I believe that the mind is separable from the body, then surely my mind, unconstrained by anything so mundane as materiality, could float away from this ostensible coil holding it in and fly into another's mind.

Indeed so, say the dualists: that is why we tend to believe in heaven or in the Platonic world of Forms. Nonsense, replies the functionalist. A mind is a mere functioning entity commensurate with the material world: it is the body's software upon which the body runs, and the separation of body and mind here is merely for explanation.

Nietzsche, Friedrich (1844–1900)

Reading Nietzsche encourages a strong impression that one should rise above the masses, discard the morality of the common herd, reject religion, sport a T-shirt announcing 'God is dead', grasp life by the horns, become an off-the-wall artist or military dictator and generally strut around with a big moustache filled with self-importance and arrogance while listening to Wagner. Nevertheless, Nietzsche himself ended up a mad cripple; like Franz Schubert, he poured out his creative talent in an expedited rush, and although no-one's quite sure whether Nietzsche was suffering from syphilis, diphtheria and/or typhoid, he collapsed in 1889 and spent the rest of his years dwindling. As with Schubert, in his phenomenal output we encounter a stretching of the human mind towards and perhaps beyond its normal capacities drawn from a precocious and brilliant foundation and cast upward and outward in a marvellous literary flow that needs to be savoured with a glass of wine and an opera to be appreciated.

Friedrich Nietzsche was born into a Lutheran family, studied theology and classical philology and following the death of his father was brought up by the women of his family and his boarding school, Pforta, Germany's most prestigious school. Either from their attentions or from a failed relationship with Lou Salomé a Russian feminist (and an unrequited one with Cosima Wagner), he became highly misogynist, despising women and arguing that they should be kept in an inferior position by masculine control: when going among women, don't forget your whip, he has his prophet Zarathustra's advice.

In some respects, we should be able to ignore the peculiar prejudices of philosophers, yet while in his penmanship, Nietzsche is vitriolic towards women, in life he was polite and gentlemanly, having been brought up well. Nonetheless and unfortunately, a despairing of womankind fits into the Nietzschean ethos – a vision of strong-willed aristocratic men running the world and trampling on the masses and women to assert their own virility and virtue, forging a new morality and a new humanity – the *Übermensch*, the Supermen. Something very far from what crippled and sick Nietzsche could ever attain. A wonderful division between his mind and his pen exudes from his biography, just like the all-conquering unmerciful emperor of war-gaming adventure and the milder, softly spoken boy who emerges from the world of his PC.

Awarded a professorship at the prodigiously young age of 24, his first work soon followed. Nietzsche was attracted by Hellenism, Schopenhauer and by his contemporary and friend, the composer

Richard Wagner – indeed, Nietzsche was for many years enamoured with Wagner, whose compositions and conversations influenced Nietzsche's early writings and, despite the dissolution of their friendship, Nietzsche never lost his adoration. The Nietzschean *Übermensch* is highly reminiscent of Wagner's Teutonic heroes, which is probably the first time in the history of philosophy that an ideal has been drawn from opera. One can hardly dare imagine present philosophers being moved by the Spice Girls. Wagner's Siegfried presents a philosophical vision of life, its cycle, its tragedies. The perfect tragedy, like the perfect man, the *Übermensch*, is when the duality of Greek spirits Apollo and Dionysus merge. Apollo stands for reason, individuality, order and mind, he is active and heroic and in embracing Apollo we can draw a veil over the tumult of life to present a more orderly vision of life; Dionysus represents primordial emotion, spontaneity, sensual abandon, the loss of individuality in collective orgiastic ecstasy, and accordingly Dionysus is terrifying, but his spirit can be embraced to reach into life's depths and horrors, indeed into nothingness. Both visions are necessary. Through art we can transfigure ourselves: the Greeks knew, as we must know, that life is dangerous and precarious, but through such art that merges Dionysus with Apollo we can assert ourselves – art is the means to metaphysical understanding, a means by which to perceive the world. Music leads us to myth, and tragedy leads us to understand that life means eventual dissolution and death; together, they form the perfect duet, a duet that enables us to fortify ourselves, if it is done properly, with philosophical intent to show us the horror of nothingness by giving us Apollo and his insistence on form and beauty as a veneer and safety line for our minds.

The Greeks, according to Nietzsche, reached their height in the Aeschylian and Sophoclean tragedies just before Socrates began philosophizing and spreading ideas to the Athenian citizens. Then the Greek ideal was dashed by Socrates' rationalizations and so too their way of looking at the world aesthetically as a means to assert their vivaciousness. Socrates wanted to explain things rationally, scientifically, and that, for Nietzsche disrupted the critical harmony and power of the Dionysian–Apollonian convergence. Socrates thereby rejected the Dionysian abandonment of reason and the peering into the abyss: instead, instinct and intuition are to be rejected in favour of rational and psychological analysis. From then on, art and all that is important to humanity would be Socratic – optimistic and rational indeed, but missing the vital component of Dionysus and authentic tragedy. Until Wagner that is. Wagner constitutes the rebirth of the Hellenic brilliance – in Wagner's operas we find the realization of life's utter futility draped once more by Apollo's comforting veil of order through music.

Nietzsche rejected Christianity as anti-life and as posing humanity's greatest danger in its exaltation of the weak and its evocation of pity as a moral aesthetic. Once we move beyond his aesthetic-metaphysical thinking, Nietzsche's philosophy and renown is dominated by his famous remark from *The Anti-Christ*, 'God is dead.' Religion provides a sop to the masses and thereby weakens the highest form of humanity that can be reached – the aristocratic ideal of unity and strength. Instead, Socrates' philosophy and that of Christianity (which borrowed intellectually from the Platonic tradition) present a false metaphysics of two worlds, this world and the other world (heaven). Such metaphysics belongs in the head, and what would the world be like if one had to cut off the head? The present, real world that we encounter is all that there is. Similarly, the state and democracy are antagonistic towards the culture that the aristocratic ideal man can reach, although they are useful in giving the masses an outlet for their energies and passions, and hence in forming a relatively solid base from which the *Übermensch* can develop.

We are asked to abandon God and to abandon the trite and vulgar in order to become the new humans who will go beyond the good and evil of traditional moralities to form their own destinies. In *Thus Spake Zarathustra*, Nietzsche waxed poetically and critically as the archetypal wise man descending from the mountain to examine

modern life. He found modernity empty and weak, his nihilism
effected an indifference to life and his morality was hypocritically
motivated by a life-destroying resentment, pity and guilt cultivated
by religion to empower the masses and undermine the great among
us; the motivated must strive to become the *Übermensch*. But such
individuals who can truly master themselves are rare and modern
culture is not a conducive breeding ground for them either.

Another fundamental element to Nietzsche's later thoughts is
his belief in the eternal recurrence: that everything that happens
will happen again, and again, and again. In a sense, this is similar to
his demand that we have the courage to peer into the abyss (but be
aware that the abyss may be peering into you, he penned), that
implies that we come to understand our life – would we think and
act differently if everything that we do would be repeated eternally? Nietzsche thought that this should be incentive enough to
strive to fulfil our potential rather than to break down at life's apparent pointlessness. The *Übermensch* ought to embrace the abyss and
the eternal recurrence.

Nietzsche's writings usher in their own nihilism, which Nietzsche
would have rejected: he sought to provide a way for humanity, or
the best of it, to assert their life force against the world, not to
abandon themselves to the worldly pessimism of Schopenhauer.
This is partly because readers can latch onto the epistemological
nihilism in his pronouncements on truth: there is no such thing
as facts, only interpretations. (But how do we interpret this statement?) Morality similarly is merely the moral interpretation of
phenomena. If facts are inadmissible and the only vehicle is our
interpretation of what we encounter, then we should embrace that
encounter: we should engage in discourse and enjoy the plurality
that conversation and philosophizing provides, instead of seeking
to master one another with particular viewpoints.

This brief review has overlooked a vast amount of Nietzsche's
thoughts, for many are captured in aphorisms; hence, the concentration has been on the intriguing side of Nietzsche's aesthetic

vision for metaphysics, one that is unique in arguing for a philosophical vision through opera.

Ontology

When we ask what is being, that is, what exists (What am I? What
is the universe? What exists?), then we enter the realm of ontology.
It is best approached by raising questions.

Do I exist? Do other people exist? Do the things that I seem to
perceive actually exist, and by that do I mean that they must exist
independently of me? A child places her hands over her eyes to
hide – the world has disappeared and so has the child from her
perspective: are philosophers similarly caught thinking so childishly,
or does the innocence of the child point to something more
profound?

I look over and see my son – it is hard to sustain an argument
that he is merely a figment of my imagination and that when I leave
the room he disappears, for he apparently leads a separate life from
me in my absence. Yet I may be continually fooling myself or being
fooled – can I be so sure of the independence of extramental
objects? Or of myself as an independent being? Or am I, and all
that I perceive as independent, nothing but a continuous swirl of
energies that happen to seem distinguishable from other things
only to our special senses (so haphazardly evolved to perceive only
certain electromagnetic frequencies)?

When I ask what exists, I am forced to consider how I come to
know about these things I perceive, which leads to epistemology.
Being and knowledge are interlinked, for something to be demands
that 'it' is, and to be an 'it' requires an acknowledgement by my
senses, mind or both. But is there a mere 'it' or a 'they'?

When I swarm my senses over the world of things around me,
can I say that there are things which are distinguishable into particulars and groups, or is all One? Is the stuff of these things material

or immaterial (figments of the mind, either my mind or The Mind of God)? And am I ineluctably led, like a moth to the flame, to accept that because things exist that God exists? This, St Anselm's Onto-logical Argument, has been highly influential: if something exists, then my understanding leads me to accept a something which is greater than all other things (the perfect being); assuredly a perfect being cannot only exist in my own mind, for it would otherwise not be perfect – so God exists. Logically, the argument leaps (Does there have to be a perfect being? Is existence a predicate?) before skipping to its conclusion, and accordingly it has its defenders and attackers, with some falling back onto what is called 'ontological commitment' – that is, avoiding the veracity of certain things, I can still claim that they possess an existence for me (or for my culture or country), and so they have a power to guide my actions.

Sometimes we are affected by an ontological commitment to dubious events or things (ghosts, UFOs, Elvis still living, government inquiries) which affect our lives, but philosophy does not retreat graciously from psychological realms here – it chases the thoughts asking about the nature of their being and the relationship of thought to action. Does that seem odd? Think of an animal – hold it there. Now, can we say that animal exists? Or, let me introduce you to Gringo, my invisible friend . . . if I am affected by mental entities, such as the number '13' or 'God' then the ontologist demands we think more about how something mental, which can affect action, can be said to exist.

At this stage, the wonderment so characteristic of the philoso-pher either immerses thought into such ponderings or pauses and retreats from ontology considering it to be the realm of poets.

Phenomenology

Phenomenology is the study of appearances, but what can philoso-phers mean when they study appearances? Philosophers are renowned for asking such awkward questions and this one is particularly peculiar – surely, the lovers of wisdom ought to be examining the 'real nature' of things, such as love, horses and beer. Some philosophers like to distinguish between appearance and reality, which suggests that what we see is not what is really there, or what is seen is not the reality of what is seen. Much literature and many movies play with the dualism that 'things are not quite what they seem'. The theory suggests that there is an underlying truth to be discerned somehow or other. Yet phenomenologists disparage such a move in preference for studying the appearances that we encounter: what else, they ask, can our senses contact?

Much of philosophy has, in the opinion of phenomenologists, apparently got itself entangled in the origins and justification of knowledge: empiricists claim that the senses are valid and what is perceived must be *real*, whereas rationalists assert that only the deductive operations of the mind make sense. Phenomenologists prefer to straddle the debate, resolve the duality between the workings of the mind and body and assert the coherency of encountering phenomena: we cannot know what things are truly like through our perception of them alone, for each change of angle provides an alternative vision of what is seen – the apparently uniform colour of 'brown' on the chair opposite me presents a range of hues. 'Brown' nonetheless belongs to a universal notion that my mind employs to distinguish brown-like articles from other coloured objects. That is, the senses do not perceive a universally acknowledgeable reality, only what is encountered personally. You will see it differently from how I see it, and who knows how the dog perceives the chair. But nor does the logico-deductive method provide a sufficient method for knowing.

A difference in opinion arises between earlier eighteenth-to nineteenth-century thoughts on the subject, and that of twentieth-century expositions. For instance, for Lambert, who influenced Kant, and who came up with the word, it means the study of consciousness. Kant asserted that it is impossible to know things-in-themselves, that is the very essence of the things we perceive, we can only know that we are; for Hegel, it is the study of things as they appear to us to gain an understanding through them to an underlying truth, which ultimately means the truth of what he terms the Absolute Spirit. Modern phenomenology begins with Husserl's endeavour to present a new method of knowing things. In this case, what we see are the appearances that our minds take up and then, when we encourage our mind to remove all extraneous elements from the picture that we have of the thing perceived, then we are in a position to gain an *eidetic* (ideal) intuition of what we hold in our consciousness. We get to know what a thing is really like through our personal intuitive grasp of what it is like: Husserl's project is also to remove anything that is not seen as extraneous – if it is not seen, then it cannot be part of the mind's study. This move implies that speculative metaphysics (what does God look like?) likewise can have no place in the mind, for it is not derived from what we encounter.

In some respects, we could take Husserl as presenting an empiricist view of entities, extending Hume's scepticism concerning extraneous conceptions of them as including cause and effect relationships; however, the emphasis is placed on what the consciousness comprehends rather than on what is 'out there', and by consciousness is meant the first-person point of view, rather than the 'scientific' third-person point of view. Turning our thoughts inward, we find that our consciousness is directed to an object, it possesses an intentionality towards it, and so our encounter with it is through our consciousness. The object may be an entity encountered, or indeed it may be a psychological state such as anger, or a memory, or a desire for something. To say that I am conscious of pain, for instance, is to assert that I am intentionally directing my consciousness towards the phenomenon of pain, that gives me an insight into Pain with a capital P. In turn, consciousness involves a variety of other experiences such as spatial and temporal awareness, and an awareness of self, others, of one's movement, of one's present situation (culturally and politically speaking, say).

Plato (428–347 BC)

Plato ('broad shouldered') was a student of the famed Socrates; he was the author of numerous dialogues in which his mentor stars vicariously embellishing Plato's own philosophy, at times doyen of theological hierarchies, the fountainhead of educational and political theories for over 2,000 years, and still worth studying for enjoyment and insight.

Plato was born Aristocles to a prominent political family in Athens in 428 BC just after the outbreak of the Peloponnesian War (431–404 BC); he saw Athens defeated by the Spartans and then lived through the political upheaval and tyranny of the Thirty Oligarchs, before democracy was reinstated and Socrates was sentenced to death by the city in 399 BC. Initially, he turned his mind to poetry but gave it up for philosophy after being introduced to Socrates; to some extent it is evident that he hankered after political influence and served twice as an adviser in Syracuse and Atarneus, but his main influence was to be gained through his political idealism as expounded in the *Republic* and the *Laws*.

As a young man, Plato travelled around the Hellenic world and Egypt. In Southern Italy, he met the Orphic-Pythagoreans who introduced him or encouraged him into a belief in the after-world and into the importance of mathematics. In 386 BC, he returned to Athens to found the first university, the Academy, which was designed to instruct people to become better citizens and statesmen; although his political influence did not achieve his expectations, the influence of his philosophical systems have not waned.

With Plato, the method of analysis is critical to his approach: this is the dialogue form in which protagonist Socrates examines others' beliefs, asking them to follow the implications of the thinking until they reach a dead-end, at which point the participant either admits defeat or goes off in a huff! Logically, this is called dialectic – a process of converging onto a truth through cross-examination. When it proceeds well, however, it tends to produce a coherent belief or set of beliefs, rather than, a critic may note, scientifically or empirically true or working hypotheses concerning nature. It may also make conclusions that become far removed from what is at stake, or what can be more simply thought of as cognitive distortions: I've failed all my exams so far, so there's no use in trying for the next one. That is, the method may produce an excellently worked out system but which has nothing to do with reality – that may also explain why Platonic thinking, like Platonic love, has much to do with the intellect and little to do with life and is of great appeal to monastic 'intellectuals', the bugbear of scientists who find much uselessness in philosophy.

Plato's philosophy was infused with the overarching importance of reason, of stretching the mind to examine ideas through examination. He argued that ideas cannot refer sufficiently to real entities, for, he thought, there was something highly lacking in entities: dialectic examination in the dialogues indicated that examples proffered always lacked a something, a *je ne sais quoi* we could say: such things only encourage philosophers! Plato reasoned that the things that we encounter, such as the beautiful girl there, or the well-proportioned table here, are indeed examples, but examples of a metaphysically higher or supernatural entity: beautiful people and well-proportioned tables are poor reflections of their true identities as found in the Forms or Ideas in the other world which he believes in. Just as the artist's rendition of the beautiful girl is a second-hand image, so is the beautiful girl a second-hand image of the Ideal (*eidos*) of The Beautiful Girl.

Philosophical reason thus leads to the mainstay of Plato's philosophy, the existence of two worlds: that is, his version of metaphysics (which asks what is the true nature of the universe) is that there are two worlds – the solid form of the world that we sense and the ethereal form of the world that we may gain quiet reflections of but which is only accessible to us once we die. This is a dualist theory of the universe for it posits two realms and it leads to his second major philosophical idea, namely that our souls are eternal and are capable of bridging the divide between the two. Plato espoused the Pythagorean doctrine of the transmigration of the soul, its rebirth and its eternal nature.

While we are physically alive we suffer from inadequate knowledge, for when we are reborn, we (conveniently) forget all that we knew in the world of the Forms and Ideas. When we do learn something, it is not learned for the first time but merely remembered or recalled – this idea has been very influential in the philosophy of education and still echoes when young students quip, 'Oh, I knew that', when something is explained. Our intellectual paucity and the relative inability of the senses to know anything for certain explains, for Plato, why we can never be contented with life. Not only that, Plato adds in a political history that echoes the myths of a prior Golden Age, whose idyllic and perfect society ours is slipping from. Imperfect creatures as we are, we are thus likely to be chained by our mediocre thinking and our senses to the world of appearances – only the philosopher can raise his thinking above the muddle of staring at what is in front of us to realize the true nature of the universe.

Plato presents a well-known allegory – the allegory of the cave. Imagine that people are sitting staring at the back of a cave, while shadows flicker on the wall, shadows which are created by a projection screen behind them, behind which objects are passed. A fire (the sun) illuminates the objects, whose shadows are then thrown by the screen onto the back wall. The philosopher is he or she who gets up to look at the screen, and who then wanders behind the screen to see the images' true source – blinded by enlightenment, he or she returns to babble about the true nature of things, much to everyone else's bemusement or annoyance.

The allegory became highly influential, but does it demand that we merely think about appearances, or does it imply that knowledge is only available to philosophers, that the rest of humanity would not get it even when it's explained to them? Thinkers who proclaim a hierarchical nature of the world in which the lowly minded remain low and subject to the intellectually inclined, naturally are attracted to the allegory that gives credence to any epiphanies that they may have had – and who then either feel sorry for the rest of us or demand that they should rule us. Given the political turmoil of Plato's youth (culminating in the Athenian democratic decision to put Socrates to death), it is unsurprising to find that Plato believes that the social world is naturally divided between those who don't get it and those who do, with the addition of a group in the middle who get it sufficiently that they will ensure that the lowly minds are policed by the laws of the higher minds.

Plato's *Republic* presents a coherent political vision for one who believes that life is an inherently corrupted version of the Perfect World of Forms and Ideas. The philosophers, they who understand that the world is dualistic and that souls are immortal (also called priests), are in charge of society. Following a very Spartan political agenda, children are taken from their parents at an early age, they are educated and then, as their talents (or lack of) begin to emerge, they are sorted out and groomed either for trade and production, for policing and social control (the 'guardians'), or for statesmanship. The statesmen's work entails securing the best that a society can be, given that it is necessarily slipping from its golden age, and this means socially engineering it to remove any possibility of further decline. The just or good society is one in which the philosopher-kings demand the removal of all forms of challenge or sources of change, including music that could prompt a lament or revolution: not a recipe for scientific experimentation and progress.

Yet is Plato a conservative? In some respects – in his political thinking – we can see that he readily fits the description, but he is also revolutionary in demanding that we (i.e. the capable) radically raise our thinking: Plato's Socrates challenges and so encourages us to challenge. It becomes the statesmen's duty to ensure that this world does not slip further into an emotive mass of whimsical fighting, bickering and war. Only the philosophically minded can raise their minds to understand the true nature of the world, which at once behumbles them in realizing how removed they are from perfection.

Political philosophy

Political philosophy examines the relationship between the individual and others: it is necessarily social in its view, demanding answers to whether society ought to respect the individual or the individual society; what rights and responsibilities can be said to exist (if at all) between individuals and people; and whether coercive structures are necessary to secure a social existence and if so, what forms should they take?

Such questions can be dizzingly broad and vast, easily falling into other philosophical realms that deal with conceptions of the self, gender and society, but always coming back to how ought the individual relate him or herself to others. Are there such things as rights, duties or responsibilities? Can they be defined if they do exist, and can they be said to belong to individuals and/or to groups? Should individuals give up power (however described in terms of rights or sheer physical ability or freedom) to others? To what extent (if any) can power over others be justified?

The anarchist proclaims the inviolability of the individual and her right to engage in social intercourse with whomever she pleases. No other has any justifiable right to rule over her or demand her obeisance or tribute. Against much of political philosophy, anarchist thought provides important role, similar to the sceptic in theories of knowledge, demanding justification at every step and usually rejecting as inadequate such moves that seek to diminish individual sovereignty.

Political theorists who justify such a move towards what we generally call government or the state do so for a variety of reasons: Hobbesians or realists typically believe that people, if not controlled by strict laws and coercive policing institutions, would shortly be at each other's throats ('where every man is Enemy to every man'

[Hobbes, *Leviathan*, I.13.62]) and a destructive vicious cycle would ensue of war and rapine: the state should thus be armed and ready to defend the peace that only it can create. Libertarians sometimes agree with the realist view but demand that the government does extend its power beyond the minimum of a protection agency. Conservatives can similarly hold a pessimistic view of human nature but will justify a grander and more interventionist stance to secure a moral order that libertarians would reject as not being the business of government. Extending the demand for justice are socialists, who generally hold that government is necessary to ensure that there is a redistribution of resources from the more able to the less able and thus can justify a range of interventions to secure that end. As the scale of intervention increases, we enter the realm of totalitarian politics – the notion that a state must control all aspects of an individual's life: totalitarian ideologies come in a variety of forms, from statist communism (as opposed to anarchic communism), theocracy (rule of the priests who define political life as serving God), and tyrannical, fascist and nationalist forms (in which a people must serve a political leader or entity absolutely).

There are other ways in which to look at political philosophy: feminism seeks to transcend traditional discourse as being peculiarly patriarchal and hence the above philosophies either need to be reinterpreted, rejected or reformed to take into account women's perspectives, needs or thoughts. Environmentalism demands that our entire political thinking be inverted to putting the earth first before humanity.

Whatever angle is taken up, political philosophy asks: what kind of life is proper, good, just, for a person among people.

Popper, Karl Raimund (1902–1994)

Sir Karl Popper was born and educated in Vienna earning a trade as a cabinet maker before migrating to England and the London School of Economics.

> My last attempt [to become a manual worker] was to become a
> cabinet maker. Physically this was not demanding, but the trouble
> was that certain speculative ideas which interested me interfered
> with my work. (Popper, *Unended Quest*, 35)

Popper initially caught philosophical attention with his *Logic of
Scientific Discovery*, which attempted to resolve a critical aspect
of empiricism concerning the logic of induction. Induction is the
taking in of evidence – data – from experiments or from experience
and then producing a theory regarding what the data imply. The
problem is how much data should one use to ensure the validity
of a theory? For Popper the inductionists had missed out a critical
element. No matter how many data one gathers, the veracity of the
principle can never be certain – for, as Hume had stressed, the next
datum may contradict the principle. A healthy scepticism is of
course useful, but inductionism left itself open to this simple criticism; Popper shifted the emphasis and, while agreeing that the
supporting data could never logically provide certainty, they could
show corroboration and that the theory should hold until it can
be falsified. That is, empiricism should justify not verifiability (the
data verify the theory) but falsifiability (the data reject the theory).
A stock example involves black and white crows: theory – all crows
are black; the evidence corroborates this but does not verify the
theory, instead we say that the theory has not yet been falsified.

This solution, for Popper, reflected scientific methodology of
examining and checking data. It also presented a useful principle of
challenging pseudo-scientific theories. Popper targeted Marxism
and Freud's psychoanalysis. Both theories could not be verified by
supporting data – and this is the general problem with pseudo-
science; but more importantly, they also could not be falsified. This
meant that they could not be deemed scientific.

Popper proceeded to bring his thinking to political philosophy
and argued that the philosophical systems of Plato, Hegel and Marx
entail a closing of society and were thus enemies to the 'open
society'. He rejected their historicism, which alluded to the future

already being mapped out: the future is open-ended and we require a wide degree of freedom to permit experimentation. The future has to be open-ended rather than closed to debate and alteration; similarly, scientists should always remain highly critical of knowledge and theories, constantly challenging the accepted to move knowledge closer to truths.

Poststructuralism

To catch a poststructuralist, you first have to catch a structuralist. In the 1960s, structuralism was one of the Parisian fashions eclipsing existentialism, having a broader appeal in areas such as anthropology, literary studies and cultural studies in which structuralists can still be found. The central idea, derived from the linguist work by Saussure, is that belief systems and cultures can be studied in the same manner that languages can be studied, namely by considering the relationship between words as they form a sentence. 'I do not understand poststructuralism' presents a meaning based on the relative position of the words; 'understand' may be replaced by a host of other words such as 'like' or 'believe', but not by other words such as 'however', 'yacht' or 'upon'. Grammatical conventions are evident, so by analogy for the structuralists, human relationships can also exhibit appropriateness and meaning courtesy of their relative positions.

If we consider social interaction, for example, in a city on a Friday night, we should be able to discern patterns and structures from the apparently disparate phenomena surveyed, for behind the exuberance and vivacity lie deeper laws regarding human myths and shared patterns that relate to other endeavours such as work, marriage ceremonies and football matches. The early structuralist and anthropologist, Lévi-Strauss argued that he observed common structures existing behind the disparate cultural practices of different communities and times, asserting the existence of the equivalent of a cultural grammar. The common functions of myths and rituals may in turn reflect the basic workings of the human mind, rather than independent forms.

The possibility of underlying laws of interaction is rejected by the poststructuralists, who accept that words mean what they do through the relations rather than with connections to reality and then deny that in discovering those relations we may learn about human nature. Poststructuralists – such as Foucault and Derrida – reject the possibility of objectivity and also of reality and truth: all is subjective, loose, spontaneous, and in flux. Here we harken echoes of Nietzsche, who held that there are no facts, only interpretations.

The poststructuralists sought to criticize everything that smacked of bourgeois society and of reality; adherents had often emerged through a Marxist phase before alighting upon the idea of deconstructing society completely, not just for the working classes. Words become laden with power structures, and hence must be revolted against. Derrida quipped, 'There is nothing outside of the text' – but what does that mean? Is it a wonderful irony to smirk over, or does it imply that a grave contradiction haunts the world in which text is real but everything outside the text is non-existent, which in turn would give text an unusually paradoxical ontological status; but, as he is thought to have meant, there is nothing outside the universe, since the universe is a text in the structuralist sense of a set of relations, then not much is being said and perhaps the ironic implication is to be preferred. The problem is that we cannot know what is being meant, for assuming that something is being meant drops us in it as far as poststructuralists are concerned, for there we go, trying to impose structures where there are none. Texts imply power relations for poststructuralists, they are to be deconstructed (including the deconstructive texts) and vaporized intellectually, just as everything else that may warrant attention – indeed, if anything gains our attention, it should be deconstructed, including ourselves. Everything becomes a fiction (including that sentence).

But of course in espousing a method of doing *something*, a principle is asserted which assumes that there are valid enterprises, for even in the hall of mirrors that poststructuralism pulls us into, there are mirrors. Although popular, criticism of poststructuralism has been severe from many intellectual angles, the most biting from scientists Sokal and Bricmont in *Intellectual Impostures*.

Pragmatism

A pragmatist is one whose actions and beliefs are chosen according to whether they are said to work. If success is not forthcoming following an act, the pragmatist drops the act in favour of another. This may seem to be very reasonable, for if I were to continue with the same action that failed each time, something would certainly seem to be wrong with the manner of my trying and that the world should bend to my endeavours. And should I alter my actions according to the situation, this would also seem reasonable in terms of means and ends: behaviour may rightly differ according to the situation – musing upon the logicality of Hegel is appropriate with a fellow philosopher or student, but not very appropriate when making love (perhaps in weird way, but I'll leave that to the fertile imagination of the reader to work out).

Nonetheless, this is not quite the whole picture of pragmatism. The coiner of the term, C. S. Pierce, argued that we should,

> Consider what effects, which might conceivably have practical bearings, we conceive the object of our conception to have. Then our conception of these effects is the whole of our conception of the object. (C. S. Peirce, *Collected Papers*, 5:402)

In other words – what is the practical benefit of holding a belief? Pragmatism implies that the successfulness of an action guarantees its 'truth'; a belief should thus be instrumental for the agent.

Whether an action is effective or not does not necessarily mean that it is true, in the sense of universally true, so pragmatists tend to avoid or to reject thinking about or describing the truth.

Consider a belief in God. For the pragmatist, there is not ultimate truth to uncover only a position to hold that has certain consequences. Imagine being an atheist and you receive a wholly unexpected visit from the Spanish Inquisition, who inquires into your belief in God. If you were a dogmatist, you would state what you sincerely believe; if you were a pragmatist, you would reply 'the one and only Catholic God, who gave his son . . .' After all, a better state of affairs would ensue by being pragmatic – unless of course, you believe that in giving up your beliefs creates a wholly unacceptable flow of consequences – reputation, integrity, honour, and so on, and that in being tortured for heresy would in some way be better.

However, what does it mean to say that a belief 'works' or 'does not work'? This presents a difficult problem, for typically a belief is about something else, and that something else may be said to work or not. For instance, I have a belief that my old laptop does not work. I take it to a specialist and she gets it working. What is the relationship of my belief to the laptop now working? I was either right or wrong depending on what the specialist has done to the laptop – I was wrong in my belief if she merely turned it on, ran a diagnostic and proclaimed it to be in full working order, but right if she had to swap the hard drive – the belief itself does not do any work.

Truth cannot stem from 'what works' as the truth depends on things (acts, events) being ratified by observation and experience. This puts pragmatism in an awkward position from which it can only defend itself by accepting a narrow version of 'truth is what works' as applied to working objects (i.e. machines). In the human or moral sphere, pragmatism logically points to an egoistic theory: I ought to act according to what furthers my interests, but here we can unravel the theory and ask questions concerning the nature of those interests – are we speaking of short-term interests? For they may not always be in one's long-term interests. And if we are speaking of long-term interests, how do we know what they are? Again, we can have beliefs about them which may or may not be correct – in some respects, only time will tell, but this is a problem for any philosopher setting off on a long journey as much as it is for the pragmatist.

If you believe yourself to be a pragmatist then, what are you saying about your beliefs?

Rationalism

Rationalism is a theory about knowledge, about how we come to know things and more importantly about how we may be certain of things. It claims that the best method of gaining knowledge about things, whether they are mental or extramental, is by using the mind and the processes of logic.

In the modern era, Descartes propounded the rationalist vision in a simplistic formula renown to many: I can be uncertain of the validity of my senses, I may be fooled by what they offer, but I can never doubt that I am thinking. Thus the initiating premise becomes the principle of the workings of the mind: given that I know that I think, my duty, as a rationalist, is then to proceed logically, maintaining a grip on the terms that I use and the connections between them, then a system of thought may be deduced. In turn, this system of thought could then be applied to various problems in philosophy such as the workings of the mind, the nature of the external world, the character of the good, the problem of beauty, or the formation of society and politics.

For many rationalists, the appeal to reason is that it is an appeal to a universally held faculty – all peoples are held to be reasoning, so, it follows, they should all agree on what is deductible from certain premises. In this regard rationalism draws heavily upon the cosmopolitan stoic ideal of one-world, one-people unhindered by local or historical bigotry. Nonetheless, there are critics of this, who contend that the process of reasoning is too saturated with cultural patterns of thinking to be or to become universal – these may be conservative thinkers who give prominence to locality or nationalists who believe that their nation should define its own logic or political system according to traditions or local circumstances. Others, who accept the universality of reason, reject that rationalism should be the sole method by which we know things and proceed – empiricists retort that knowledge can only be gained from the senses in the first place, while compatibilists prefer to mix sense with some mental sensibility.

Rationalism is criticized for potentially being disconnected from the reality of the extramental world and for seeking to demean the complexities of the universe to logical analysis, whose terms and connections can be culturally and philosophically loaded words. Logicians may seek to avoid this problem by reducing logical statements to mathematical language that betokens no dissent or ambiguity, but such adventures in philosophy rarely produce anything of worth to the broad and deep waters of human culture, thought and vision. Nonetheless, if ambiguities are kept to a minimum, the rationalist may respond that philosophy can proceed deductively, step by step, as mathematics does.

Rationality and reason possess the same root, the Latin *ratio*. To act rationally implies to act reasonably as well, but there is often something else implied in reasoning that is lacking in acting rationally when used by some thinkers. This is because rationality can be used to mean 'acting in one's interests', which entails such a breadth of action that all living entities can be said to be rational. It is in the mitochondria interests to respire, so they have found a means by which to ensure a cosy environment to replicate and respire, namely cells. It is in the interests of many plants to have a dormant period, or ants to form colonies, or rabbits to burrow. But we should discern function from purposive action, for possessing a function (e.g. a DNA strand replicating) does not necessarily imply that the entity possess interests – a stone that rolls down the hill following a downpour can hardly be said to be following its interests (although some have argued that they indeed do).

If rationality implies pursuing acts conducive to betterment, we can compare it to acting irrationally, which may include wishing things were better, or acting on faith or luck: again, there are interesting nuances here, I may be acting rationally in believing that my luck or God has held out for me in the past, and so why, on inductive reasoning, should it fail now? However, 'wishing' suggests a partial or absolute renunciation of any consideration of how things are and what I ought to do to achieve my goals. Do other animals wish? Or is wishing merely an extended form of associating? In Wittgensteinian mode, does my horse, in his world, look forward to me coming to feed him, and does he look forward to me coming next Wednesday? How can I know what his world is like and what reasoning he performs?

Others may prefer to focus on the associative or behavioural patterns that derive from instincts. Yet we may think of instincts as being rational, for, if they are truly embedded instincts, then they may be said to have satisfied the criteria of Darwinian evolution and hence be inherently for the benefit of the holder whether it is a human or an amoeba. David Hume argued that reason is the slave of the passions, but what if the two are entwined in a mutual dance? Rejecting the implied dualism, we can bring into account the homeostatic mechanisms of the body with the emotional responses and urges we possess and note that perhaps from an evolutionary perspective that they have rational roles to play. However, that may place our thinking with Leibniz and his notion that everything that happens must be for the best, which often it is (apparently at least) not. Genetic evolution theories acknowledge that some instincts may be subsumed into a being's behaviour, predispositions or physical appearance, which no longer provide beneficial functions and so may be termed irrational – these can ultimately lead to extinction.

Properly speaking, acting rationally should be a minor premise in any description of human action: what is more important is the means available by which we judge the success of failure of our actions. The faculty of reason – the ability to seek truth – does not imply that every single thought and action is rational in the sense of being able to achieve the end aimed at, but rather action (means and ends) are subject to critical considerations. Here we can either assert the need for ends to be rational, which usually means reflecting on our natural requirements, or, dismissing the judging of ends in favour of focusing on the means. When I commence an undertaking, my actions can be judged for their conduciveness to attaining my goal: I thereby am acting rationally when my means do indeed attain my goal, *ceteris paribus*. Or my ends may be judged as being conducive to a separate standard, such as my general well-being, or that of my society or planet. However, the problem that runs here is whether the ends can in turn be truly said to be rational.

Focusing on rationality alone presents an easy target for critics of human actions. Game theorists, for instance, enjoy dismissing human rationality, usually to reject economists' premises that people act rationally. The move is fallacious, however, for the choice-matrixes presented (such as the Prisoners' Dilemma) are mere games and not reflective of life's multifarious means and aims: in the Prisoners' Dilemma and other games, if the values are changed, the outcomes change. Such games attempt to show that if individuals act rationally (pursuing their own interests), then all agents will suffer. Such games strike one as unreasonable in the sense that they are missing something critical.

Reason

Be reasonable – an often heard plea or command, but what does it evoke – to use reasoned thinking or to become more pliable or to live the rational life that is our human inheritance? There is much to unpack here.

Compare reason to faith: faith demands that we accept theories or stories without evidence or without logicality – for example, Santa getting down all those chimneys around the world. What would reason do in contrast? Check the facts, follow the logic used closely, relate the assertion to experience, evaluate against other validated theories. It is less clear with our use of emotions: emotions can provide quick analyses of situations or of people, sometimes working with reason and perhaps forming a fundamental rock upon which reasoning must take place – hence Hume's quip that reason is the slave of the passions. But for dualists, reason should be wholly separable from the emotions and be able to work independently of them.

Reasoning can imply deducing arguments from premises and ensuring their validity, such as when I claim: 'If it snows, it will be cold; it is snowing, therefore it will be cold.' Someone who has never experienced snow or even cold can still accept the logic of the argument. There may be no truth to the argument but there is at least validity. Reasoning can also be inductive, the method that dominates scientific reasoning. 'This banana is bent, the second banana is bent, the third, and so on for several thousand. Therefore all bananas are bent.' On second reflection, we may retort, but aren't there straight bananas? I have never seen a straight banana, but from what I know of biological diversity, it is always possible that one exists somewhere. This encourages us to think (reason) about the nature of induction a little more. Can I present a valid inductive argument as I can a deductive argument? Since an inductive argument moves beyond working with the definitions and chasing conclusions from what is already given, it cannot be valid as such; instead, it points to an empirical truth, which entails problems of verification, falsification and probability that many of the great analytical philosophers (e.g. Russell, Wittgenstein) have worked on.

Nonetheless, reason implies living according to reasoned out arguments – being rational, but what does that mean? When a parent demands that you be more reasonable, does it imply that you should merely acquiesce with their interests and requests, or does it mean that you should pursue a reasoned out moral programme in which the principles are concluded to be universally binding, as Kant would have it? If you are asked to be reasonable, you need to draw out the implied premises but also consider the capacity for someone to be reasonable. Asking a baby to be reasonable is an unreasonable request – but why is it unreasonable? Because we have learned that babies are incapable of reasoned arguments as evinced by a lack of speech. Yet that does not mean to say that they are incapable of understanding, making themselves understood, and associating events and results: in a baby's actions, are we witnessing a primitive form of reasoning and when we compare babies with the higher animals, can we say that they share reasoning abilities? We can detect a complicated quagmire ahead, but much of the swamp is generated by vaguely implied definitions, which can be moulded to suit certain philosophical (or political) programmes.

In some respects, reasoning implies a multidisciplinary activity, drawing on inductive and deductive processes while testing conjectures with imagined scenarios and then, sometimes, producing a package – an argument or command or desire – that can be pronounced or merely toyed with in the mind.

Relativism

When we utter the phrase, 'when in Rome, do as the Romans do', we are suggesting a belief in moral relativity; similarly, if we say, 'well, that may be how you see things, but we (or I) see things differently', we are also presenting a relativist theory, this time about knowledge. In both cases, thought's conclusion is assumed to be relative to person, location and/or time – that is, the nature of the good or truth is context or agent dependent and is not impartial or objective and hence scientifically or logically deducible.

The moral to 'do what the Romans do' does indeed suggest changing one's moral code to that of the people around, and there may be good reasons for doing so. The reciprocal of offering good hospitality is of course being a good guest, which implies learning and adapting to local conventions. Nonetheless, if those conventions breach deeply held personal values hospitality in turn must accommodate the guest – such as acknowledging a Muslim's time to pray or a vegetarian's desire to avoid meat dishes. But the concept 'deeply held personal values' also implies a relativistic trump card – these are *my* values which are to be held as sacrosanct and to which all must bend. Ethics demands that we think further – are such values truly good values, do they have any moral import that is, or are they merely whimsically held ideas to which the individual tenaciously holds. After all, what would we think of a guest who believed that it is acceptable (to him or her) to speak offensively of women, other religions or political beliefs, or refused to accept a dish? Naturally, a second invitation would not be forthcoming for etiquette – the gentle rules that act to smooth social intercourse – would be broached.

Yet, if one is 'in Rome', should one always follow the crowd? The great Roman Stoic, Seneca, certainly thought not – the crowd produces disturbing and dangerous effects, and the wise man ought to remain aloof to ensure that his reasoning is not affected detrimentally, and his reasoning will guide him to universal codes of right and wrong. Arguably, relativism provides just as swift a path to the renunciation of personal moral authenticity as does blind obedience: the quip, 'whatever goes' is barely sustainable logically and morally. It is not the case that 'whatever goes' for that implies contradicting acts become of similar worth or value either for the same individual at different times or different people at the same time. Can, for instance, the targeting of civilians in war ever be justified? Only by stretching the imagined contexts so much that the innocent targets merge into legitimate targets. For example, consider a problem familiar to just war ethicists: civilians are strapped to devices such as tanks that are in themselves legitimate targets – in effect, in such circumstances the civilians become conscripted into the military and hence militarized into becoming justifiable targets in war: their deaths are always regrettable but understandable, just as is the death of an unwilling conscript following an aggressive and unjustifiable policy of invasion. But the core value is that non-combatant life remains the standard by which military action be judged.

The same applies to epistemological relativism, which claims that *knowing* is peculiarly individual or collective. It runs into the same logical problems as moral relativism, but is often more swiftly challenged by the reality to which all must eventually bend dogma and whimsicality: if I believe the physical world is amenable to my wishes, I am soon disappointed (usually as a child, but it is incredible at times how people in power can remain attracted to a childish belief in omnipotence ignoring laws of economics or rising popular resentment for instance). Arguably, there is only physics – not African, Japanese, women's or Christian's physics, for the scientific method demands the universality of method and results, so if one group or individual finds something experimentally interesting, his or her method should be repeatable.

Nonetheless, relativism seems to defend an impassable principle that in dealing with the individual in terms of his or her health or mental state, there can be no impartial and random repeatable trials – each presents symptoms unique to that person, for in acting upon the individual a host of particulars are invoked: unique physiology, peculiar mind-set, personal reactions to treatment, diet, lifestyle, and so on, all unrepeatable. But even here, the universalist may reply that indeed that may be so – universally, each person should be treated (or taught) in the unique manner that suits them.

Religion

While God would seem the logical centrepiece of the philosophy of religion, there are other aspects that gain our attention and which should work equally well for those who reject monotheism (or theism in preference for 'spirit').

What status should religion have in relation to other forms of knowledge? The scientist, for instance Richard Dawkins, would prefer that the arguments of religion be treated analytically, logically and empirically, so if religion offers a creationist theory of the universe, then it should be tested along with other competing theories of the origins of the universe.

Historically, in breaking from the political grip that the Western churches held for many centuries, modern philosophers from the seventeenth century onwards preferred to demote theology, returning in some respects to Plato's subtle challenge to religion: are things good because God tells us that they are good, or are they good in themselves? It is a provocative question for if God could readily change the nature of the good, this presents some interesting issues for why would God thus change his mind as well as epistemological considerations concerning how we might know if God had changed his mind.

Some may claim that they personally 'know' God. But when asked how, they may revert to holy texts that have been collected and passed down; yet texts present issues of comprehension, focus, emphasis and problems of translation. Or they invoke their heart or mind – they personally 'know' God through their emotions. Such claims to epistemic privilege are rarely granted by most religious authorities – only the more individualistic Protestant sects of the Christian church seek to justify personal knowledge of God through feeling or just knowing. However, inconsistent or contradictory 'messages' rather diminish the epistemic value of such utterances as, 'I know that Jesus commands me to live in poverty.' Extraordinary claims require extraordinary justifications and these are never forthcoming.

Beyond the big questions concerning the nature of God and the nature of the universe and of possible Heavens, there is the question of grace. Are some people destined to reach God and Heaven, or is it through moral action alone that determines who gets to Heaven? Others reject the possibility that a person could, through her own efforts, determine whether she got into Heaven or not, in favour of giving God full control who passes and who is rejected – this is what is meant by God's grace.

In the realm of ethics, religious thinking has had an enormous influence on the notion of good and evil. Sin is deemed to be breaking God's laws or turning from His moral stance – for some this is a mere convenient means of maintaining social order and its relation to theology can be severed; others though are plagued by their innate evilness, a view propagated by various religions through interpretations of scriptures and through educational philosophies. As a philosopher and a father, I find it difficult to see sin in a child, but I can see its benefits for those who would prefer to control others through invoking their guilt and hence their obedience.

Rousseau, Jean-Jacques (1712–1778)

Jean-Jacques Rousseau was one of the most colourful characters of philosophy. In embracing at what times can only be called a contrarian attitude, we understand Rousseau better if we see him as an able essayist, one whose influence stems from his breadth of discourse and his wit, seemingly untied to a unifying doctrine. In an age of powerful but tenuously justified monarchies, he penned a republican tract; while intellectuals were becoming increasingly atheistic, he wondered if he was the only person who believed in God; the author of a critically influential tract on an ideal education for a young boy, he deposited his own children in the care of charities; a proponent of the individual having to bend his will to that of the 'general will' of the public, he fled for his life from the authorities he aggravated. Indubitably, his philosophy clashed with life at various points, which speaks volumes of either his manner of living or his philosophy.

Rousseau hailed from Geneva, but most of his life was spent among the French. For a while, he sought exile from his enemies (real and imagined) in Britain and spent some time with David Hume, but by then his persecution obsessions had made him unsociable to Hume and other hosts; he was most content residing in the countryside far from condemning authorities. As one would imagine, he was never an easy guest with many people – Rousseau cultivated a curious vision of his personality that we read of in his *Confessions*, at times rather arrogant and egoistical and yet so humbling and self-effacing, but it is still hard to dismiss the wonderful prose and humour that flows from his pen.

In his educational and political writings, the common theme is the rejection of the artificial trappings of urban life with its fashions and contrived etiquette in favour of a more natural existence, one that keeps us connected to nature. *Émile* teaches us that a child should develop and grow according to his proclivities: he should not be forced to learn things which he is not ready to learn, but his education should nonetheless be subtly guided to enable him to learn as if it were all his own doing. In many respects that is also how Jean-Jacques envisioned politics – life is so much better when we do not crowd upon one another and when we can exude our individuality without treading on others.

> Men are not to be crowded together in ant-hills, but scattered over the earth to till it . . . Of all creatures man is least fitted to live in herds. (Rousseau, *Emile*, 26)

The rural life suits man much better, he advised: to know man as he naturally is, the philosopher should not look in the cities. Accordingly, Rousseau rejected progress through scientific enlightenment, instead he claimed that progress involves rejecting modern life and returning to the life of the 'noble savage'.

Rousseau was not the first to hark on about how noble savages were supposed to be, the idea had been bandied around following

European explorers' tales of North American Indian peoples living what they considered a purer life than city dwellers or those in the feudal orders back in Europe. However, Rousseau's critique caught intellectual attention and earned him patronage from those wealthy enough to feel guilty for something. The noble savage supposedly lives closer to nature and does not fall prey to the trappings of the modern world, *ergo*, he is supposedly happier. In some respects, Rousseau's argument is useful to remind us that material progress does not necessarily entail a happier population, but it also falls prey itself to a romanticization of what can be a thoroughly hard life unsuitable for many who have been born and bred in more comfort. More importantly though, for what Rousseau developed, is that this archetypal natural man does not know property – there is no 'thine and mine' in this idyllic world, nor family, nor common languages or anything communal. Rousseau imagined man wandering around minding his own business, until someone somewhere comes up with the idea of property: then everything changes as people fence off their land and impose their will upon their property by excluding others; from thence they need protection from marauders and thieves and so a state becomes necessary – and the decline into internecine warfare is inevitable. Man, for Rousseau, is hence freest in the era predating civilization and prior to the construction of laws and property, with which begins all the social arrangements that are characteristic of civil life: family and property, and 'the source of a thousand quarrels and conflicts.' Modern man, he famously declared echoing Vico, is born free yet is everywhere in chains, that is, in the civilized life he has made for himself.

From a Golden Age of peace and individuality, modern man has fallen into the morass of the present; accordingly, Rousseau appealed to man's more primal instincts or emotions, notably to his natural capacity for sympathy as the vehicle for his proper enlightenment from the artificiality of modern predicaments, and implicatively away from war and political strife. Sympathy, or compassion, draws us into the fold of others' lives and predicaments and thus promotes a sense of community and love for others; it is just a shame that he could not cast aside his own selfish pursuits when looking at his newly born children (if that is, he did indeed produce any – one never quite knows with Jean-Jacques).

Compassion, he argued, is the binding instinctual emotion that civilization smothers with reason and philosophy; although there are exceptional circumstances in which a man has to act to preserve himself. The distancing of man from his proper morality is a product of too much reasoning, too much discussion and thought. He decried the intellectual who removes himself through rationalizations from his fellow man. The trappings of civilization keep man from his innate compassion for others: it follows that those less affected by the ruse of civil virtues are closer to the natural state and are more compassionate people.

The primordial existence that Rousseau invokes is known as the 'state of nature', and it is a philosophical tool that we encounter in Hobbes and in Locke. Hobbes believed the state of nature to be an unpleasant realm in which life would be solitary, poor, nasty, brutish and short; Locke thought that it would be a generally pleasant state of affairs whose anarchy would work very well for humanity were it not for a few bad eggs; Rousseau went one step further than Locke and thought that the anarchy of solitary noble savages wandering around would be ideal. Nonetheless, social pressures emerging from the invention and expansion of property encourage people to devise a government in what is known as the social contract; predominantly, Rousseau saw the pressures forming because of the lack of mutuality in social intercourse – he accepted an ancient fallacy (propagated by Aristotle, for instance) that one man's gain is another man's loss. Rousseau may have read it in Montesquieu, but it is an unfortunate theory that besets thinking: the alternative is that one man's gain in trade is not necessarily another's loss and may indeed be his gain too, for otherwise people would not trade. What is now a commonly accepted principle of economics has sadly not transported well into philosophical circles and even today many intellectuals make Rousseau's mistake: could he have continued to argue for the state's development if he recognized that trade and voluntaristic arrangements tend to be mutually beneficial?

Nevertheless, the state is 'consequently the best calculated to promote peace, and [is] the most suitable for mankind'. (*Discourse*, 72) The formation of the ideal state should be through the concord of all citizens who realize that through the state they may achieve not only the security of their liberties but also the exercise of their moral rights. However, their rights do not remain inalienable (as in Locke's theory), instead they are given over to the community (rather than the government as in Hobbes's theory: indeed, Rousseau's theory is one of a populist Leviathan). Ethically, within the community, the individual wills what is best for the community as a whole, for the 'general will', and thereby a universal code for social existence is produced. The general will is necessarily that which is for the good of public overall, so if an individual demurs, he must be 'forced to be free'. This rather paradoxical claim, which reverberates in Orwell's doublespeak in *1984*, implies that the recalcitrant cannot truly know his interests, in as much as they should merge with his fellow citizens. The general will becomes an ideal that states should aim for – the best being run along Swiss (particularly Genevan) lines in which the public turn out to vote *en masse* (well, at least the men did in his day).

Yet the notion of 'forcing people to be free' can so easily be turned by those who pretend to have secured the will of the people, but who in fact merely represent their own interests or some minority ideology. Of this Rousseau seems to be aware: the state emerges as a dream of liberty, which only produces man's enslavement: 'All ran headlong to their chains, in hopes of securing their liberty.' (*Discourse*, 99) The state thus creates an uneasy power – able to secure the peace and freedom of the people yet so quickly may it turn against them.

Anticipating the general premise of Hegel's theory of the belligerent state, Rousseau noted that for a state to know itself, it must compare itself to others, and whereas man tends to rest, eat and sleep, states must be in constant motion: a state 'without motion would be dead', he surmised. ('L'état de guerre', 192) States must be vigorous entities, and smaller states more so than larger ones, although there are limits to the growth of larger states, for they soon are burdened by their own weight and fall into disease and perish. But if we were to draw the conclusion from Rousseau's *Social Contract* that the general will would be a pacific institution, his notes in *L'état de guerre* teach otherwise, for the active, vigorous, indeed aggressive state's direction is determined by nothing other than the general will. If the public possesses no courage or heart then the state correspondingly has no life. The implication is that the evolution of the state encourages warfare between states: of this Rousseau was all too aware, yet he was not a world government theorist, for in commenting upon an earlier writer, L'Abbé Saint-Pierre's vision of a united Europe under one government, Rousseau rejected the idea as absurd and unworkable.

An uneasy balance exists in Rousseau's writings: the anarchic individualism of the noble savage is replaced by a conformism characteristic of government. The individual must relinquish an element of freedom to secure the peace that government provides, but on the international scene, Rousseau deprecated the aims of world governments or international federations: the anarchy of international affairs cannot be overcome.

Rousseau's clearer writings on the joys of a simpler existence remain pertinent and current. He has been blamed for the French Revolution (unlikely) and later revolts (more likely). Pursuing some of Rousseau's ideals, various movements have sprung up in the past two centuries, whose members seek to level man's achievements, to rekindle the customs, and even the languages of their forefathers, to rekindle the echoes of a Golden Age of innocence and purity, when man was wise rather than knowledgeable. Some strands of Rousseau lend themselves to anti-intellectualism or anti-industrialism, which are expounded in environmentalist and anti-capitalist organizations.

Russell, Bertrand (1872–1970)

Bertrand Arthur William Russell was a prolific philosopher writing on a variety of subjects including education, marriage, religion and war; his philosophical fame however rests on his work on mathematics and logic, which spills over into epistemology and metaphysics. Russell lived for ideals as much as he did for philosophy, and while we can spot forgivable changes and inconsistencies emerging over his long career, we can generally only admire his fortitude and example: he opposed Britain's engagement in the First World War and served time in prison; he stood for women's enfranchisement; he campaigned for nuclear disarmament and eugenics. He earned the Nobel Prize for Literature in 1950 for his *History of Western Philosophy*.

In 1901 Russell devised a paradox, which still attracts attention. George Cantor had developed what is now called 'naïve set theory' elements of which we learn in schools through Venn diagrams; Russell, who read mathematics at Cambridge, conjectured that the Cantor's logic implies that some classes must contain themselves. For instance, the set of abstract objects is itself an abstract object, so it should contain itself; more entertainingly is the problem of the barber associated with Russell's paradox. The barber of a village shaves only the men who do not shave themselves. That seems appropriate. But then who shaves the barber? If he does shave himself, then he shaves one person in the village who shaves himself, so breaching the set's rules; if he does not shave himself, he should go to himself for a shave! The self-referring paradox is ancient: Eubulides asked, 'A man says that he is lying. Is what he says true or false?' So the statement 'He is lying' is true only if it is false; it is false only if it is true.

Paradoxes generated by arguments are considered true and whose deduction leads to a valid conclusion, but that the conclusion is either a contradiction or is bewildering to our intuition. If a theory produces a paradox, something may have gone wrong in the theory, which is what Russell believed with Cantor's logic. For a decade he worked with Whitehead on what both hoped would resolve such paradoxes – the *Principia Mathematica*. They sought to replace set theory with a theory of types in which statements about statements are said to belong to a higher level of sets than simple statements about things. A hierarchical system of cataloguing would remove problems of what to do with the set of sets: each level must not contain elements from other levels. This is often summarized in forms such as 'the set of cows is not itself a cow.' So the self-referring statement cannot be contained in the same class. (But paradoxes continue to buzz our minds – controversy remains both regarding the nature of paradoxes and the various attempts to resolve them.)

In 1905 Russell published a short article, 'On Denoting', in the journal, *Mind*. It has become a seminal article, inaugurating analytical philosophy, a term used by G. E. Moore. Russell drew from the great logician Frege's works, who is held as the father of modern logic; Frege believed that to ensure deductive proofs were tight, a formal language of unambiguous symbols should be used. The clarity necessitated in removing the ambiguities commonly associated with words motivated Russell's analytical programme. For Russell, understanding could be improved if philosophers focused on language and broke wholes into pieces, reducing concepts into constituent parts. There are three kinds of denoting: denoting something that does not refer to anything presently existing (e.g. the present [2008] King of the United Kingdom); a denotation denoting something that exists now (e.g. the present President of the United States); or it may denote ambiguously – a man implies any man. Some symbols do not mean anything by themselves but when put back into a sentence – I saw the present King of the United Kingdom – it possesses sense but then is either true or false. Analytical philosophy thus proceeds to exchange ambiguity found in propositions into alternative descriptions.

Like many logicians, including Leibniz, whom Russell studied in detail, he believed that a thorough going revision of our arguments could not only reduce confusion but also help us to understand the structures of the world better, analogous to how a knowledge of the chemical elements enables us to understand compounds. The theory, termed logical atomism, suggested then that as we resolved sentences into their components, we would discover the basic referents of the world being employed – the things that we are acquainted with, as Russell put it.

Russell was liberal yet politically elitist at times dallying with eugenics, racism and social engineering: Heidegger was not the only philosopher to ally himself with haughty extremism.

Sartre, Jean-Paul (1905–1980)

Jean-Paul Sartre is entertaining – at times one can hardly take him seriously but his imaginative descriptions, influenced by phenomenology, become indelible. Sartre was a prolific writer, a problem not helped by taking uppers with his coffee; he was polymath in the humanities, a rare philosopher who penned novels, plays, literary criticism as well as political commentaries. Influenced by Husserl's phenomenology and encouraged into further examination over a glass of wine with Raymond Aron, who explained that philosophy could be about a glass of wine, Sartre developed into one of the prominent defenders of existentialism. Although a tentative figurehead of the French resistance, Sartre could not actually make up his mind which side of the resistance to support, so he opted to write. In 1943 he completed his *Being and Nothingness*; after the war he tried to merge existentialism with humanism, and while dallying with communism, he thought he could merge the individualistic thrust of his existentialism with the popular communist ideology in his *Existentialism and Marxism*.

Sartre initially sought to extend phenomenology (the study of appearances) to the imagination but saw imagination not in the traditional sense of a collection of ideas but in a more radical light as a distinctive mode of intentional consciousness. In directing consciousness into the imaginative world we find our freedom, Sartre argued; consciousness is free from restraint in that regard – it is purely for-itself (*pour soi*), in the sense that it does not exist for anything else and is not an actuality that can be empirically validated like that of an object. Consciousness is intentional (one of Husserl's terms), which implies that it is always directed towards something – I am conscious of the smell of peppermint tea; but I can also direct consciousness inward into my imagination.

Taking up an old metaphysical problem of what defines Being, Sartre claimed that Being just is. He divided Being into the Being-for-itself, which is conscious, and the Being-in-itself, which is not conscious. This is not an ontological duality, however, for Being supports the Being-for-itself or the 'nothingness' of conscious. In reflection, consciousness attempts to become its own object, just like it perceives any other object, but in doing so consciousness realizes that it is nothing – it is not an object, an in-itself.

Yet the nothingness of consciousness is not a bad thing for Sartre, for herein he found freedom. His notion of freedom is an existentialist conception, which sees freedom as the ability to define one's essence, spontaneously and undetermined by other factors or people. It is a strict libertarian view of free will that sees the force of freedom presented in act. I am fully in control of my next action, and therefore I am in control of defining my essence. What Sartre meant by this is that my essence – my human nature – is not predefined and which therefore would define and determine my character. The nothingness of *pour soi* ensures that ultimate freedom, since it hangs upon nothing physical except pure Being.

People do not like being 'condemned to be free'. It entails too much responsibility and since that frightens some, they revert to beliefs in determinism, that is, to holding on to a belief that they are not really free but that society, God, or nature determines their character. Sartre was disparaging of such people – they are 'bastards' for living in 'bad faith'. Liberation comes from realizing one's freedom (and metaphysical responsibility) to define oneself. 'You're free, you choose', is the strong implication.

In defining my own freedom, I must relate to the world of things. This relationship, including the connection to all my prior acts, Sartre called one's facticity. It is a useful term, if we imagine the immediate matrix of sensations of other things around us – the phenomena that we perceive – as well as the actions and events that brought me to this particular moment in space-time. However, other people upset this pure world of me and my things (they are my things, because I perceive them, so I own them in a metaphysical manner). Once another appears on the scene, my freedom is thwarted, for she perceives what I see, and since I recognize her as another consciousness, I realize that she too determines the things around her – but these are the same things that I owned just a minute back, so my cosy world is demolished, fractured by this Other, capitalized for metaphysical importance.

The relationship between two consciousnesses is one of war; Sartre embellished upon Hegel's master–slave thesis in his descriptions of how I try to overpower her and she overpowers me. At each moment, my freedom to define myself is threatened by this Other and can only be truly maintained by excluding the Other, which since that is nigh impossible, means that we're all doomed to a combat for dominance.

The Other becomes a 'mediator between myself and me' so I am 'ashamed of myself as I *appear* to the Other' (*Being and Nothingness*, 222). And therein lies the danger of falling into living by what others expect of you – the route to bad faith. Hence a waiter in a café is merely acting *for* others, he has in acting put on a show for what others expect of him. The Other provides the Look, which puts my world into a spin, for she can perceive me metaphysically naked, demoting me to a mere object; I must therefore try to re-ascend to the status of a *pour-soi* and not an *en-soi* – hence the inevitable struggle between consciousnesses. Such relationships pepper Sartre's work.

In later writings Sartre tried to merge existentialism with Marxism (it was fashionable at the time) but despite the radical sounding nature and implications of his moral philosophy at times, he tended to return to a homely ethic of being nice to others for they will be nice to you.

Scepticism

A sceptic takes a critical attitude, but to what extent? In being critical of life, others, philosophies or the sciences, is there any standard which the sceptic must ultimately defer, or is the sceptic merely an intellectual free-falling into a black hole, destined never to offer anything useful to debate, love or knowledge? Proponents, however, enjoy the sceptical attitude as being a positive force for either change or sharper thought.

Scepticism can be construed either as a strong scepticism meaning that I challenge any and every piece of knowledge presented, or, more interestingly, in a weak sense as an attitude towards knowledge. For instance, how can I be sure that my senses are indeed correct? In watching sceptics' videos of the terrorists' attacks on New York in 2001, I am asked to reject the official story in favour of another one that supporters believe is more credulous. But in shifting my mind from one story to another I must retain a sceptical attitude of course – do the 9/11 sceptics' own versions make any more sense, and what criteria should I invoke to establish which account 'makes sense'? If I end up chasing theory after theory and secure no connection to truths, I easily end up shrugging my shoulders indifferently thereby rejecting any sense of truth.

Accordingly, most sceptics tend to be weak sceptics on that account: they seek to avoid epistemic nihilism and invoke a standard by which to judge evidence: hence the command to look with one's own eyes and follow one's own judgement of the facts. However, critics argue that the senses can be fooled notably at critical times. Consider varying eyewitness accounts of a famous encounter between Wittgenstein and Popper involving a poker at a talk on knowledge of all things.

At this point, some philosophers drag us back from justifying perception to forming our beliefs on what we believe: rationalism proceeds by asserting the validity of the mind's internal operations, notably logical deductive operations from certain axioms: I can be certain that if A > B > C then A > C. However, empiricists retort that the rationalist programme is no defence against the sceptic, for rationalists' axioms are questionable in their own right, just as Euclid's mathematical axioms were challenged by Riemann. Rationalism rests on presenting certain axioms from which to deduce inferences; the axioms do not have to relate to the real world.

Alternatively, all of my thoughts and experiences may be produced by a clever wi-fi device (the latest incarnation of Descartes's demon that tormented his self-certainty). But is such a move fair? We can retort that either dismissing the obvious (I can see *something* even though I may be mistaken in my knowing what it truly is, or I know that I personally am thinking) is a philosophical *non-sequitur*, an annoying irrelevancy that hinders proper epistemic expansion, or that it is self-refuting or circular: I don't believe that I am the originator of my thoughts, who does not believe this? So I must exist, which is the conclusion Descartes held on to. Hegel rejects this as a shallow argument, arguing that knowledge of the self is dependent on knowing that other egos exist: self-consciousness exists only in being recognized – 'being-in-itself and being-for-another are one and the same thing.' Hence others do exist. Wittgenstein takes another tact asserting that the very certainty that I possess basic *means* of knowing is sufficient to quieten sceptics: similar certainties begin to form a scaffolding, a means by which to guide our ascent to knowledge, rather than knowledge itself – hence, his argument goes, the scaffolding is not subject to sceptical quizzing.

Above all, the sceptic wishes to challenge the validity of the mundane trust that we place in ourselves, and especially that which we place in the care of others (religious leaders, politicians, medics, government officials, commercial marketing, etc.), and so to pursue that challenge inexorably: nothing should be sacred to the sceptic, for only by constantly challenging and rechallenging cherished beliefs and assumptions can there be a possibility of progress. The impetus gained implies a movement towards a truer state of knowledge rather than perhaps the True state of knowledge, which, for many thinkers such as Popper, may never be attainable: hence the importance of philosophy to guide our questions and thinking.

Schopenhauer, Arthur (1788–1860)

Immanuel Kant divided the world between the phenomenal world of appearances and the noumenal world of things-in-themselves; the latter we are incapable of knowing – they are forever beyond us. Schopenhauer, however, pursued Kant's duality to unfurl the thing-in-itself as 'Will'. Not a friend of his living at the bottom of his garden, but the will that resides in each of us, the commander-in-chief of our cerebral forces, that which readies us to do its bidding.

Initially destined to follow his father into business, Arthur decided to pursue the more fruitful path of professional philosophy – neither the first nor the last philosopher to have disappointed his parents, Aquinas did the same.

Schopenhauer's initial work *The World as Will and Idea* barely sold. Biting comments made about Hegel and Fichte did not enamour his peers towards him – he even set himself up in competition for students by lecturing at the same time as Hegel at Berlin University – and failed. He sloped off to pen more essays. One 'On Women' is rather chauvinistic (he did have a sarcastic mother): women remain children all their lives, nothing good has come of them, they may pity the suffering more than men but that is because they are weak. It may explain why Schopenhauer seemed to prey on much younger consorts. Philosophically, he struggled to gain a reputation; a series of popular essays, good conversation and wit finally merited him fame during the last decade of his life; indeed, in his essays, he underlined the importance of etiquette, of being well mannered and well-turned out, and for thinking for yourself (always a good idea).

At Weimar he met an Oriental scholar, Friedrich Mayer, who introduced him to Indian thought and Schopenhauer went on to combine his Kantian insights with Indian philosophy. Suddenly Schopenhauer thought he could find a way through the impasse that Kant's noumenal world, the world of things-in-themselves had presented to philosophy. Your self has two aspects to it, for Schopenhauer: your phenomenal self, that which you perceive the world with, which you sense that you belong to and which works its way through the world, and the noumenal self of your will. The phenomenal world is the world of perception, but philosophical reasoning begins when we grasp the argument that 'the world is my idea' – that all that I perceive is merely done through my senses and is known to me as ideas. That the world is idea was explored by Berkeley and by Hindu Vedanta philosophy.

> Birth and death belong merely to the phenomenon of will, thus to life; and it is essential to this to exhibit itself in individuals which come into being and pass away, as fleeting phenomena appearing in the form of time. (Schopenhauer, *The World as Will*, 355)

Everything possesses a momentum which Schopenhauer preferred to call Will; all is subject to this living movement – thoughts, needs, desires. Consider your reasoning – the manner in which you think things through (hopefully logically): reason, for Schopenhauer, was a mere tool for the Will, an instrument for satisfying our needs; reason can only work when it gains knowledge (it must receive before giving) and knowledge is the servant of the Will. As such, reason cannot untangle what is behind the veil of things – an intuition is required, but whence the intuition? It emerges with perception and reason, standing between them as it were, playing between them to secure an intuition that there are things-in-themselves lying behind the particular individual entities that we perceive with our senses. What can we intuit? Intuition presents that flash of inspiration elucidating something – that all is subject to Will.

However, Schopenhauer's solution to Kant's unknowable noumenal world is not just a form of vitalism (the theory that there is a *something* that separates life from non-life), for he extended Will to include non-living matter as well. This presents numerous problems, for how can matter be said to possess 'Will' power? Schopenhauer accepted the problem but prefers to keep with the notion; however, it is interesting that in the Chinese, *Wu Li*, according to Zukav, means living energy and suffuses both 'inanimate' and 'animate' matter – the Tai Chi masters assuming no distinction between organic and non-organic matter.

Will, poor lad, cannot find happiness, it has no end, it is ceaselessly striving – the pursuit of happiness is a mere dalliance, which cannot rid the striving of its inevitable failure and boredom. Death pervades and we can only surmount the Will by denying it – by denying the internal life force that tempts you to eat and to enjoy pleasures.

In time, Schopenhauer gained a reputation for pessimism emphasizing the natural evil of the world and the need for an ascetic existence (give up your worldly goods). If asceticism is none too appealing, then you can turn to art, although this is the inferior path as it is more temporary. Within art, be aware, tragedy is the highest form of art that shows us the real nature of the world (and so he influenced Richard Wagner, who influenced Nietzsche) – poetic justice, in which the bad characters get their comeuppance presents a false view of the world; in Schopenhauer's reality, the world for people is one of suffering. In tragedies, the suffering reaches its ultimate pinnacle – death, and death is the release. His pessimism concluded that it would have been better not to have been born. Now where's my black gothic cape and dark make-up?

On a relatively lighter note, Schopenhauer wrote a wonderful little essay on the annoyance of noise – how the cracking of whips would disturb his thoughts and how the crackers should be whipped themselves, for their horses do not obey their habitual cracking and the only effect is to put people off thinking. Today he would have railed against mobile phones and muzak.

Science

Science means knowledge and so is intimately connected with epistemology, the study of knowledge in which we look at meaning, reference and truth. Science deals with the physical world, covering chemistry, physics and biology. In terms of results, science has been immensely successful; doubters only have to look around and focus for a few minutes on the products visible including this book.

In that respect, science's epistemology has been successful: its successes have naturally attracted attention and philosophers and other intellectuals have attempted to replicate the methods for their own areas, but such a move implies that the scientific methods are universal in application, which is not necessary. The scientific method is one of testing a theory by experimentation and being able to replicate that experiment and get the same results; conclusions drawn are tentative, given that experiments are often highly contrived. Nonetheless, the immense quantity of work that has been based on controlled and repeatable experiments builds up to an impressive edifice – not one that is dogmatic though, for the scientific method demands a healthy scepticism to ensure that what is understood today is always up for revision tomorrow.

The philosophy of science discusses problems such as induction and deduction, the status of causation in events, and the role of the mind and senses in understanding the issues to be researched. When an experiment is repeated is the result being verified or does it stand until falsified, as Popper proposed, and so can we speak of truth in science? What is proof and what are its criteria?

Science should always be distinguished from the scientific community, the people and personalities, the laboratory assistants and innovators. People are prone to err, to alter results to suit their own interests or budgets, or to pursue a dogma allegedly under the aegis of science. So long as others adhere to the scientific method, problems created by biased or doctored results, scientific propaganda, pseudo-scientific theories and unscientific claims should be unmasked. However, there is a concern that the politicization of science in which governments and large businesses fund projects – such as mass vaccinations – will act to undermine the attempts of authentically motivated researchers and hence corrupt the method in favour of politically favourable results, akin to the trappings of theological control in sixteenth-century Europe and creating a medical–industrial establishment whose relationship to power is similar to that of the military–industrial establishment. Optimists may believe that the 'truth will out' but that is not necessarily the case when so much in this world depends upon human endeavour and courage.

Kuhn argues that science works within paradigms – sets of beliefs regarding nature and method, which are periodically shattered by innovative thinkers and a new paradigm emerges. It is a popular but not untested theory: Kuhn does not just stress the sociological forces at work within the scientific community but he raises this to describe science itself – that is, what is true in science *depends* upon the social paradigms, not the scientific ideas themselves and how they relate to the facts and events that they seek to explain: it is the people and the force of numbers that form a paradigm, which will be self-perpetuating till overthrown by another, dissenting group, whose numbers eventually reach a critical mass. Each scientific establishment rewrites history as it were. Popper on the other hand, presents a critical view of science that permits any to question the validity and truths of the scientific community rather than merely accepting that the truth is relative to the scientific community *per se*. Anybody may present a theory and that theory is then subject to falsification – that is, it is to be tested and its falsification will justify its rejection. People change their view of the world, not because the scientific establishment has changed personnel, but because they are persuaded of a new way of thinking; for Kuhn, the community reaches a limit to its vision and a new vision and community are required. These are radically differing views not just of what constitutes science but also how science progresses.

In a sense, we can see how the two philosophies clash over 9/11 issues: for Popper, each theory presented ought to be falsifiable, and once falsified rejected; for Kuhn, who supports a Platonic view of science (that it should be used to keep the people content), the official theories form the paradigm, for no-one else is qualified to challenge the orthodoxy – only the experts may pronounce – so long as their power or numbers are sufficient that is. Popper would have been satisfied with the plurality of web-based journalism, which opens up society for perennial criticism, while Kuhn would have been keen to control it.

Popper and Hayek both railed against the abuse of science in the sense of it being used as an inappropriate method in other subjects. Scientism is the theory that all human (and animal) acts and events can be reduced to scientific study as used by the natural scientists. The case of medicine can provide a powerful example to consider here to encourage thought. In laboratorial conditions, the effect of a drug on a culture of cells may be observed, analysed, and the experiment conducted by different researchers under similar conditions. If the results tally, then it can be agreed that the evidence sustains a certain hypothesis. Now translate that drug to child – reductionist thinking assumes that the effects on the child's body can be extrapolated or be assumed to be analogous to the effects on the cell culture, yet the child is not a laboratory (physically, never mind morally), for a myriad of other issues emerge that act to overwhelm the simplicity of a cause and effect relationship tested in artificial conditions. The child is a living and dynamic organism whose cells are constantly striving to reform a healthy environment and to reproduce, abetted by the child's own interaction with his environment, nutrition and even attitude; this would suggest that an interdisciplinary approach to medicine should be part of its scientific remit.

Holistic approaches are often rejected by those who demand an application of the scientific method in medicine, yet employing and observing the same drug on two different people will produce different effects, since their particular conditions, nutrition and mindset cannot be held constant. Accordingly, medical practice reverts to statistics correlating the performances of drugs and treatments, which implies that simple cause–effect relationships are hidden by averaging procedures.

The morality of scientific issues is vast – ranging from fluoridation of water, mass vaccination programmes and genetic engineering, to the moral responsibility of scientists and whether government should be permitted to direct or control science and its results. Arguably, if it did, I would not have been writing this on a laptop!

Self

When 'I' is distinguished from 'we' the philosophy of self begins and so too the amusement: Who am I? What am I? Can 'I' be seen? Can 'I' be recorded or empirically verified? Am 'I' a figment, an imaginative device, a cruel trick of the gods? Accounts of the self have implications for a vast range of philosophy, particularly ethics, for if I should pursue the good life, what is the 'I' doing the pursuing?

Some may claim that the ego is not at all distinguishable from 'we' and this is not on the most obvious retort of checking oneself in the mirror: some such as James entertain a Hindu belief in the ego's ability to transcend its own particular existence and to feel the greater spirit from which all are derived. Accordingly, authentic behaviour consists in transcending self-interest to further the greater good of the universal spirit.

If we take up the reductionist baton, philosophical issues still arise. At the heart of the self (as a mind = brain) is the ego, the irreducible I which is the depository of all personal experiences (i.e. felt by this particular individual) and the formation of internal wishes, ideas, desires, fears, emotions and actions. But discerning what the self is still an infuriating game, like capturing 'now' in time: am I the same self as I was yesterday? What ties me to my former (or future) selves? Is it merely neuronic pathways? While some brain neurons live for a long time, some die and some new ones develop, so where does that leave 'me'? Should I stop worrying about who is worrying about these questions and immerse myself into life anyway? That wouldn't be very philosophical though – keep thinking! And who is doing the thinking?!

Hume rejected the existence of an unchanging self, and argued that while it can be said that we have a personality, the self is illusory in that it is merely a bundle of continuous and fleeting perceptions and that the association of those perceptions (in the same body) forms a self. Some may argue that the self thereby changes according to context, similar in some respects to how Wittgenstein saw language changing according to the particular game being played: here is my academic self, here my fatherly, here my husbandly, here my tutorial self. However, if the self is just a fleeting flow that differs from that of yesterday, then what ties the 'I' of today with the 'I' of yesterday – I acknowledge myself through time, as other people apparently do, so what constitutes this selfish bedrock upon which dreams exist? I can alter the attitude that

I present other people and even myself, here jovial, here serious, here inquisitive, here lamenting. In each case there is an 'I' working, one that accumulates sensations, fantasies, thoughts and broader experiences, and which is governed in turn by this complexity. Perhaps the self is like a vast and eclectic music collection: different but all music.

Sex

A panoply of thoughts – religious, secular and hence philosophical – pervade thinking about sex. Sexual activity rates high in specific moral discourses. Arguably, the reason appears to be that taboos have arisen concerning the consequences of certain forms of sexual behaviour which human interaction over many generations have developed into conventional rules. The piercing of those rules by philosophy brings their character to the fore and we can thus engage in disputes regarding the purpose of sex (reproduction, pleasure, political control), the age and/or nature of consent, promiscuity, homosexuality, erotic or pornographic art or media.

When we initially think of philosophy and sex it is the ethical matters that rush to the fore: should rules be imposed on certain kinds of sexual activity and if so upon what grounds? Libertarians decry any form of prohibition that acts to interfere with the volitional choices of adults: they provoke us to think about taboos or acts deemed illegal such as calling for the legalization of prostitution, homosexuality and pornography which they deem victimless crimes.

Literature is often a good source of philosophical examinations of libertarian (or indeed libertine) ethics: Nabokov's *Lolita*, for instance, presents a literary exploration of a world in which some barriers to adult–child sexual relations are removed, while De Sade provokes thought on sexual acts and religion. Naturally, this position demands consideration on what forms adult and/or volitional status – is a drunk person culpable or accountable for his or her acts? Or to what extent should the effects on innocent parties be curtailed (e.g. restraints on televised images or adverts)? Conservatives of various political hues tend to highlight traditional mores concerning sexual behaviour as such rules are seen as either promoting certain values or virtues or as encapsulating the wisdom of the ages on the consequences. Some acts are deemed absolutely immoral and hence prohibitable as they are presumed to degrade the dignity of the people engaged; other acts are to be eschewed as they imply deleterious consequences for the individuals concerned or for the greater society affected: that promiscuity leads to a higher prevalence of disease or emotionally damaged offspring, for instance.

But the philosophy of sex also deals with behaviour. The range of behaviour that slides into sexual is evidentially complicated in its subtleties that permit the philosopher to raise what are often implicit forms to an explicit level and this encourages analysis of sexual behaviour as well as identity replete with political or aesthetic implications. Does the naked form present a sexuality or is that only when the viewer becomes engaged in perceiving the naked form sexually? Political exegesis of the varying expositions of this kind of thinking also lead us to examine the nature of power and sex: are women deemed sex objects because they are politically weaker, or does political weakness stem from a systemic cultural degradation of the female form?

In a free world, how should relations between consenting adults proceed – would the institution of marriage or of monogamy make any sense, or is there, as some believe, a natural biological tendency to forge long relationships (hetero or homosexual), which act to sustain health and happiness both individually and consequently socially too, as well as the pursuit of pleasures, that overwhelm attempts to redefine human sexuality according to rationalist criticism?

Often in the philosophy of sex, the emphasis is placed on initiating or on acting out sexual desires; sometimes, thought is stretched to pregnancy and birth but often, in traditional writings, as a warning to imprudent permissive behaviour on the part of the woman. Feminists have applauded the emergence of modern contraception as giving women freedom to enjoy sexual activity on par with men, perhaps though with a de-emphasising of the beauty and natural role of a pregnant woman and the act of childbirth: while sex in the West has become generally promoted by secular individualism, birth has ironically become institutionalized, even nationalized, but resoundingly medicalized.

Part of the philosophy of sex can thus stretch to follow through initiation and act to consequence and to pull the various strands of thinking on sex and childbirth together – birth can be seen as the completion of the reproductive cycle that sex initiates.

Socrates (469–399)

Socrates presides over Western philosophy both in terms of his character and his philosophical conversations. He never committed anything down, but his dialogues with Athenian citizens were written up by pupil-followers such as Plato and Xenophon. Plato's account of his thoughts dominates philosophical analysis and one has to remember that in reading Plato's dialogues that it is his rendition of his tutor, a rendition that naturally becomes less Socratic and more Platonic as Plato's great mind unfolds and matures.

Initially, stocky, strong, pug-nosed Socrates was a sculptor, but his friend Crito encouraged him to further his philosophical thinking, so Socrates studied under Archelaus and Anaxagoras. He married Xanthippe, sired three boys, fought in the Peloponnesian War but in peace became popularly known and was for the most part well-liked as a compassionate and venerable man who emphasized toleration and *sophrosyne* (self-control). He practised his philosophy in the market place in the sense that he discussed human affairs, justice, the soul, as well as knowledge as he meandered through the streets and in the *agora*. He brought philosophy down from the heavens to and the ordinary man, and it is from this revolutionary perspective that Plato and other followers of Socrates bring philosophy to bear on life and what we can know about it and what we ought to do. According to legend, the priest at Delphi called him the wisest man in Greece; hence he set about finding out why that was the case and realized that his wisdom was based on his ignorance – while others professed to knowledge, which his analysis soon found to be wanting, Socrates maintained that he really knew nothing.

A strong theory that emanates from Socrates' own thinking (as far as we can tell) is that one cannot knowingly do wrong. If you know what the right thing to do is, then you will do it; there can be no quibbling. This form of moral determinism was criticized by Aristotle as being rather naïve – he countered that people can knowingly do wrong, because they may be morally weak.

However, Socrates' forthright analysis of everything under the sun soon gained him enemies who trumped up charges that he was corrupting the youth of Athens and introducing new gods into their pantheon. At his own trial, Socrates' magnanimity shone brightly: he refused assistance from his friends and defended himself capably, but his humble defence (he argued that after all, 'he knew nothing') irritated the judges and they sentenced him to death by drinking hemlock. He accepted the sentence and refused offers of escape because, he argued, who but the gods knew whether life or death was better.

From what we learn of him through Plato's dialogue, *Phaedo*, Socrates also wanted to try death to learn what he may learn. He died 30 days after his trial, a period that allowed his friends to reason with him and to discuss many ideas. Socrates' noble bearing and death prompted the Athenians to regret their decision (a common occurrence with the Athenians at the time) and the prosecutors fled or took their own lives, and one was killed. Years later, Aristotle fled from Athens so that the Athenians would not sin against philosophy one more time.

Soul

Realizing that we die, we wonder what happens to us, whether we possess an eternal thing called a soul that lives on afterwards in the happy hunting grounds or Elysium or which is judged according to our deeds and either sent onward and upward to heavenly bliss or downward into hellish depravity. Sceptics assert that the desire for immortality is mere wishful thinking on our part and a refusal to acknowledge that once we are dead the game is over. Of course, proof of the soul's immortality or of the existence of another place where we all end up is non-existent and logical arguments that seek to deduce either are notoriously leaky or circular, which encourages many of us to assert that 'we'll find out when we are dead'.

On the other hand, it is evident that our existence is characterized by a continuity of personality that many are happy to describe as a soul, as something that is behind our will, our thinking, our emotions – that which gives us life; it is often described as possessing irrational and rational components. Aristotle defined the soul as such and as the substance and energy form which animates the living thing (any living thing); it is immaterial but is coterminous with the body and cannot exist without it. In contrast, Plato's asserted that the soul is not only eternal but also that it is subject to rebirth – a mystical belief that seemingly emanated from the East (India) and through the early Hellenic thinkers and the Pythagoreans. Buddhists and Hindus notably claim that the soul is reborn again and again (*samsara*) until a higher form of enlightenment is achieved through bodily discipline and is allowed to be removed from the divine recycling programme. Christianity rejected reincarnation but drew heavily on Plato's theory that the soul is released into a separate realm, called Heaven: as a realm of punishing our mundane deeds, Hell was a later addition, arguably, as a reminder to Christians to behave in life.

Do other living creatures possess souls, as Aristotle thought? Most Christian thinkers rejected the notion preferring to assert a hierarchy of life from plants through to animals to soul-possessing humans to bodiless souls (angels) and then to God, the Absolute Soul. Descartes however stirred controversy by asserting that animals, and our bodies, were mere machines: the soul is an immaterial and separable substance that can body-hop, the implication goes, as well as enjoy an eternal existence. Construing animals as machines caused a reaction which rekindled vitalist thinking, that all living entities are somehow different from immaterial entities perhaps because of the existence of a soul but that the soul and body are one and inseparable. Panpsychists argue that souls are everywhere – in rocks as much in amoeba and you and I; such thinkers tend to accept idealism in which all is said to be One – one vast immaterial spiritual.

While early modern philosophers felt the need to agree in the existence of soul from social or political pressures or mere force of habitual indoctrination, by the nineteenth century, atheists and sceptics were stripping the concept apart with Ryle arguing that it is merely a 'ghost in the machine', a non-existent imaginative creation of our mind.

Spinoza, Benedict de (1632–1677)

Benedict (né Baruch) de Spinoza of Amsterdam, belongs to the philosophical fallout from Descartes's writings, but while admiring Descartes, Spinoza also sought to differentiate himself from Cartesian philosophy. Spinoza was an original and broad thinker, maturing in Judaism and its education, rejecting it in favour of what can be loosely termed secular Christianity, but broadly proposing an unorthodox vision of God and religion. He lived frugally making lenses, with much of his work being published after his death from phthisis – the old name for tuberculosis.

The influence of Descartes's methodology is immediately recognized in Spinoza's *Ethics*, which is set out in the manner of a Euclidean

exposition of arguments from a series of axioms. Geometry was
highly popular among intellectuals – Hobbes had an epiphany
reading Euclid, and it seemed that deductive mathematical methods could explain not just the natural universe (it was the time of
Copernicus and Galileo) but also be extended to explain human
nature, ethics and politics. Indeed, a passion for mathematics in
philosophy can be traced back to Pythagoras and Plato and the
general encouragement of rationalist philosophers who believe
that the universe is knowable to our thinking minds.

> I do not attribute to nature either beauty or deformity, order or con-
> fusion. Only in relation to our imagination can things be called
> beautiful or ugly, well-ordered or confused. (Spinoza, *Correspon-
> dence*, Letter XV)

Spinoza began the *Ethics* with a series of arguments on God,
mind, bodies, emotions, human bondage and freedom; the particular propositions are deduced from a series of definitions and axioms. The purpose was to define what makes us happy, and for
Spinoza, that is when we secure the passions and emotions under
rational control. The deductive method proceeds tightly, but if the
definitions are unstable or open to criticism, the arguments too will
wobble. Beginning rather than concluding with God separates
Spinoza from Descartes (who begins with his own mind) and Aquinas (who begins with sensations of things); yet God's role in his
philosophy then presents very different implications. Spinoza was a
monist: all is attributable to God both logically and causally: 'I mean
that which is in itself, and is conceived through itself.' The one substance is eternal and infinite. It has to be infinite, for if substance
were finite, it could be acted upon by another substance, but ultimately, there is only one thing that underpins everything and that is
God, a being absolutely infinite.
   Herein begins the controversy, for while his definition of God is
traditional, he believes that Descartes and his predecessors did not
understand infinity meant that God was also indivisible. God is an

extended thing – He reaches out into everything that is finite; this is similar to how a pantheist looks at the world and some have held Spinoza to be a pantheist. Extending into the universe – God is in effect Nature, we see that there are two divine attributes, which remain substantially the same (God), but are defined by us as body and mind. Body and mind are not opposing descriptions but describe, with different language, two different attributes or modes of God's extension into the universe.

That God is Nature may seem not to be very radical – it has a New Age or Cabalistic quality to it (the latter being a Judaic mystic tradition with which Spinoza was familiar) for those who relate Nature to Spirit, but traditionally for the scholars and theologians, God was held to exist outside of the universe – He created it after all. For Spinoza the world we encounter nature is unified; in turn, this implies that everything is determined, which means that there is no room for freedom of will.

Contrary to Descartes, Spinoza affirmed that the mind is the body: there is no problem concerning how the mind operates on the body, or vice versa. On perceiving water the body is affected by its physicality and so affects the mind (today, we would say the light rays reflecting off it affect our eyes' cones and rods and a nervous signal is posited in the brain). The mind in turn holds the impression upon the body and the impression of the thing perceived: sensory perception alone is thus an inadequate tool for learning about the world, one has to include mind, otherwise, sensations are likely to be haphazard and not prove very adequate for knowledge, for there is a lack of rational order upon them. Once commonalties are apprehended by the mind, then adequate ideas can be produced from which a system of definitions and propositions may be inferred. From such ideas, we can also intuit a relationship between their essences and that of God, but how that is to happen Spinoza does not clarify.

Spinoza's political theory is reminiscent of his contemporary Hobbes's: because most people are affected by their blind passions, they require a strong government to keep order, so justice can only exist under government. Government must be strong, but it must not interfere with freedom of thought. He accused the clergy of manipulating people through fear and superstition; he denied the soul's immortality, free will, and hence moral responsibility and he also began examining the Bible as a text. The synagogue excommunicated him and controversy was generated across Holland following the publication of his *Theological-Political Treatise*, which argued for freedom of thought and of philosophy against the establishmentarianism of the clergy.

However, Spinoza does provide humanity with some control over their lives insofar as we reject the passions and emotions. The greater the control that we impose upon the emotions with our reason, the freer we are; if we relinquish ourselves to the passions, we are in effect slaves, bound to the fortunes of the passions and their effects. Control comes from learning about adequate ideas, particularly coming to understand the effecting control of the passions, will help a person gain more control: the 'free man' is one who has liberated himself from the power of the passions to control his life, an echo of the Stoic philosophy, but one that was to enthuse the German romanticists and idealists whose idealization of living naturally and discarding moral conventions. A fashion that resurfaced in the 1960s.

Stoicism

'Live according to nature', is the Stoics' ethos. That implies nature is something we can learn about and, proceeding logically, apply what we learn about the world to our own lives. At once Stoicism demands the highest from human capacity and a humility and fortitude in understanding our meagre position in a vast, ordered universe. It was the guiding ethic of Rome's philosopher-emperor, Marcus Aurelius, and we still hear its echoes today.

Stoicism was developed by Zeno of Citium, Cleanthes and Chrysippus, the last forming a consistent philosophy that afterwards found great favour with Roman thinkers, who were able to ally its moral emphasis on duty and submission to the given order to Roman martial and imperial values; the philosophy has three phases – early, middle and late – which are denoted as its journey from Greece to Imperial Rome and then to late Rome; most of the early texts have been lost and research has focused on secondary and later writings.

Stoic philosophy divides into three: logic, ethics and physics: all are deemed equal, but emphatically Stoics demand that we live according to our ideals, rather than muse upon them.

The world according to the Stoics is material and rationally ordered: nothing incorporeal exists. This implies that the soul and the body are not dual entities but are one and the same. The world is thus a coherent unity: it possesses a logical structure and that structure is knowable. The Stoic universe is also divinely ordered by a higher intelligence: God is a rational force acting upon a material force giving matter air and fire (what we would perhaps call energy); when combined, matter can produce life and soul, and, following Aristotle, the highest form of life is human life as it is rational, albeit in a pale version of the divinity's. Not only is the universe material, the Stoics held that its unfolding is preordained – fated – and said to recur in cycles: God – as elemental fire – will at some future date destroy the world and then recreate it, and everything that has happened will happen once again. This is the doctrine of eternal recurrence, toyed with by Nietzsche in the late nineteenth century and is a peculiar, untestable doctrine – indeed a myth – but one that resurfaces in some of the implications of multiple universe theories.

We learn about the world through the impressions we receive upon our blank minds (cf. Locke), and truth is the correspondence of our impressions to the world we perceive, a theory that stirs much controversy, for it rejects the Platonic vision of ideal forms and Cartesian deductive constructions. These impressions have to be clear but they are also subjective, for they are based on what I feel by virtue of the impressions I receive, not what is there to be felt. The observer and the observed meld in a way that anticipates quantum physics thinking; Stoic epistemology also rejects reductionist thinking, of focusing on a single part of nature (the human eye) while ignoring all the parts that connect to it (the face, the mind, the body, the view). It therefore seeks a grasping, apprehensive, *cataleptic* impression – derived from an object, accurately representing the object, and stamped on the senses.

Since the world is rationally ordered and people are rational beings, it follows that, ethically, the life proper to humanity is one of acknowledging your role relative to the universe and to your own nature. This creates an awkward knot: to understand the inevitability and omnipresence of the laws of nature is to recognize that your life is similarly subject to the great laws governing the unfolding of the future; your actions are predetermined and thus fated. Stoics argued that authenticity stems from accepting that fact, rather than permitting free will presumably which could endanger the universe; that is why they sought to repress emotion, which distracts the mind from its higher purpose of recognizing its innate humble nature!

By assenting to obey nature and learn its laws, a person can become virtuous. Virtue is deontological – duty oriented – and based on education, as I need to mentally mature to know my humble role and accept the way of things. Happiness thus comes from obedience to nature rather than the pursuit of ephemeral pleasures, and wisdom can only come from straining to apply our reason to the world (and thereby acknowledge our humble position therein). The ephemera of life possess no value whatsoever to the Stoic, hence he or she is indifferent to pain, poverty, and even death.

Fortitude, benevolence, indifference and self-sufficiency characterize the Stoic; but most importantly, one should live by one's philosophy; indeed, Epictetus argued strongly that living is more important than reflecting.

Time

What is time, the philosopher asks? A measurement of change or duration, most have replied. 'But to whom?' retorts Einstein. Relativity theory shattered the classical conception of absolute time and introduced time dilation, but physics has yet to disentangle some of the oldest problems concerning time: was there a beginning to time, and if so, what happened before that? For there to have been a beginning implies that there was a prior event or cause that produced time, as we are now aware of it.

Philosophy demands that we consider carefully such questions, for they can easily drop us into contradictions: for example, in our daily thinking we assert strong propositions that time can be objectively or publicly measured and that it only flows one way, via the now. Yet the notion of the 'now' presents itself as an awkward logical complexity – the now is forever disappearing in front of us, or as some would hold, within us.

We may be looking at time completely wrongly: time just is, and we progress through it (in our own relative frames of reference) and have come to be aware of our progression, just as if we were forever walking along a path of space-time. If so, why are we all apparently 'progressing' through time: why can't we turn around and walk the other way, or stop, or is the question an imponderable inference of human language? Nonetheless, Einstein's theory of relativity implies not only can time be warped, but that it could also fold back on itself, so time-travel becomes possible. And hence the philosopher is not quietened: questions on how should we deal with time-travel furthering much amusement.

> What, then, is time? As long as no one asks me, I know; but if someone asks me and I try to explain, I do not know. (St Augustine, *Confessions*, Book 11)

Defining time requires defining the background definitions with which we define time, while avoiding circular definitions: for example, 'time is change', and 'change is what happens over time'. Wittgenstein criticizes language – there is no problem concerning time, he says, only verbal problems that can be surmounted; from physics, Edward Witten's M-theory implies that space and time may not exist at some infinitesimal but fundamental level. Neither satisfies all: for Aristotle time is not just something that we count in observing change, but the 'something in change' that allows us to count. This forms the basis of physical conceptions of time used in the sciences. Isaac Newton claimed that time is independent of change and indeed of the universe, whereas Einstein explained that time's progress is relative to the observer, which implies that the ticking of a watch depends on the speed at which the watch is moving: the faster its wearer is travelling, the slower time proceeds relative to other observers.

Even with a grasp of relativity theory, the philosopher notes that we still rely on perceptions of change to understand time. Does that mean that an absence of change implies an absence of time? If there is no perception of time, does time still exist? Bradley says no – time is indefinable and unreal. Whereas Augustine conceives time as purely mental or psychological (and experiments confirm that we possess an ineradicable internal 'clock'), Kant argues that time is a necessary experience of consciousness, a category that we place upon the world: both concur that time is psychological rather than objective – an internal experience rather than something we can point to and say, 'that is time'. Bergson explains that we are not passive objects to time's passing, but that we live through time, which gives rise to the phenomenological study of la durée (duration). Certainly, our consciousness of change is linked to how we understand time; hence it appears that sometimes it flows quicker than at other times. But we are then aware of the passage of something, which brings us back to physical time of the scientists by which we can both gauge our procession and the change in other things through time.

Are the past and the future real? To some only the present can be real, since that is all that we experience. That either means the past and future do not exist in some meaningful way and hence we would not have much to talk about, or the past is a separate category 'was once real' and the future 'yet to be real' both implying that the past and future are not real. This raises some interesting problems: we are constantly aware of the inexorable advance of the future hitting our senses every moment as it were, but does that mean the future is constantly being formed momentarily or spontaneously before it is experienced, which would imply that a probe able to jump ahead into the future would not find anything (and could not therefore jump into 'the future')? That seems rather dubious, for what has been is readily recognizable as existing in the past (and can be physically identified as having existed), so why should the future be presently non-existent? Whitehead argued that the future is real, but the present actual: the real becomes the actual through a creative process, which presents a semantic distinction certainly, and not one satisfactory to critics.

Now, the cup of coffee you may need to make to ponder time further: does it presently exist? We know that it *will* exist and therefore *will have existed*, semantically speaking, but philosophically what kind of existence do things in the future have? Are they the same as present and past objects, or are they forever real but not actual? And what of my choice to make the coffee, when did that arise? Was it always there, awaiting, deep in my past, my ownership of it? Conceiving time is similar to visualizing a four-dimensional object: a quintessentially slippery process.

Truth

'What is the truth? Is mine the same as yours?' mocks Pontius Pilate in Webber and Rice's *Jesus Christ Superstar*. It is a fitting beginning to any discussion on truth, one that niggles the brain: does Pilate mean that there are many different truths – as many as there are individuals? Or does he mean that he has beliefs about truths, which is perhaps all that we can produce in life for the truth is forever unattainable? On the other hand, in general discourse we often assume the existence of certain truths, such as there is a dog on the chair: either there is a dog there, or there isn't. That is different from a belief statement: 'I believe that there is a dog on the chair', which is open to verification according to the imagery and relevant prepositions presented. I may be wrong in my belief (because of a hallucinogenic or drunken state, myopia, or perceptual confusion – I only caught a sideways glance as I passed the chair).

Even if there *is* a dog on the chair, what does that mean philosophically? The words I utter are mere conventions so it is not the words themselves that create the truthfulness of the proposition: if we reject the contrivance of language, the statement boils down to a phrase written symbolically as p is true, or, for those who want to secure an even finer statement: p.

You find a lot of ps and qs in logical discussions about truth – the reason is that the writers want to get to the bottom of philosophical problems by ejecting useless or distracting vocabulary in a quest to make certain parts of philosophy more akin to maths – this was one of Leibniz's hopes; p can include complex relationships as well as simple ideas, and if rejected gains the lovely symbol ¬p (not p: that is, that proposition we're on about, called p for short, is actually false).

Once I utter a proposition 'p' it still remains to be argued as to how it can indeed be true or false. Is it 'p is true to me'? This is a problematic move, for what does the addition of 'to me' imply? Either it means that I create the truth just as we imagine God could create truths if He were all powerful, or it means that 'I believe that p is true.' But belief is different from something being so (or not being so). Philosophy demands more from us: if p is indeed true (there *is* a dog on the chair, as we normally understand that statement), then is it true because we all agree on there being a dog on the chair. Or is it true because it is true regardless of whether we agree or not?

One may retort that things that are true are true to all people concerned, and Pilate's subjectivist jibe should be rejected, or is it indeed the case that what I perceive or think only I can pronounce on, and so long as my beliefs cohere in my mental demesne, then they must be true? That is, where am I trying to anchor my statement – in the halls of my consciousness or in an extramental reality? If the latter, how do I know whether the reality that I imagine exists really exists? If the truth is that which agrees with reality, we take it as indicating something factual and objectively assessable. This is the correspondence theory of truth – 'that dog is muddy' corresponds with the dog indicated possessing the attribute of being muddy. But what of 'all fiction is true'? – an entertaining little number that is immediately perplexing and paradoxical, except that what I write as fiction is necessarily true, as it corresponds to the material in my head (of which I am conveniently the only witness). Fiction aside, after much coughing and spluttering from some philosophers, when I say that 'the dog is muddy' corresponds with the fact that 'the dog is muddy', we would seem to be getting somewhere – but do we? P is p, because p is p; so we're back to just p and we may be getting p'ed off.

Accordingly, philosophers are encouraged to develop deeper explanations as to why p is indeed p (or ¬p), which chase us into other realms notably metaphysics, ontology and epistemology. If p is true, then there must be something about p that exists independently of belief, wisecracks or emotions, and something about our thinking or uttering p that can connect to the reality, however understood, of p being true: empiricists implore that our senses form the conduit, while rationalists propose that it is our ability to deduce that is critical; mystics prefer to delegate to other supernatural powers to inform them of the connections: either way, we are still in need of a good p.

Universals

Universals bedevil philosophy. They are, simply put, words that identify a group of particular entities or instances, but simplicity, while not necessarily wrong, attracts philosophical attention as much as complexity does: for instance, once we utter a universal term, are we now indicating the existence of something over and above the particulars that it groups? Dualist thinking allows that it does: if we speak of 'man' in the traditional sense of meaning 'men and women', it follows that there is something existing, man, which exists over and above the individuals that belong (have belonged, will belong) to the group. Plato's philosophy claims such a duality – that there is a world of ideal forms, drawn from the concept of universals, as well as a world of particulars and the phenomena that we see around.

For Plato, universals exist in their own realm, whereas his student Aristotle rejected the dualism preferring a realistic notion that universals do exist, it is just that they exist in particular entities. For example, when I see Mr Hobbes, my dog, he is said to possess – and I am capable of perceiving or knowing this – a dogginess that each instance of a dog also possesses. Both Plato's and Aristotle's theories imply that universals do exist and that they are discoverable; but we also know that sometimes we get classifications wrong – biologists sometimes have had to shift one species from one category to another. Does that mean, contrived labels apart, that the plant has been discovered to possess a universal that was for a long time mistaken, or that the universal of which it was said to belong is a mere categorical class of our making? The realist tradition with regard to universals assumes that such things are there; nominalists reply that the labels are merely names and that since names are conventional labels there is nothing special in the idea of a universal.

Nominalists baulk at the reification – of making something into a *thing*, in this case of an abstract noun into an existent – as potentially committing a fallacy, but the Platonic tradition retains supporters both in secular and especially in theological thinking: God is for religious believers the most obvious 'existing' universal entity: one who is all-present, all-knowing and all-good. The Platonic argument is that the particular things that we see are shadows of the universals, whereas the empirical tradition (emanating from nominalism to some extent) substantially expanded by Locke for instance claims that the universals are shadows of the particular existents that I perceive – they are mere abstract tools, created by grouping the impressions in my head that I have had of similar entities (e.g. this table and that table, and that one over there – to make the abstract 'table'). I can only perceive particulars and, as the empirical philosophy is expanded, the implication follows that all my ideas are necessarily reducible to particulars.

Such reducibility creates its own problems. The mind drives towards integration – of pattern forming and grouping things, which encourages Kantian supporters to argue that universals are innate categories of the mind that impose mental structures upon evidence. According to this conceptualism, universals are mental products – they do not exist in the sense that Platonists think nor are they non-existents in the sense that the nominalists or strict empiricists believe: they exist as conceptual tools. The concept 'dog' exists in my head as a useful tool to recognize dog creatures – which allows that I may be mistaken in assuming your pet was a dog (I mistook the particular as belonging to the group) as well as for altering the conceptual boundaries to include new or hitherto unrecognized creatures as dogs (shih-tzus?). This draws upon the Aristotelian legacy of finding commonalties between members of a group to form a group, a process which is flexible for it is innately fallible and groupings can be arranged according to political, aesthetic or moral criteria and which may thus be subject to forms of propaganda: think about how some peoples have been and still are categorized by elites or their enemies.

Utilitarianism

'How should I act?' demands ethics. Why, by ensuring that you maximize your pleasure, replies the hedonist; by living for your neighbour, replies the Christian. Live for your neighbour's pleasure, asserts the utilitarian. This caricature (by Rand) of utilitarianism is not far from its essence, that before you act you should consider the impact of your action upon the rest of the world – and some utilitarians such as Peter Singer ask not just to think of your human neighbours, but also the animal kingdom and even the planet.

Utilitarianism proposes that an act should aim to maximize the greatest good for the greatest number. It is a consequentialist philosophy that looks to the results of actions rather than at the actions or the agents themselves. The developer of modern utilitarianism was Bentham, who argued that life is governed by pleasure and pain and that the good life is thus the pursuit of pleasure and the minimization of pain, which sounds like hedonism, but Bentham added a new twist: pleasure and pain could, he mused, be calculated in what is known as 'felicific calculus', of examining a pleasure's intensity, duration, fecundity (fruitfulness in encouraging other pleasures), purity, certainty and propinquity (nearness). Here the troubles begin but let us consider what the thrust of utilitarianism means in practice.

Consider a play on Hugo's *Les Misérables*: Marius is about to kiss Cosette, when he does his pain/pleasure reckoning. If he kisses her, he will enjoy the experience and so, he presumes will she. But can he rely on this presumption? Cosette looks as if she wants to be kissed but she may prefer to hold hands or to share a meal. Should he ask her what she would prefer and could he be sure that she replies honestly? On the other hand, a new figure emerges: the face of Eponine. Thinking of her, Marius realizes that kissing Cosette would break Eponine's heart, and so he should recalculate whether the benefits from the kiss now outweigh Eponine's pain. And what if he dismissed Cosette in favour of Eponine, is there a chance that her happiness would overwhelm Cosette's forgiving sadness and his own melancholy? If so, then he must foreswear Cosette.

But what of honesty and sincerity? Apparently they are not important in utilitarianism. Some utilitarians may hesitate at the apparent facetiousness here and reply that the morality of utilitarianism is supposed to be legislative choices – it is not for the mundane issues of life. However, this retreat is not sufficient, for it would have to explain at what point mundane issues become important: matters of the realm involve just as many mundane decisions as everyday life can involve highly consequential ones. Instead, the calculating of outcomes must precede and invade every aspect of human life; this contradicts the deontologist, who looks at the rightness or wrongness of actions in themselves, and the virtue theorist, who prefers to ask 'what kind of person will I be if I so act?'

Bentham's utilitarianism is notoriously egalitarian, which worries those who believe that some acts are intrinsically better than other acts: Bentham allowed push-pin to be of equal worth to poetry if it produced as much satisfaction, but other utilitarians, particularly Mill, were not pleased, and utilitarianism divided into what are now know as act and rule utilitarianisms. Act utilitarianism says we should consider each act on its pleasure-inducing merits, whereas rule utilitarianism implies that over time, experience will enlighten us as to the benefits of certain forms of behaviour which should thusly become rules. Such rules may be taught to new generations as having produced overall long-term benefits, even though they appear to not to do so in the short term: thus Marius should be faithful to his love for Cosette, for experience would underline the need to follow his heart in love rather than a superficial penny counting procedure in the moment. Similarly, the rule utilitarian stipulates that honesty is always the best policy despite the immediate and perceivable beneficial consequences of truth avoidance.

Reckoning the pleasure and pain accruing from an act is notoriously difficult for the individual, so what can be made of utilitarianism's principle that people's happiness and misery be added? Can

Marius truly compare the love two women hold for him and then proceed to account the profit and loss from kissing Cosette? Critics may maintain that pleasure is intimately subjective and while it can be ordered (I prefer red wine to beer to white wine), it cannot be quantified, as Bentham would wish, into what are called *utils*, or units of utility: red wine equals 40 utils, beer 20 utils, white wine 5 utils. But does that mean I truly prefer red wine over white by a factor of eight? And what would I say of a kiss? And what would the response be with my loved one if I admitted that a kiss gave me 230 utils of pleasure? If pleasure is purely subjective and preferences ordinal, then the utilitarian felicific calculus fails.

Secondly, what of its principle of securing the greatest good for the greatest number? Why the greatest number? If the greatest number sought your destruction, would the force of numbers make it a moral enterprise? Mill recognized the implications of this and argued that just as 99 men do not have a right over 1, nor does 1 have a right over 99: he sought to temper Bentham's raw utilitarian calculus by extolling the pleasurable benefits that ensue from the higher intellectual pursuits, for, as he wryly observed, it is better to be a dissatisfied Socrates than a satisfied fool.

The criticisms bite and force retractions that lead utilitarians back to supporting traditional morals. However, one remaining philosophical premise to Bentham's utilitarianism needs addressing: in the calculus, each is to count for one and no more than one. When levelled against legislation, the principle demands that the voice (or noise) of the loud few should not offset the quieter members of the civic order. This is a radical demand indeed, for often political philosophies proceed as if the voices of some (the elite, rich, poor, religious, educated, working class, certain racial types, men, women, tribes, and so on) should have more weight than others, which the Benthamite utilitarian cannot condone, and when harnessed to liberalism with its emphasis on the rights of the individual (against the crowd or crown) then we can witness utilitarianism's influence in history and the attempted overthrow of political privileges.

War

War is a seemingly ubiquitous constant throughout human history. It certainly gets coverage because of the noise, violence and repercussions that it produces. Because of its frequency some philosophers have fallen into thinking war is inevitable. Others disagree and indicate that the blame for war lies with certain causal factors that either can be controlled or their effects mitigated. War is certainly a philosophical problem – it is not the monopoly of historians or strategists, for the philosopher can raise some very interesting questions concerning its nature.

What is war; can it be defined, and if so, how? What causes war; what is the relationship between human nature and war – does human nature necessitate war, or only its response to certain sociological or environmental conditions? War has been blamed on human nature (or genes these days), on our innate disposition to own or to control our fellow people, on economic circumstances, on types of political constitution; or in the ideological realm on religion, nationalism and forms of totalitarianism.

If we turn to ethics and politics, we can ask whether war can ever be justified, and if so on what grounds? Who should declare war? The individual who is aggressed against, or does its collective nature demand a political sovereign's legitimization? And if war be justified morally, should certain acts of war be impermissible as breaching basic human standards or rights? Can morality even intrude into war's realm? Just war theorists think so and propose that various conventions have emerged over the centuries that act to limit, on mutually agreeable criteria, the breadth and violence of war: others retort that gentlemanly or honourable conduct in war is typically adhered to only in wars between culturally similar groups and that when it suits military leaders, no quarter is more the fashion. Do the ends of war justify the means used? For many aggressors, ennobled by a crusading ideology, that has often been the case – yet philosophically justifying the supremacy of one ideology over another is devilishly difficult: it invokes the issue of what constitutes a value as well as the more obvious problem of the right of one group of people to impose on another their way of life.

The pacifist rejects the justification of war on any grounds but leaves us disconcerted as to what ought to be done with those who do find pretexts for imposing violence on those who would prefer to turn the other cheek. Realists reject pacifism as implausibly idealistic in favour of sustaining a country prepared to fight off invaders or deter those who would even deign to consider attack; they may even allow for pre-emptive or aggressive war to secure peace. In between are many variations on justifying war to some extent or less, grappling with the kinds of warfare envisaged – the weapons, tactics, purposes.

Wittgenstein, Ludwig (1889–1951)

Ludwig Wittgenstein enters twentieth-century philosophy with the attitude of the boy calling out that the Emperor has no clothes. Into philosophy he stumbled, being diverted from a career as an engineer, and quietly he produced a revolution: his declaration that there are no philosophical problems only linguistic ones has reverberated loudly since. Not quite as loudly as Nietzsche's 'God is dead' for the death of philosophy would rather put a damper on things for some of us, but one cannot study philosophy without reading and then returning to Wittgenstein for clarity and insight. Incidentally, little Ludwig apparently attended *Realschule* with Adolf Hitler. He also enjoyed relaxing watching cowboy movies.

There are two periods to Wittgenstein's philosophy: the early period is found in the *Tractatus Logico-Philosophicus* and the later found in the *Philosophical Investigations*. The early position expands on seven sentences – each sentence is unfolded for further meaning and elucidation in the manner of an itemizing catalogue. Each line in turn demands the fullest of our attention – there is not a slow construction of a philosophical vision here that we may enjoy

as we may the unfurling of a good mystery: Wittgenstein demol-
ishes that from the start. The *Tractatus* is not easy reading either;
personally, I find the best place to read it is in the bath – failing that,
the shower.

How do we know the world? Only through language, Wittgenstein argues. Anything present to the senses becomes linguified so
to speak, which raises the alternative perspective of how language
enables us to represent the world. In the *Tractatus* the thesis is that
language ought to represent the world closely: the constituents of
a sentence connecting to that which they refer. Exceptions include
logical connectives (and, or), which act merely to assist language
work. What is uttered should be logically consistent but it should
also produce a picture of the world (the so-called picture theory
of language). Impressed by how a model of an accident can represent the accident, Wittgenstein believed that language too acted
as a picture or model and can represent reality; beyond the pictures
it can produce (which must equate to things seen), there can be
no cognitive meanings. When constructed properly, a proposition
is either true or false – it 'shows what it says': if it is true, it depicts
correctly a state of affairs. In saying 'there is a dog in the room' I am
saying that there is state of affairs such that there is a dog in
the room. The essence of a proposition is thus that 'this is how
things are'.

> The limits of my language mean the limits of my world. (Wittgenstein,
> *Tractatus*, 5.6)

Necessity is logical for Wittgenstein – that is, it does not refer to
the reason why things ought to happen. Only the relationship
between words create necessity, but tautologies (things necessarily
true) really do not say anything and so are 'senseless'. Contradictions similarly say nothing of the world, their truth conditions are
contradictory. Nonsense on the other hand is created when an
utterance relates to nothing, particularly in attempts to define

'being', 'I', 'fact', and so on; 'Where *in* the world is a metaphysical subject to be found?' One should reply to someone uttering metaphysical propositions that 'he [fails] to give a meaning to certain signs in his propositions'. That is the job of philosophy, for 'what we cannot speak about we must pass over in silence'.

Having completed the *Tractatus* (while serving in the Austrian army during First World War) Wittgenstein believed that he had solved philosophy's problem(s) and he retreated from formal philosophy to teach children in a rural school for a few years. He was cajoled back into philosophy after encountering the Viennese Logical Positivists, who were developing some of the themes of his work; he acknowledged that there was indeed more to be done in philosophy and over the next few years, he rethought his general vision and in 1945 produced the *Philosophical Investigations*.

Before, Wittgenstein's mission had all the trappings of a rationalist attempt to solve philosophy's problems, akin in many respects to trying to prove God's existence through logic and language alone. The result was abstract, removed from what he later saw as the use of language in everyday life, although the irony at the end of the *Tractatus* is delightful – once you've understood it, you'll not need it, so like a ladder that has enabled you to climb to a vista, you can then kick it away. He dropped some of his earlier theses (such as words representing things) but the motivation in the *Investigations* remained the same: to examine language and mind and to elucidate the limits of philosophy and to pursue the demand to express oneself as clearly as possible. Why? To secure knowledge; but that security depends on the language that I am using – the rules of the language game that I enter in speaking and writing produces my vision of the world and through that game and its rules I must seek to make myself understood. There are a multiplicity of games though – each with its own set of rules, connected only by a 'family resemblance' as it were; there is the game of telling a joke, ordering a meal, describing an event, asking a question, and so on: hence his later emphasis on language in use rather than language abstracted from use. Consider a word as a set of symbols: 'girl' for example, how does the set of characters relate to the actuality of a girl (whom we may point to and say, 'this is what I mean')? Only through being used – the word cannot relate to anything if it is not used.

Wittgenstein also sought to remove the solipsist from philosophy. The solipsist is one who believes that only she exists – everyone else is a figment of her imagination. Avoiding that conclusion motivates much philosophical discussion and Wittgenstein presented his version: the solipsist necessarily engages in a public, communal language game for she cannot produce a private language of her own, or at least one that carries any meaning. He denies that language can be private. To be wrong in my pronouncement that 'I am in pain' seems nonsensical, so the first-person, solipsist, privileged view is shaky. We may believe that to feel a sensation provides an example of an inalienable privacy; but how could I assure myself that the sensation that I am presently feeling (and keeping to myself) is the same as the one that I felt yesterday (and kept to myself)? I make a note of the sensation with an 'S'; but what good would that do, for if I attempt to compare S1 with S2, what criterion of correctness do I have to allow me to connect the Ss together as being of the same type? By invoking the term 'sensation' as in I am having this sensation (pain), I am necessarily employing a commonly known word, without which I cannot proceed. So the apparent logical loop that is effected by the solipsist comes to naught: expressing the idea 'I know that I exist' invokes a host of communally derived words and their images. Any private experience that I have (an impression of something leaning against me) presupposes a shared public world that provides us with the means of understanding what I am doing or feeling.

> It makes sense to say about other people that they doubt whether I am in pain; but not to say it about myself. (Wittgenstein, *Philosophical Investigations*, I.246)

Since language is used, it is critical for us to return notions back to their proper 'homes'; so instead of denying metaphysical statements as unverifiable (God exists is a meaningless sentence because 'God' is unverifiable, so you may as well be saying 'Vup' exists), Wittgenstein prefers us to remove the nonsense that can be created by words such as 'knowledge', 'being', 'object', 'I', 'proposition', and so on in favour of 'clearing up the ground of language on which they stand' (*Investigations*, I.118). But where does knowledge begin? Can we express certainty? Empiricists argue that we gain our certainty from sense impressions (I feel the fire's glow), idealists from the internal obviousness of my mind (I know I'm thinking at least), but both claims are insufficient for Wittgenstein, for both rely on the certainty of the mind's internal contents which ultimately produce an unwarranted solipsism with which his refutation of private language deals.

So whence certainty – is it at all possible? From the opposite view, consider doubt. Wittgenstein notes that if I doubt my hands then continue to use them, then I am not really doubting their existence; more importantly (for Descartes could reply, I mean to doubt theoretically), doubts require grounds for doubting, that is a mastery of the language game which is presupposed. One cannot proceed by doubting one has hands unless one knows the meaning of having hands in the first place. Some things just cannot be doubted, about which we cannot be mistaken, such as the existence of external objects. I may make false judgements about what I identify but I thereby can be corrected – which assumes a basis upon which corrections can be made. Certainty stems from a deeper level than thinking or sensing, it is not the product of empirical or intellectual inquiry but the very foundation of our researches; the propositions that we use are gained through living them – they are not learned or experienced as such, they are inherited, 'swallowed down' as it were, indeed through observation and instruction but Wittgenstein prefers not to use the word 'learned'. It is not as if we learn single propositions at a time, but we gain an overview of the whole system – of the language game that is being employed. So when I say, 'run over there', you glimpse what is meant by my command from acknowledging what game we are playing from what you have previously understood. But whence original understanding? From acting – from observing and following the actions of others.

In a sense, and this is what some but not all critics hold, the later Wittgenstein converges onto a behaviourist thesis of mind, that is what can be known of your mind can only be ascertained by your behaviour – by your rule following. But how do we get to know the rules and can we know if we were to diverge from them? By engaging in life – engaging in the customs and forms of culture that underpin our rules. These overlap and integrate through meaning and intention. For instance, in your home, asking 'Is the kettle hot?' may imply a rule to check whether the kettle is hot or not in case a younger sibling scalds himself; while the same question in our friend's household may imply a rule to make a cup of tea. How do I, as a guest, know what is meant in each house – only by residing there and coming to terms with the rule's meaning. We can only make sense of what is uttered through the context of background assumptions upon which the utterance is made. I can of course help to alter the rule, so when I'm in our friend's house, I may reject the rule and proclaim, 'yes, indeed, the kettle is hot', forcing a restatement of what was intended.

From the *Tractatus*'s conclusions, one naturally imagines a much quieter (and peaceful) world but before we all close our mouths and consider what can actually be said, one must not forget the straining of music and poetry that sometimes helps us learn about the world; in some respects the *Investigations* return us to familiar territory – the world-view of people and whether those views make sense or are just ways of doing things. Philosophy did not die with Wittgenstein of course; there are problems to grapple with in ethics, politics, aesthetics, religion, mind, language, mathematics, and so on – indeed, these are philosophical problems, and chasing those problems returns us to the problems of philosophy itself.

Zen

An A–Z of Philosophy requires a contribution from the letter Z; after much wrangling, the top slot went to Zen, an appropriate final entry. Other contenders include Zeno's paradoxes (Achilles and the Tortoise), Zhuangzi or Zero.

The original Zen proponent was Bodhidharma, who allegedly spent 9 years gazing at a wall (Who fed him and when did he relieve himself?). Zen is a form of Buddhism which stresses the importance of meditation (*zazen*) and by the dropping of secular desire the vision that may be gained of the world as beautiful and the true nature of the self. For Buddhists, desire – the passions that prompt us to seek things – is the cause of suffering, so if we can transcend desire we lose our self. Like Sartre's vision of consciousness as nothingness, Buddhism holds that the substantial self is an illusion; reality is similarly phenomenal – we see appearances rather than truths, so any perspective is as equally valid as any other is. Indeed, we gain strong glimpses of Buddhist thinking coming through to the West via Schopenhauer in recent times but also possibly through Heraclitus and Pythogoras in ancient times – Heraclitus' city of Ephesus was a cosmopolitan trading port with access to eastern routes and he exiled himself to the hills to live naturally before returning to sit (and die) on a dung heap.

Meditation implies that by focusing the mind on 'nothing', a state of enlightenment can be gained – for the religiously inclined this may present a path to know Buddha or God. Nonetheless, since what becomes known at these deeply moved psychological states differs among practitioners, philosophy and the logical pursuit of knowledge is not thereby rejected to sift through the interesting results from the delirious. For the non-religious, meditation is useful as a means of calming the mind, reducing the noise and stress of modern life, reasserting a balance in the mind/body, or plainly for relaxation: and philosophical insights may also be enjoyed.

Zen oriented meditation can thus be seen as healthy in itself or as a means to a chosen end – indeed, one can imagine Aristotle enjoying contemplation through meditation. Perhaps he did. It would make a good Philip Glass opera.

Further Reading

A non-exhaustive and perhaps highly peculiar further reading list – explore as you wish.

Absolute

Ayer, A. J., *Language, Truth and Logic* (London: Gollanz, 1955)
Sprigge, T. L. S., *The Vindication of Absolute Idealism* (Edinburgh: Edinburgh University Press, 1983)

Action

Davidson, Donald, *Essays on Actions and Events* (Oxford: Oxford University Press, 1980)
Mele, Alfred (ed.), *The Philosophy of Action* (Oxford: Oxford University Press, 1997)
Thomson, Judith Jarvis, *Acts and Other Events* (Cornell: Cornell University Press, 1977)

Aesthetics

Eco, Umberto, *On Beauty: A History of a Western Idea*, trans. Alastair McEwen (London: Secker and Warburg, 2004)
Kant, Immanuel, *The Critique of Judgement*, trans. J. C. Meredith (Oxford: Oxford University Press, 1964)
—*Observations on the Feeling of the Beautiful and Sublime*, trans. John T. Goldthwait (London: University of California Press, 1991)
Plato, *Symposium and Phaedras*, trans. Benjamin Jowett (New York: Dover, 1993)
Santayana, George, *The Sense of Beauty: Being the Outline of Aesthetic Theory* (New York: Dover, 1955)
Scruton, Roger, *Art and Imagination* (London: Methuen, 1974)

Tolstoy, Leo, *What Is Art?* (Indianapolis, IN: Bobbs-Merrill, 1960)

Analytical philosophy

Cf. Russell, Wittgenstein

Animal rights

Nozick, Robert, *Anarchy, State, and Utopia* (New York: Basic Books, 1974)
Scruton, Roger, *On Hunting* (London: Yellow Jersey Press, 1999)
Singer, Peter, *The Expanding Circle* (Oxford: Oxford University Press, 1981)

Aquinas, Thomas (1225–1274)

Aquinas, Thomas, *Selected Philosophical Writings*, trans. Timothy McDermott (Oxford: Oxford University Press, 1998)
—'Summa against the Gentiles', in *On Ethics and Politics*, trans. Paul E. Sigmund (New York: W. W. Norton & Co., 1988)

Aristotle

Aristotle, *The Complete Works of Aristotle*, ed. Jonathan Barnes, two volumes (Princeton, NJ: Princeton University Press, 1995)
—'Politics' in *A New Aristotle Reader*, ed. J. L. Akrill, trans. T. A. Sinclair and T. J. Saunders (Oxford: Clarendon Press, 1992)

Augustine

Augustine, Saint, *City of God*, trans. Henry Bettenson Withan (London: Penguin, 1984)

Being

Barnes, Jonathan, *Early Greek Philosophy* (Harmondsworth: Penguin, 1987)

Heidegger, Martin, *Being and Time*, trans. J. Stambaugh in *Martin Heidegger: Basic Writings*, ed. David Farrell Krell (New York: Harper Collins, 1993)

Plato, 'Parmenides' in *Plato: Complete Works*, ed. John M. Cooper, trans. Mary Louise Gill and Paul Ryan (Indianapolis, IN: Hackett Publishing, 1997)

Sartre, Jean-Paul, *Being and Nothingness*, trans. Hazel E. Barnes (Northampton: John Dickens & Co., 1972)

Belief

Cf. Hume, Kant, Aquinas

Griffiths, A. Phillips (ed.), *Knowledge and Beliefs* (Oxford: Oxford University Press, 1967)

Bentham, Jeremy (1748–1832)

Bentham, Jeremy, *Introduction to the Principles of Morals and Legislation* (New York: Dover, 2007)

Clark, G. Kitson, *The Making of Victorian England* (Cambridge, MA: Harvard University Press, 1962)

Mack, M. P., *Jeremy Bentham: An Odyssey of Ideas* (New York: Columbia University Press, 1963)

Rothbard, Murray, *Classical Economics*. (Cheltenham: Edward Elgar, 1995)

Berkeley, George (1685–1753)

Berkeley, George, *The Principles of Human Knowledge* (London: William Collins Sons and Co., 1972)

Causation

Mises, Ludwig von, *Theory and History* (Auburn, AL: Ludwig von Mises
    Institute, 1985)

Conscience

Butler, Joseph, *Five Sermons* (Indianapolis, IN: Hackett Publishing, 1983)
Dostoevsky, Fyodor, *Crime and Punishment*, trans. Jessie Coulson
    (Oxford: Oxford University Press, 1980)
Locke, John, *An Essay on Human Understanding* (London: Everyman,
    1993)
Shaftesbury, A. A. C., *Characteristics of Men, Manners, Opinions, Times*
    (Cambridge: Cambridge University Press, 1997)
Smith, Adam, *Theory of Moral Sentiments* (Indianapolis, IN: Liberty
    Classics, 1982)

Consciousness

Dennett, Daniel, *Consciousness Explained* (London: Penguin, 1991)
Hopkin, Michael, 'Implant Boosts Activity in Injured Brain', *Nature*, 448
    (1 August 2007) 522
Nagel, Thomas, 'What Is It Like to Be a Bat?' in *Mortal Questions*
    (Cambridge: Cambridge University Press, 1979)
Priest, Stephen, *Theories of the Mind* (London: Houghton Mifflin, 1991)

Continental philosophy

See Sartre, Heidegger, Hegel.

Crime and punishment

Mill, John Stuart, 'Speech in Favour of Capital Punishment' in *Applied
    Ethics*, ed. Peter Singer (Oxford: Oxford University Press, 1988)

Rothbard, Murray, *Ethics of Liberty* (London: New York University Press, 2002)

Tolstoy, Leo, *The Kingdom of God Is Within You*, trans. Constance Garnett (New York: Cassel, 1894)

Descartes, René (1596–1650)

Descartes, René, *Key Philosophical Writings*, trans. Elizabeth S. Haldane and G. R. T. Ross (Ware, Herts: Wordsworth Editions, 1997)

Education

Palmer, Joy A., *Fifty Major Thinkers on Education* (London: Routledge, 2001)

Plato, *The Trial and Death of Socrates*, trans. G. M. A. Grube (Indianapolis: Hackett Publishing, 2000) p. 39

Winch, Christopher and John Gingell, *Key Concepts in the Philosophy of Education* (London: Routledge, 2005)

Egoism

Hobbes, Thomas, *Leviathan* (ed.) Richard Tuck (Cambridge: Cambridge University Press, 1996)

Hume, David, *Enquiry Concerning the Principles of Morals* (Indianapolis, IN: Hackett Publishing, 1983)

Mandeville, Bernard, *Fable of the Bees*, two volumes (Indianapolis, IN: Liberty Classics, 1988)

Rand, Ayn, *Virtue of Selfishness* (New York: Signet, 1964)

Smith, Adam, *Theory of Moral Sentiments* (Indianapolis, IN: Liberty Classics, 1982)

Empiricism

Popper, Karl R., *Conjectures and Refutations* (London: Routledge and Kegan Paul, 1963)

Priest, Stephen, *British Empiricists* (London: Penguin, 1990)

Environmentalism

Pepper, David, *Modern Environmentalism: An Introduction* (New York: Routledge, 1996)

Epistemology

Hume, David, *Hume's Treatise*, ed. L. A. Selby-Bigge and P. H. Nidditch (Oxford: Oxford University Press, 1978)

Russell, Bertrand, *The Problems of Philosophy* (Oxford: Oxford University Press, 1980)

Ethics

Aristotle, *Nichomachean Ethics*, trans. Sir David Ross (Oxford: Oxford University Press, 1992)

Bentham, Jeremy, *Introduction to the Principles of Morals and Legislation* (New York: Dover, 2007)

Lewis, C. S. *The Abolition of Man* (London: Fount, 1979)

Smith, Adam, *Theory of Moral Sentiments* (Indianapolis, IN: Liberty Classics, 1982)

Evil

Aristotle, *Nichomachean Ethics*, trans. Sir David Ross (Oxford: Oxford University Press, 1992)

Augustine, Saint, *City of God*, trans. Henry Bettenson Withan (Penguin: London, 1984)

Leibniz, Gottfried Wilhelm, *Theodicy* (Chicago: Open Court Publishing, 1988)

Locke, John, (1690) *Two Treatises on Government*, ed. Peter Laslett (Cambridge: Cambridge University Press, 1997)

Nietzche, Friedrich, *Genealogy of Morals*, trans. Douglass Smith (Oxford: Oxford University Press, 2000)

Rand, Ayn, *Virtue of Selfishness* (New York: Signet, 1964)

Existentialism

Cf. Heidegger, Sartre
Sprigge, T. L. S., *Theories of Existence* (Harmondsworth: Penguin,
 1985)

Feminism

Walters, Margaret, *Feminism: A Very Short Introduction* (Oxford: Oxford
 University Press, 2005)

Free will

Kane, Robert, *The Significance of Free Will* (Oxford: Oxford University
 Press: 1996)
Pink, Thomas, *Free Will: A Very Short Introduction* (Oxford: Oxford Uni-
 versity Press, 2004)

God

Cf. Augustine, Aquinas
Hume, David, *Hume on Human Nature and the Understanding*, ed.
 Antony Flew (New York: Collier Books, 1962)
Paley, Rev. William, *The Works of William Paley, D. D.*, five volumes
 (London: William Baynes and Son, 1825)

Hedonism

Bentham, Jeremy, *An Introduction to the Principles of Morals and
 Legislation* (Oxford: Clarendon, 1996)
—*Introduction to the Principles of Morals and Legislation* (New York:
 Dover, 2007)
Carson, Thomas L., and Paul K. Moser, *Morality and the Good Life*
 (Oxford: Oxford University Press, 1997)

Feldman, Fred, *Pleasure and the Good Life: Concerning the Nature, Varieties and Plausibility of Hedonism* (Oxford: Clarendon, 2004)

Nozick, Robert, *Anarchy, State, and Utopia* (New York: Basic Books, 1974)

Sidgwick, Henry, *The Method of Ethics.* (London: MacMillan & Co., 1911)

Hegel, Georg Wilhelm Friedrich (1770–1831)

Hegel, G. W. F., *Hegel's Phenomenology of Spirit*, trans. A. V. Miller. (Oxford: Oxford University Press, 1977)

—*The Philosophy of History*, Trans. J. Sibree. (New York: Prometheus Books, 1991)

—*The Philosophy of Right*, trans. S. W. Dyde. (New York: Prometheus Books, 1996)

Horstmann, Rolf-Peter, 'Hegel', in *The Shorter Routledge Encyclopedia of Philosophy*, trans. Jane Michael-Rushmer (London: Routledge, 2005)

Houlgate, Stephen (ed.), *The Hegel Reader* (Oxford: Blackwell, 1998)

Norman, Richard, *Hegel's Phenomenology* (London: Sussex University Press, 1977)

Plant, Raymond, *Hegel* (London: Phoenix, 1990)

Singer, Peter, *Hegel* (Oxford: Oxford University Press, 1983)

Heidegger, Martin (1889–1976)

Heidegger, Martin, *Heidegger: Basic Writings*, ed. David Farrell Krell (New York: Harper Collins, 1993)

History

Collingwood, R. G., *The Idea of History* (Oxford: Oxford University Press, 1946)

Gardiner, P. L., *Theories of History* (New York: Free Press, 1959)

Marx, Karl, *The 18th Brumaire of Louis Bonaparte* (New York: Interna-
tional, 1963)
Popper, Karl R., *The Poverty of Historicism* (London: Routledge and
Kegan Paul, 1976)

Hobbes, Thomas (1588–1679)

Hobbes, Thomas, *Behemoth or the Long Parliament* (London: University of Chicago Press, 1990)
—*De Cive* (Montana: Kessinger Publishing, 2004)
—*Leviathan*, ed. Richard Tuck (Cambridge: Cambridge University Press,
1996)
Martinich, A. P., *Hobbes: A Biography* (Cambridge: Cambridge University Press, 1999)

Hume, David (1711–1776)

Hume, David, *Enquiry Concerning the Principles of Morals* (Indianapo-
lis, IN: Hackett Publishing, 1983)
—*Hume's Treatise*, ed. L. A. Selby-Bigge and P. H. Nidditch (Oxford:
Oxford University Press, 1978)

Intuition

Bergson, Henri, *Introduction to Metaphysics*, trans. T. E. Hulme (Indianapolis, IN: Hackett Publishing, 1999)
Moore, G. E., *Principia Ethica* (Cambridge: Cambridge University Press,
1959)

Justice

Nozick, Robert, *Anarchy, State and Utopia* (New York: Basic Books,
1974)

Rawls, John, *A Theory of Justice* (Oxford: Oxford University Press, 1988)

Rothbard, Murray, *The Ethics of Liberty* (London: New York University Press, 2002)

Kant, Immanuel (1724–1804)

Kant, Immanuel, *Critique of Judgement*, trans. J. C. Meredith (Oxford: Oxford University Press, 2007)

—*Critique of Practical Reason*, trans. Werner S. Pluhar (Indianapolis, IN: Hackett Publishing, 2002)

—*Critique of Pure Reason*, trans. Norman Kemp Smith (London: Macmillan, 1970)

—*The Moral Law*, trans. H. J. Paton (London: Hutchinson, 1972)

Kierkegaard, Søren Aabye (1813–1855)

Kierkegaard, Søren Aabye, *Either/Or*, trans. Alastair Hannay (London: Penguin, 2004)

—*Fear and Trembling and the Book on Adler*, trans. Walter Lowrie (London: Everyman's Library, 1994)

Language

Cf. Wittgenstein

McGinn, Colin, *Making of a Philosopher* (London: Simon & Schuster, 2002)

Leibniz, Gottfried Wilhelm (1646–1716)

Leibniz, Gottfried Wilhelm, *Philosophical Writings*, trans. Mary Morris and G. H. R. Parkinson (London: J. M. Dent & Sons Ltd, 1973)

—*Theodicy: Essays on the goodness of God, etc.*, trans. E. M. Huggard (London: Routledge, 1951)
Voltaire, *Candide* (New York: Modern Library, 1915)

Locke, John (1632–1704)

Locke, John, *An Essay Concerning Human Understanding* (London: Penguin, 1997)
—*A Letter Concerning on Toleration* (Indianapolis, IN: Hackett Publishing, 1983)
—*Political Essays*, ed. Mark Goldie (Cambridge: Cambridge University Press, 2002)
—*Some Thoughts Concerning Education,* eds. W. John and Jean S. Yolton (Oxford: Clarendon Press, 1986)
—*Two Treatises of Government*, ed. Peter Laslett (Cambridge: Cambridge University Press, 1963)
Moseley, Alexander, *John Locke* (London: Continuum, 2007)

Logic

Hodges, Wilfrid, *Logic* (Harmondsworth: Penguin, 1977)
Kneale, William and Martha, *The Development of Logic* (Oxford: Clarendon Press, 1984)
Priest, Graham, *Logic: A Very Short Introduction* (Oxford: Oxford University Press, 2001)
Strawson, P. F. (ed.), *Philosophical Logic* (Oxford: Oxford University Press, 1967)

Love

Cf. Aristotle, Plato
Branden, Nathaniel, *Psychology of Romantic Love* (New York: Bantam, 1985)

Marxism

Böhm-Bawerk, Eugen, *Karl Marx and the Close of His System* (London: Merlin Press, 1949)
Marx, Karl and Friedrich Engels, *The Communist Manifesto* (Oxford: Oxford World Classics, 1998)
—*A Handbook of Marxism* (London: Victor Gollancz, 1935)

Materialism

Cf. Hobbes
Ball, Philop, *The Elements: A Very Short Introduction* (Oxford: Oxford University Press, 2002)

Mathematics

Beckmann, Petr, *A History of π (pi)* (New York: St Martin's Press, 1971)
Seife, Charles, *Zero: The Biography of a Dangerous Idea* (London: Souvenir Press, 2000)

Metaphysics

Ayer, A. J., *Language, Truth and Logic* (London: Gollanz, 1955)
Hegel, G. W. F., *Hegel's Phenomenology of Spirit*, trans. A. V. Miller. (Oxford: Oxford University Press, 1977)

Mill, John Stuart (1806–1873)

Mill, John Stuart, *Autobiography* (New York: Columbia University Press, 1944)
—*On Liberty* (London: Longmans, Green and Co, 1884)

—*A System of Logic, etc.* (London: Longmans, Green and Co., 1884)
Rothbard, Murray, *Classical Economics* (Cheltenham: Edward Elgar
    Publishing, 1999)
Thomas, William, *Mill* (Oxford: Oxford University Press, 1985)

Mind

Priest, Stephen, *Theories of the Mind* (New York: Houghton Mifflin,
    1991)

Nietzsche, Friedrich (1844–1900)

Nietzsche, Friedrich, *Beyond Good and Evil*, trans. Robert C. Holub
    (Oxford: Oxford University Press, 1998)
—*The Birth of Tragedy and the Genealogy of Morals*, trans. Francis
    Golffing (New York: Doubleday, 1956)
—*Thus Spake Zarathustra*, trans. Thomas Common (New York: Modern
    Library, undated)

Ontology

Cf. Heidegger
Grossman, R., *The Existence of the World: An Introduction to Ontology*
    (London: Routledge, 1992)

Phenomenology

Cf. Continental philosophy
Scruton, Roger, *Modern Philosophy: An Introduction and Survey*
    (London: Sinclair-Stevenson, 1994)
Thénevaz, Pierre, *What Is Phenomenology?*, ed. James M. Edie (Chicago:
    Quadrangle, 1962)

Plato

Plato, *Plato: Complete Works*, ed. John M. Cooper (Indianapolis, IN: Hackett Publishing, 1997)

Political philosophy

Kymlicka, Will, *Contemporary Political Philosophy* (Oxford: Oxford University Press, 2002)

Moseley, Alexander, *Introduction to Political Philosophy* (London: Continuum, 2007)

Popper, Karl Raimund (1902–1994)

Popper, Karl R., *The Open Society and Its Enemies*, two volumes (London: Routledge, 1990)

—*The Poverty of Historicism* (London: Routledge and Kegan Paul, 1976)

—*Unended Quest: An Intellectual Biography* (Glasgow: Fontana, 1976)

Poststructuralism

Belsey, Catherine, *Poststructuralism: A Very Short Introduction* (Oxford: Oxford University Press, 2002)

Sokal, Alan and Jean Bricmont, *Intellectual Impostures* (London: Profile Books, 1999)

Pragmatism

Murphy, J. P., *Pragmatism: From Pierce to Davidson* (Boulder, CO: Westview Press, 1990)

Peirce, Charles Sanders, *Collected Papers of Charles Sanders Peirce*, eight volumes, ed. Charles Hartshorne, Paul Weiss and Arthur W. Burks (Cambridge, MA: Harvard University Press, 1931–1958)

Rationalism

Cf. Descartes
Hayek, Friedrich, *The Counter-Revolution of Science* (Indianapolis, IN: Liberty Press, 1979)

Reason

Mises, Ludwig von, *Human Action* (London: William Hodge & Co., 1949)
Rand, Ayn, *Philosophy: Who Needs It?* (New York: Bobbs-Merrill, 1988)

Relativism

Nagel, Thomas, *The View from Nowhere* (Oxford: Oxford University Press, 1986)
Wong, David, 'Relativism' in *A Companion to Ethics*, ed. Peter Singer (Oxford: Blackwell, 1997)

Religion

Dawkins, Richard, *The God Delusion* (London: Black Swan, 2007)
Lewis, C. S., *Mere Christianity* (London: Fount, 1997)

Rousseau, Jean-Jacques (1712–1778)

Rousseau, Jean-Jacques, *Confessions*, trans. anon., ed. P. N. Furbank (London: Everyman, 1992)
—*Emile*, trans. Barbara Foxley (London: Everyman, 1969)

—*Social Contract and Discourses*, trans. G. D. H. Cole. (London: Everyman, 1993)

Russell, Bertrand (1872–1970)

Russell, Bertrand, *The Impact of Science on Society* (London: Routledge, 1976)
—*The Problems of Philosophy* (Oxford: Oxford University Press, 1980)
—*Unpopular Essays* (London: George Allen & Unwin, 1950)

Sartre, Jean-Paul (1905–1980)

Sartre, Jean-Paul, *Being and Nothingness*, trans. Hazel E. Barnes (Northampton: John Dickens & Co., 1972)

Scepticism

Cf. Descartes, Hume, Popper, Wittgenstein
Fuller, Steve, *Kuhn versus Popper* (Cambridge: Icon, 2003)

Schopenhauer, Arthur (1788–1860)

Schopenhauer, Arthur, *Essays and Aphorisms* (London: Penguin, 1970)
—*The World as Will and Idea*, trans. R. B. Haldane and J. Kemp (London: Kegan Paul, Trench, Trübner &Co, 1910)
Zukav, Gary, *The Dancing Wu Li Masters* (New York: William Morrow and Co., 1979)

Science

Cf. Popper
Williams, Roger J., *Biochemical individuality* (New Canaan, CN: Keats Publishing, 1998)

Self

Beauvoir, Simone de, *The Second Sex*, trans. H. M. Parshley (New York: Vintage, 1952)

Descartes, René, *Key Philosophical Writings*, trans. Elizabeth S. Haldane (Ware, Herts: Wordsworth Editions, 1997)

Gaarder, Jostein, *Sophie's World*, trans. Paulette Møller (London: Phoenix, 1994)

Hume, David, *Hume's Treatise*, ed. L. A. Selby-Bigge and P. H. Nidditch (Oxford: Oxford University Press, 1978)

James, William, *The Varieties of Religious Experience* (London: Longmans, 1902)

Sex

De Sade, Marquis de, *Philosophy of the Boudoir*, trans. Joachim Neugroschel (London: Penguin, 2007)

Posner, Richard A., *Sex and Reason* (Cambridge, MA: Harvard University Press, 1997)

Scruton, Roger, *Sexual Desire: A Philosophical Investigation* (London: Continuum, 2006)

Vannoy, Russell, *Sex without Love* (New York: Prometheus, 1980)

Socrates

Cf. Plato, Aristotle, various histories of philosophy

Soul

Cf. Plato, Aristotle, Aquinas.

Ryle, Gilbert, *The Concept of Mind* (New York: Barnes & Noble, 1970)

Zukav, Gary, *The Dancing Wu Li Masters* (New York: William Morrow and Co.: 1979)

Spinoza, Benedict de (1632–1677)

Spinoza, Benedict de, *On the Improvement of the Understanding; The Ethics; Correspondence*, trans. R. H. M. Elwes (New York: Dover, 1955)

—*Spinoza's Ethics and 'De Intellectus Emendatione* (London: Everyman, 1910)

—*Tractatus Theologico-Politicus; Tractatus Politicus*, trans. R. H. M. Elwes (London: George Routledge and Sons, undated)

Stoicism

Inward, Brad (ed.), *The Cambridge Companion to the Stoics* (Cambridge: Cambridge University Press, 2003)

Sellars, John, *Stoicism* (Chesham: Acumen, 2006)

Seneca, *Letters from a Stoic*, trans. Robin Campbell (Harmondsworth: Penguin, 1982)

Time

Augustine, *The Confessions*, trans. Philip Burton (London: Everyman's Library, 2001) p. 271

Callender, Craig and Ralph Edney, *Introducing Time* (Royston: Icon Books, 2002)

Mermin, N. David, *It's About Time: Understanding Einstein's Relativity* (Oxford: Princeton University Press, 2005)

Truth

Hospers, John, *An Introduction to Philosophical Analysis*, 2nd edn (London: Routledge and Kegan Paul, 1967)

Universals

Cf. Truth, Aristotle, Wittgenstein

Utilitarianism

Bentham, Jeremy, *Introduction to the Principles and Morals of Legislation* (Oxford: Clarendon, 1996)

Mill, John Stuart, *Utilitarianism and Representative Government* (London: J. M. Dent & Sons, 1929)

Singer, Peter, *The Expanding Circle: Ethics and Sociobiology* (Oxford: Clarendon Press, 1981)

Smart, J. J. C., and Bernard Williams, *Utilitarianism: For and Against* (Cambridge: Cambridge University Press, 1987)

War

Clausewitz, Karl, *On War*, trans. Colonel J. J. Graham (London: Routledge and Kegan Paul, 1968)

Moseley, Alexander, *A Philosophy of War* (New York: Algora, 2003)

Robinson, Paul, *Military Honour and the Conduct of War* (London: Routledge, 2006)

Walzer, Michael, *Just and Unjust Wars* (New York: Basic Books, 1977)

Wittgenstein, Ludwig (1889–1951)

Wittgenstein, Ludwig, *On Certainty*, trans. G. E. M. Anscombe and Denis Paul (London: Harper Torchbooks, 1972)

—*Philosophical Investigations*, trans. G. E. M. Anscombe (Oxford: Basil Blackwell, 1978)

—*Tractatus Logico-Philosophicus*, trans. D. F. Pears and B. F. McGuinness (London: Routledge, 1999)

Zen

Sekida, Katsuki and A. V. Grimstone, *Zen Training: Methods and Philosophy* (New York: Weatherhill, 1975)

Other sources always worth referring to either to get started or to check a different perspective are:
The Internet Encyclopedia of Philosophy, www.iep.utm.edu
The Oxford Companion to Philosophy, ed. Ted Honderich (Oxford: Oxford University Press, 1995)
The Oxford Dictionary of Philosophy, Simon Blackburn (Oxford: Oxford University Press, 2005)
The Pan Dictionary of Philosophy, Anthony Flew (London: Pan, 1984)
The Shorter Routledge Encyclopedia of Philosophy, ed. Edward Craig (Abingdon: Routledge, 2005)
Similarly, histories of philosophy are invaluable:
Copleston, Frederick, *History of Philosophy*, volumes 1–7 (New York: Image, 1985)
Kenny, Anthony *A New History of Western Philosophy* volumes 1–4 (Oxford: Oxford University Press, 2007)
Russell, Bertrand, *History of Western Philosophy* (London: *Philosophy*, George Allen and Unwin Ltd, 1947)
Scruton, Roger, *Modern Philosophy: An Introduction and Survey* (London: Sinclair-Stevenson, 1994)

List of Entries

Index of Names